Re

THE UNIVERSITY OF
WINCHESTER

Martial Rose Library
Tel: 01962 827306

Religion, Culture, and Public Life

Series Editors: Alfred Stepan and Mark C. Taylor

The resurgence of religion calls for careful analysis and constructive criticism of new forms of intolerance, as well as new approaches to tolerance, respect, mutual understanding, and accommodation. In order to promote serious scholarship and informed debate, the Institute for Religion, Culture, and Public Life and Columbia University Press are sponsoring a book series devoted to the investigation of the role of religion in society and culture today. This series includes works by scholars in religious studies, political science, history, cultural anthropology, economics, social psychology, and other allied fields whose work sustains multidisciplinary and comparative as well as transnational analyses of historical and contemporary issues. The series focuses on issues related to questions of difference, identity, and practice within local, national, and international contexts. Special attention is paid to the ways in which religious traditions encourage conflict, violence, and intolerance and also support human rights, ecumenical values, and mutual understanding. By mediating alternative methodologies and different religious, social, and cultural traditions, books published in this series will open channels of communication that facilitate critical analysis.

After Pluralism: Reimagining Religious Engagement
Edited by Courtney Bender and Pamela E. Klassen

Religion and
International Relations Theory

Edited by Jack Snyder

COLUMBIA UNIVERSITY PRESS

NEW YORK

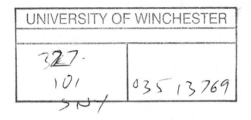

Columbia University Press
Publishers Since 1893
New York   Chichester, West Sussex
Copyright © 2011 Columbia University Press

Library of Congress Cataloging-in-Publication Data
Religion and international relations theory / edited by Jack Snyder.
        p.   cm. — (Religion, culture, and public life)
Includes bibliographical references and index.
ISBN 978–0–231–15338–6 (cloth : alk. paper) —
ISBN 978–0–231–15339–3 (pbk. : alk. paper) — ISBN 978–0–231–52691–3 (e-book)
1. Religion and international relations. I. Snyder, Jack L. II. Title. III. Series.

BL65.I55R453 2011
201'.727 — dc22
                                                    2010033152

Columbia University Press books are printed on permanent
and durable acid-free paper.
This book is printed on paper with recycled content.
Printed in the United States of America

References to Internet Web sites (URLs) were accurate at the time of writing.
Neither the editor nor Columbia University Press is responsible for URLs
that may have expired or changed since the manuscript was prepared.

CONTENTS

Religion and International Relations Theory

1. INTRODUCTION

JACK SNYDER

Since September 11, 2001, religion has become a central topic in discussions about international politics. Once Islamic terrorism put religion in the international spotlight, this realm suddenly seemed to teem with lively issues: the foreign policy predilections of the Christian Right for Israel and Southern Sudan, the complications of faith-based Western activism abroad, the Dalai Lama and Falun Gong as potential destabilizers of officially atheist but increasingly neo-Confucian China, and the Myanmar military regime's fear of a potential alliance of Burmese monks and international refugee organizations. Perhaps religious international politics had been there all along, but it suddenly became harder to ignore.

And yet the main canonical works of international relations theory, which continue to shape much empirical academic work, hardly mention religion. A handful of new works, most of them by the contributors to this volume, have begun to show how international relations scholarship can be turned to face this new issue, but most commentary about religion and international affairs remains in the realm of current events talk, area studies, or comparative domestic politics.[1]

One reason for this neglect is that mainstream international relations scholars find it difficult to integrate religious subject matter into their normal conceptual frameworks. The foundational statements of the three leading paradigms—by norms that originate from nonreligious sources, but as Toft's chapter on war shows, norms with divine authority may produce different kinds of commitment. For these reasons, a conventional theoretical tool kit that is limited to the mundane politics of states and nations may struggle to comprehend the role of religion in international relations.

Though broader than politics, let alone international politics, religion has implications for virtually every basic concept in those fields. Religion may affect, for example, who the actors in world politics are, what they want, what resources they bring to the tasks of mobilizing support and making allies, and what rules they follow. Religion may shore up the state-centered international order as it is conventionally understood and help to explain it, but it may also work at cross-purposes to that order. Religion helped to forge the system of sovereign states, yet cuts across it. Religion can help to legitimate state authority, yet may also undermine it. Religion may help to delimit the territorial boundaries of a state, yet also creates loyalties and networks that cross boundaries. Religion may reinforce ethnonational identity, bridge the gap between national identities, or divide a nation. Religion may facilitate otherwise improbable coalitions or wreck otherwise obvious ones. Religion may affect politics by shaping its organizational and network structures and by affecting its values and motives.

Some of these diverse and pervasive effects of religion might be grasped within conventional frameworks for studying international politics, but the contributors to this volume warn that a too literal application of routine methods can yield cartoonish, distorted interpretations. Religion straddles our usual methodological divides. It plays a role in constituting actors and systems of action, and it also constrains or enables actors' behavior. Religious actors can be strategic and calculating, and at the same time influenced in politics by their conception of the divine and the sacred. Conventional power calculations and religious purpose may simultaneously play a role in judgments about alliance and enmity.[9] Whichever approach a scholar chooses to conceptualize religion's place in international politics, it needs to be fully sensitive to these distinctive characteristics.

RELIGION AND PARADIGMS OF INTERNATIONAL RELATIONS

Religion has unquestionably been among the most fundamental phenomena structuring human relations throughout history, so it is reasonable to ask whether religion itself might serve as a point of departure for a new paradigm of international relations. The category of religion, especially if it is defined to encompass the varieties of secularism (as some authors do in this volume), is more broadly applicable across time and space than liberalism. At the same time, it has more empirical content than the primarily ontological category of constructivism. Both points speak in favor of religion's utility as a substantively interesting, wide-angle prism for theorizing about international relations. Despite this, religion per se cannot succeed as the core of such a paradigm.

The attempt that comes closest to enthroning religion as the central category for understanding international relations is Samuel Huntington's thesis of a clash of civilizations.[10] Huntington defines the fault lines of civilizations substantially in religious terms and argues that these boundaries will mark the main lines of contention in international relations in the coming era. Arguably, his views constitute a paradigm, one that is no more time-bound than liberalism.

The problem, though, is empirical. Huntington himself admits that lines of conflict and cleavage are typically more intense between political and cultural groups within civilizations (states and nations) than they are between civilizations. States, which are organizations that seek to monopolize violence and make public rules within a specific territory, have for some centuries shown themselves to be the indispensable units for organizing security and public administration. Recently, scholars and public commentators have debated whether globalization and other transnational processes, including religious ones, are altering the dominant position of the state in the international system. The predominant view in this debate is that, while transnational actors and processes may now loom larger in states' calculations and in shaping the environment in which states act, states continue to "set the basic rules and define the environment within which transnationals must function," as Stephen Krasner has argued.[11] Most of our contributors proceed from this assumption.

Nations, whether based on ethnicity or on common historical and institutional experiences, are the cultural units that link people to states. Religions, in contrast, are cultural units that are typically mismatched with states because they are usually nonterritorial, often too large in scale, normally lacking congruity with the boundaries of a state, and ideologically aimed at goals other than state sovereignty. Religion may matter a great deal for some processes and outcomes in world politics, but as long as nation-states are the main units of territorial security and administration, religions will exert an effect on world politics mainly through the preferences, power, perceptions, and policies of states and state-seeking nations. Huntington's clash of civilizations thesis, like any paradigm of world politics that centers on religion, is empirically unsatisfying for that reason.

A more productive approach would be to explore the ways in which religion may constitute and influence the state in world politics. Religion has shaped the formation of the state system, sometimes informing the cultural self-conception that makes a nation distinctive, influencing what nation-states want, and generating subnational and transnational actors that occupy part of the landscape in which states operate. In these ways, religion shapes processes that are close to the core of existing international relations paradigms that have the state as their basic unit.

Consequently, it will be worthwhile to consider how religion can be integrated into these existing paradigms without violating their essential assumptions. In developing scientific theories, there are moments when an effective strategy requires keeping the core assumptions of the theory few in number and homogeneous in kind in order to focus on deducing general conjectures about a small number of foundational questions. However, in applying the insights of the theory to a diverse range of empirically specific circumstances, it is necessary to relax this vigilance and introduce complementary elements so long as they meet three basic standards of progressive extension of a theoretical paradigm: namely, the added elements do not contradict the core assumptions and logic of the theory; the extensions are not loosely connected to the core but grow directly out of core questions; and new conceptual elements explain many new facts while adding only a little complexity to the theory. I want to explore whether religion meets those criteria as a complementary element in existing international relations paradigms.

It may seem a procrustean exercise to force religion to fit into paradigms that have resolutely ignored or rejected a role for it. Upon closer inspection, however, each of the three reigning paradigms offers solid bedrock on which to build a framework for studying religion and international relations. The best point of departure is in accounts of the origins of the interstate system. The realist Stephen Krasner writes, for example, about the aftermath of Europe's wars of religion and the emergence of rules of state sovereignty regarding the regulation of religion. Constructivist John Gerard Ruggie writes about the central role of the Catholic church and monasteries in the "heteronymous" international system of the late Middle Ages, a system that was in his view neither a monolithic hierarchy nor an anarchy of disconnected territorial units. Constructivist Daniel Philpott explains the role of the Protestant Reformation in the transformation of that order into the Westphalian sovereignty system. Even liberals could look to the Reformation period as a precursor to the politics of popular accountability in government, given the rising political role of literate urban middle classes,[12] the "priesthood of all believers" as a precursor to the Enlightenment and human rights thinking,[13] and the wars of religion as precursors to the formation of national identities and the idea of popular national self-determination.[14]

As these examples show, adding religion to mainstream international relations theory should be neither a matter of merely adding an explanatory variable to the existing list nor of adding the niche topic of transnational religion as an additional outcome to be explained, but of asking how religion helps to constitute the core assumptions in each of the major disciplinary paradigms. What is at stake is nothing less than the way international relations scholars conceptualize continuity and change in the international system. I want to undertake this task here not because I think that international relations theory must necessarily be contained within the three conventional paradigms, or indeed any set paradigms. Instead, I do this because many scholars gain inspiration from the paradigms and use them to structure their research on issues large and small, including war, peace, cooperation, economic integration and autarky, alliances, and governance, that have been central to all the paradigms. For those scholars, I want to explore how a more explicit focus on religion can enrich their paradigmatic insights, starting with the particularly hard case of realism.

RELIGION AND REALIST THEORY

Kenneth Waltz says that he leaves culture (and therefore religion) out of his structural theory of international politics not because it is substantively unimportant but because building a parsimonious theory requires focusing only on core assumptions about the relationship of "structure" to "process".[15] However, even by this stringent criterion, a case can be made that realists should pay closer attention to religion's role in constituting the international system's structure and shaping action within it. To show this, I will begin with the checklist of central elements that Waltz says structures politics in any international system.

I start here because the parsimonious hard core of structural realism stands out most starkly in Waltz, whose writings therefore constitute the most difficult test for the integration of religion into the semi-core layer of realist theory directly adjacent to the hard core. Although such moves have sometimes been criticized as theoretically degenerative, they have been made by almost everyone who has tried to adapt structural realism for use as a theory of foreign policy in specific situations, including Robert Jervis (who added offensive and defensive military technology to the concept of the security dilemma in anarchy),[16] Stephen Walt (who added perception of threat to balance of power theory),[17] Randall Schweller (who allows for theoretically exogenous variations in state goals),[18] defensive realists (who bring in ideology and domestic politics to explain anomalies that diverge from sound realist strategy),[19] and neoclassical realists (who show how domestic political and ideological mobilization to face international challenges can divert foreign policy from the expectations of more parsimonious realist theory).[20] These elaborations on core realist theory are theoretically progressive insofar as they are parsimonious and shed light on realism's core causal mechanisms, such as the security dilemma in anarchy and the balance of power. Some of them explain how the anarchical system gets structured, whereas others explore the effect of actors' preferences and perceptions on their choice of strategies under anarchy. By these standards, religion, too, can successfully contribute to elaborating realism's core insights.

Waltz defines a system's structure in terms of the principle by which its units are organized, their functional differentiation, and the distribution of power across them. Religion matters for all three. For good measure, I add a discussion of religion and "the national interest," a quintessential realist lodestar.

THE ORDERING PRINCIPLE OF THE INTERNATIONAL SYSTEM

Waltz begins with the basic principle that orders the political system—how the units are arranged relative to each other. He offers two possibilities: hierarchy, a system of rule-governed authority relations between units, and anarchy, a system in which units seeking to survive lack any authority above them to set and enforce rules or guarantee agreements between them. Empirically, he notes that politics within states is normally hierarchical, whereas politics between states is normally anarchical.

Realists typically hold that international politics has been anarchical since time immemorial. All the basics are already in Thucydides. Even in the Middle Ages, when lip service was paid to the pope and wars were sometimes justified as crusades, realists typically argue that all the key players in the international system—whether principalities, city-states, knightly orders, or monasteries—behaved like self-help units using force opportunistically to survive and prosper in the absence of reliable rules enforced by a system-level sovereign.[21] While the size and internal organization of units has varied over time, states, empires, castellated manors, fortified abbeys, and ethnic groups in failed states all remain in the grip of the basic ordering principle of international anarchy.[22] In principle, realists admit that anarchy could give way to hierarchy—for example, if a single unit, such as the ancient state of Chin, should conquer the rest of the relevant actors in an interacting system[23]—but they find this empirically rare and logically unlikely because the basic ordering principle of anarchy tends to be self-perpetuating through the mechanism of unit self-help and the balance of power.

Realists tend to treat religions as hypocritical, marginal, or irrelevant to politics insofar as units of all kinds, whether secular or religious, must act the same way if they are to play an effective role in international politics. Such a dismissive view is unwarranted. Religion may play a decisive role in determining the ordering principle of the system in the first place, as well as significantly influencing the behavior of units in the system once it is constituted.

This should not be surprising for realists, given their emphasis on the state as the central unit of international politics. From a Weberian standpoint, states are organizations that monopolize legitimate violence within a territory, and religion is often the trump card in claims to social legitimacy. How those trumps are dealt out and reshuffled can profoundly shape the nature of the international system.

It is true that most of history has been ordered as anarchy, but not all of it. Hierarchically structured empires like Rome and ancient China have sometimes subordinated entire regions, interacting strategically only with isolated, peripheral barbarians incapable of coordinating a policy of balance of power.[24] Macrohistorical sociologists Michael Mann and Rodney Stark show how religions facilitated the collective action and legitimacy that such civilization-sized, multilinguistic empires needed to survive and prosper.[25] The size and shape of the empire could depend heavily on which social networks were amenable to penetration by the empire's religious ideology. The rise of a new religion, such as Islam, could directly give rise to a new empire, and a schism within religion, such as the Protestant Reformation, could break down imperial hierarchy and return it to anarchy. Materialists may try to reduce these dynamics to some underlying military or economic determinant, but it is not clear that such historical reductionism is empirically convincing.[26]

Moreover, not all anarchies are systems of sovereign states. John Gerard Ruggie identifies a distinct pattern of international order, which he follows the historian Friedrich Meinecke in calling heteronomy, a system of multiple relationships of normative obligation that cut across territorial boundaries. In this system, hierarchical ties of religious and feudal obligation to persons and organizations coexist with simultaneous obligations to a territorial authority in anarchy. Wars occur, and the goals of security and domination motivate action, but who is on what side, and what they are fighting for, cannot be fully understood without appreciating the intricate web of religious and social obligations.

Religion helps to order the system. Moreover, change in religion can disorder and reorder the international system. The Reformation touched off civil wars within the Habsburg Empire and other territorial jurisdictions, which spread through transnational networks linking like-minded actors with common strategic concerns in different territorial entities.[27] Territorial leaders prospered when they could harness popular religious enthusiasms to their purposes, and conversely, religious groups survived only if they received backing from a territorial unit. This dovetailing of strategic and religious logic, combined with the military and ideological stalemate between Catholicism and Protestantism, led to the Westphalian sovereignty system. In this sense, the anarchical European states system enshrined in realist balance of power theory was constituted in part through the dynamic of religious schism.

Religion not only plays a central role in constituting the basic ordering principle of the system, but it can also shape specific behavioral choices and patterns within an ordered system. This is most obvious in a system like Ruggie's heteronymy, where lines of transnational religious authority directly shape the allegiances and goals of armed actors, but religion can also shape behavior in pure anarchies. For example, offensive and defensive realists disagree at the margins about the relative merits of more and less aggressive tactics under strategic uncertainty. Consequently, it seems highly possible—and completely compatible with realism—that different religious cultures might develop different strategic cultures that shape choices within this band of ambiguity. Indeed, Monica Toft shows that Islamic strategic culture, when confronting contemporary processes such as popular self-determination, is measurably more bellicist than average.[28]

On the other hand, religious affinity need not always trump realist strategic calculation when they are in direct conflict. Shia militias sometimes help each other against Sunnis and Americans, but sometimes work with Sunnis or Americans against rival cosectarians. Sometimes birds of a feather flock together, but when cosectarians are the most urgent threat, the enemy of my enemy is my friend, no matter what his religion. This realist dynamic should not be confused, however, with the tendency for fraternal competitors to "fly apart" in ideological movements that can inherently have only one authority, such as the Soviet Union and China under Communism and the Syrian and Iraqi Ba'ath socialists.[29] These communities of belief and legitimacy fight because they share a common culture, not because culture is hypocrisy.

DIFFERENTIATION OF UNITS

Waltz uses the concept of differentiation in a limited way, focusing only on the question of whether the units in a system have specialized functions. In hierarchies, the units do participate in a functionally differentiated division of labor; in anarchies, they do not, because a substantial degree of self-sufficiency in the territorial state improves its chance of survival. Functional differentiation means interdependence and therefore vulnerability, which states in anarchy seek to minimize.

Ruggie's critique of Waltz pushes toward a deeper conception of differentiation, based on Émile Durkheim's distinction between primitive, functionally identical units, differentiated only by territory, and more advanced, functionally differentiated units participating in an interdependent division of labor within a larger territory. This echoes the distinction in modernization theory between undifferentiated *Gemeinschaft* (or traditional society) and differentiated *Gesellschaft* (or modern market society). Following Durkheim, Ruggie says that the increasing "dynamic density" of growing population and economic activity in late medieval society broke down political and economic barriers between small, undifferentiated local units and led to the creation of modern states with an interdependent division of labor on a larger territorial scale.[30]

Before modernization, political authority was not as sharply differentiated from religious authority. Kings ruled by divine right and wielded religious authority over their subjects, and popes and abbots had their own military "divisions." After modernization, secular political authority became more differentiated from religious authority organizationally and conceptually. Legitimacy of rule emanated from the self-determining people or nation, or at any rate from the claim to rule on their behalf. The state often stripped religious organizations of their temporal powers. In some countries such as France and Turkey, differentiation took the form of laicism—opposition between state and church. In others such as the United States, differentiation took the form of the appropriation of a least-common-denominator generic religiosity by the state and even-handed toleration of religions, which were pushed into the private sphere.[31]

This secular differentiation of politics from religion has had profound consequences for international politics. As Anthony Marx has argued, the wars of religion following the Protestant Reformation were simply a transitional stage on the way to the wars of secular nationalism that began with the French Revolution and continue down to the present.[32] Gellner remarks that for Durkheim, society worshipped itself covertly through its religion, whereas under secular nationalism society dropped all pretense of the sacred and began to worship itself "brazenly and openly."[33] Most realists accept that nationalism is a supercharger of international competition, though they see it as heightened in states that occupy a particularly vulnerable position in the international system.[34] The new scholarship of secularism, including secular nationalism, emphasizes that secularism is defined through its stance toward religion and is best understood as a type of belief system that occupies the same category as religion.[35]

More specifically, secular nationalism is also important to contemporary international politics because of the backlash against it in many developing societies, including Islamic and Hindu ones, which see secular nationalism as a European import that failed to create a working state and instead brought a corrupt, alien form of rule. In its place, religious nationalists, sometimes mislabeled religious fundamentalists, are seeking to replace it with a more authentic, more effective state-building ideology. This contributes to the zeitgeist of a clash of civilizations that has so marked international politics over the past decade or more.[36]

DISTRIBUTION OF POWER

Waltz's third defining element of an international system is the distribution of power across its units, in particular the number of great powers. Waltz's view of power tends to be quite materialist, but there is no reason that it has to be. Any sociologically sophisticated theory of social power has to recognize that power, including material power, rests on some combination of coercion, legitimate authority, persuasion, and mobilization of support. Religion might be central to generating power by almost any of these means. Most obviously, religious enthusiasm has been an effective motivator of military rebellion in times and places as diverse as the phenomenally deadly millenarian Christian Taiping Rebellion in nineteenth-century China, Europe's devastating wars of religion in the sixteenth and seventeenth centuries, as well as Islamic jihadi fighting today.

Religious actors might deploy their own distinctive instruments of power to try to accomplish the same objectives that secular actors seek through different means. Democratic regime change, for example, has been a goal sought in different settings over the past two decades by means of military intervention, economic sanctions, secular persuasion, and liberation theology. According to Samuel Huntington's list of causes of the "third wave" of democratization in the 1980s, transnational religious trends, especially in the Catholic Church, were among the most central and efficacious.[37]

Religion may delimit the scope of an actor's power or influence which tools can be deployed in which social settings. NGO campaigns against female genital cutting, for example, have found that the same techniques that work in Christian communities get nowhere in otherwise similar Muslim communities unless the local imam agrees to tell his followers that cutting is not required by the Koran. Likewise, military occupation may produce worse outcomes in alien religious communities.[38] Furthermore, power may be used less discriminately across religious lines. Suicide terrorists seem more willing to use deadly force against civilian targets of a different religion, for example, because they are more likely to see the victims as less than fully human.[39] However, Alexander Downes's study concludes that targeting of civilians is not more likely across civilizational divides, which he codes largely by religion.[40]

INTERESTS

Unit interests are not explicitly listed as a system-defining element in Waltz's theory, in part because the overriding interest in survival through self-help is seen as a direct implication of anarchy as the system's ordering principle. However, Waltz acknowledges that states can and do seek a range of goals from mere survival to system-wide domination.

Waltz does not attempt to subsume variation in goals under his structural theory, leaving open the possibility that interests might vary with unit characteristics such as religion. However, variation in interests is a more central problem for Waltz's structural theory than he admits. A state's drive for hegemony is the mainspring that animates the balance-of-power dynamic at the heart of Waltz's theory, and religion could be one possible motivation for such expansion. In this sense, religion could be one of the stimuli that set his systemic processes in motion.

Other realists, most notably offensive realist John Mearsheimer, try to explain this variation in goals based on the state's position in the international system. For example, does the state have a chance to solve its security problems by becoming a regional hegemon? But if regional homogeneity of religion affects the feasibility of achieving such hegemony, because people may not balance as forcefully against culturally similar conquerors whose rule they might be willing to accept, then religion would be a strategically significant structural property of the system.

Moreover, survival-seeking behavior in the international system will depend on the actors' theories of what it takes to survive. Religion (or secularism) can affect this in diverse and significant ways: which allies can be trusted; is international rivalry a Manichaean identity struggle or a limited Lockean competition; what kinds of actors should be acknowledged as having the standing to participate in international relations? Waltz says that the population of states adapts to the systemic requirements for survival through a combination of natural selection and socialization to the system by experiencing rewards and punishments for behavior. However, he admits that selection is the less-common mechanism, since states rarely die. Insofar as socialization is the more prevalent, though more ambiguous, mechanism of adaptation, this leaves considerable latitude for interpretation of rewards and punishments through the prism of culture, including religion. Some of Toft's arguments about the greater war-proneness of Islamic societies may operate through this mechanism.

Finally, Waltz writes as if the national interest of a state in survival in its existing form can be taken for granted. But empirically, we know that the nation-state is not an unproblematic billiard ball. The interest of the state as a territorial administrative unit is often in a vexed relationship with the interest of the nation as a cultural (sometimes religious-cultural) unit. When administrative boundaries are mismatched with ethnic or religious boundaries that define political identities, all hell breaks loose, as exemplified in the Thirty Years' War, pan-Arabism between 1947 and 1973, and political Islam more recently.[41]

In sum, religion has played a central role in processes that lie at the core of the realist conception of international politics: the ordering of the system itself, the nature of its units, their power and interests, and the strategies through which they seek to achieve those interests.

RELIGION AND CONSTRUCTIVIST THEORY

Constructivist international relations theory would seem to provide friendly terrain for the role of religion in international politics because of its emphasis on ideas, norms, identity, and culture. Although no single work captures constructivism's full intellectual diversity, Alexander Wendt's *Social Theory of International Politics* comes closest to being its canonical text. Neither the term *religion* nor any specific religions appear in the book's index. This is not accidental. While Wendt notes that the domestic-level cultures that units bring to the international situation matter for the development of international-level culture, his main interest lies in the way that units create international-level "cultures of anarchy" through their interactions. His prominent version of constructivist theory is therefore not the most religion-friendly statement of this approach. Even so, his widely used categories do seem to offer a role to religion in thinking about international culture.

Wendt distinguishes three cultures of anarchy: the Hobbesian war of all against all; Lockean self-interested competition restrained by the recognition of sovereign units' right to exist; and Kantian friendship expressed as the expectation of mutual non-violence. It is easy to imagine how different expressions of religion could have an elective affinity with these different cultures of anarchy (setting aside the question of causal direction): Hobbesian enmity coinciding with Manichaean religion; Lockean restrained competition coinciding with religion-based rules of restraint in warfare; and Kantian friendship based in religious (or secular) tenets of common identity or altruism. This kind of hypothesis might not hold up under serious empirical scrutiny, but at least superficially it seems loosely consistent with Toft's findings about the Hobbesian war-proneness of transitional Islamic societies, the historical link between the Catholic just war tradition and the development of Lockean international laws of war, and the role of religious dissenters in the development of Kantian international ethics. Another hypothesis might be that Hobbesian cultures of anarchy spread during the early mobilization phase of a proselytizing religion (early Islam or the Protestant Reformation), Lockean cultures emerge in the wake of their routinization, and Kantian ones are associated with the differentiation of state power and religious authority.

Within each of the three cultures, Wendt discusses three successively deeper degrees of the internalization of culture based in turn on force, price, and legitimacy. Each of these might have its expression in terms of religion (again setting aside the question of which is cause and which is effect). Thus, a shallow internalization of a culture of anarchy based on the recognition of force would fit with an Augustinian-style religious doctrine of the "two kingdoms" of the sacred and the mundane. A somewhat more internalized culture of anarchy based on the costs and benefits of self-restraint would fit with the acceptance of rules based on religion (or on secular philosophy) that regulate in-group/out-group comity, hospitality, and conflict. Both Islam and secular international law have such rules. A more deeply internalized culture of anarchy legitimated by the sacred would fit with religions or secular philosophies that merge morality, identity, and cosmology with war, peace, or global human rights. Examples of the latter could include Hobbesian warrior cults or Kantian Mennonite pacifist humanitarians.

Wendt's final theoretical move is to posit four "master variables" that may change the culture of anarchy by undermining egoistic identities and promoting collective ones: namely, interdependence, common fate, homogeneity, and self-restraint. Religion might be relevant to all four. Cultural interdependence might be enhanced by networks of theological diffusion, persuasion, and emulation. An example would be the role of networks of transnational diffusion in creating Protestant collective identities that led to the Lockean Westphalian culture of anarchy. A sense of common fate might arise from being attacked by a powerful religion-based aggressor. Homogeneity may be enhanced by the emergence of a common religious identity. Finally, self-restraint could be enhanced by religious rules of behavior toward in-group members or toward all humans. In contrast, self-restraint might be lessened in periods of mass religious mobilization, such as the Protestant Reformation or the recent surge in political Islamism. These of course are all empirical conjectures, which might be wrong. Buddhist philosophy emphasizes generalized self-restraint, for example, but Theraveda Buddhist–dominated societies such as Sri Lanka and Thailand have behaved coercively toward religious minorities.

In short, a prism that focuses on religion might add a great deal to constructivist theorizing about international relations despite the absence of an explicit discussion of anything religious in that approach's most prominent theoretical text. If Wendt's state-centric approach has room for religion, other constructivist approaches that focus on transnational processes or domestic sources of foreign policy can accommodate religion even more easily by tracing the impact of religious norms, identities, and principled networks. Margaret Keck and Kathryn Sikkink note the role of missionaries as the "norms entrepreneurs" of the nineteenth century, for example, in the anti–foot binding campaign in China.[42] (In our own volume, Michael Barnett examines the religious ideas that underpin contemporary secular humanitarianism.) Martha Finnemore and Gary Bass are debating the extent to which the impulse for humanitarian intervention was limited to sympathy for co-religionists in the nineteenth century, and consequently whether today's more universalistic humanitarian discourse constitutes a fundamental change in norms.[43] Neta Crawford notes the role of religious arguments in changing norms regarding colonialism and slavery.[44] Alastair Johnston and David Kang note the role of Confucian ideas in Chinese military strategy and in the exercise of regional Chinese political hegemony.[45] Thus, a constructivist look at religion and international relations encompasses not only those obviously norm-infused issues such as human rights but also military relations between the great powers.

Daniel Nexon's chapter in this book, however, warns against a simplistic treatment of religion as a pat identity furnished with essentialized norms and values. Instead, he uses the example of the politics of the Reformation to show how religion works as a complex discursive field in which political claims play out in a process that involves religious conviction and strategic calculation in a shifting configuration of transnational alliances. His approach draws on constructivism—indeed it would not be possible without the notion of the social construction of political reality through discourse—but it cannot be reduced to reified norms, identities, ideas, and symbols. In a sense, Nexon is being truer to the original insights of constructivism than are such reifiers when he points out that wine in transubstantiation was not just a *symbol* of Christ's blood for the religious state builders; their belief that it really *was* his blood affected the political implications of the Reformation.

This raises important substantive questions for research on religion and international politics. Does the divine character of norms in religion-based transnational advocacy networks, for example, make them work differently from superficially analogous secular norms? How is social construction different when it ascends to the plane of the sacred? All of the chapters in this book engage this question.[46]

RELIGION AND LIBERALISM

Like Wendt's paradigmatic statement of constructivist international relations theory, Michael Doyle's foundational articles on democratic peace and liberal international relations theory make no mention of religion except for a throwaway remark about the elected "theocratic" regime of the Boers.[47] This might not surprise those who see liberalism as a thoroughly secular ideology and thus antithetical to religion. However, the equal and opposite cliché may be more compelling: liberalism arose in the wake of the Protestant Reformation and the Protestant ethic of the capitalist middle class. As Hurd points out in this volume, much liberal Enlightenment thought was grounded in a Christian form of secularism. In international affairs, Protestant dissenters operating in the conducive environment of Protestant-dominated liberal democratic hegemonic states were in the vanguard of the peace and free trade movements and the movement to suppress slavery.[48] Hence, in this view: no Reformation, no liberal peace. The liberalism of revolutionary France is the exception that proves the rule: a Catholic society that undergoes a laicist rejection of religion fails to institutionalize liberal democracy, turns instead to populist nationalism, and tries to conquer the world.

What are the implications for liberal international relations theory of the view that liberal secularism has strong religious roots? Liberalism's trademark claim, that liberal democracies do not fight wars against each other, has various explanations, most of them traceable back to Kant. Democracies are prudent because the average citizen who bears the cost of war constrains the government. Democracies are free-trading, so have incentives not to disrupt beneficial commerce. Democracies have an open marketplace of ideas, so they make better-informed choices and are easier for outsiders to understand and trust. Finally, democracies share a common identity and sense of political legitimacy, so they do not consider each other to be a threat. Insofar as we agree with Hurd that Kant is a forerunner of what she calls "Judeo-Christian secularism," this might strengthen the genealogical claim that the democratic peace should mainly be understood in terms of liberalism's normative roots in religion rather than in terms of mechanical procedures of electoral accountability and checks and balances. This in turn could have implications for efforts to promote the spread of democracy and expectations about how likely it is the democratic peace can be extended. Africanists, for example, are debating whether simply holding elections in illiberal societies can contribute to the development of democratic accountability and its benefits for social peace, or whether the whole package of Kantian preconditions, including deeply rooted normative change, is needed for the democratic miracle to happen.[49]

One reason that some liberal international relations scholars have underestimated the role of religion is that they implicitly accept the liberal modernization theory of political development—namely, that historical modernization is a linear process in which liberal formations such as capitalism, secularism, and democracy all progress together.[50] In this view, religion drops out of the equation as societies become more modern and democratic. The current resurgence of politicized religion shows, however, that political development produces multiple modernities.[51] In some of these trajectories, frustration with unresponsive secular government stimulates increasing pressure for mass political participation. When the political consequences of mass movements of this kind spill across international boundaries, this becomes a lively subject for international relations theory. A properly broadened version of liberalism, as the international paradigm that addresses political development and the emergence of modern regime types, is highly relevant to understanding these societal trends and their consequences for global politics.

Not all scholars working within the liberal paradigm have left out religion. Andrew Moravcsik, for example, includes religious identities in his characterization of the liberal paradigm as a source of societal groups' preferences or interests.[52] This straightforward approach should work well for many purposes.

NEOLIBERAL INSTITUTIONALISM

Religion has a less obvious connection to the other branch of the liberal paradigm of international relations, the neoliberal institutionalism of Robert Keohane. His foundational *After Hegemony* stresses the role of multilateral institutions in facilitating cooperation among states by reducing information asymmetries, coordinating bargains across issue areas, and magnifying the long-term reputational consequences of short-term opportunism.[53] This highly rationalistic book makes no mention of religion.

And yet if we step far back and look from Max Weber's vantage point, religion constitutes one of humankind's earliest steps to rationalize and institutionalize society. In place of the patent irrationalism of shamanism and witchcraft, religion proposes an intellectually coherent interpretation of natural, supernatural, and social reality, and creates a specialized institution to carry out religious ritual and to transmit and develop religious doctrine. Religious organizations were thus forerunners of modern bureaucratic secular organizations. They carried out political and economic functions, and in some societies and issue domains, they still do.

Neoliberal institutionalism is concerned with international organizations, which are of course secular, notwithstanding the religious roots or character of some quasi-official NGOs like the Red Cross and Red Crescent. Even so, Michael Barnett and Martha Finnemore describe the authority and power of international organizations in terms that sound more characteristic of religious organizations: delegated authority (viz., divine right), moral authority, expert authority (viz. specialists in ritual and doctrine), the power to classify the world, the power to fix meanings, and the diffusion of norms.[54] In areas such as human rights, international organizations—for example, the International Criminal Court—compete directly with religious organizations in attempts to classify behavior, affix meaning to it, and promote norms. Michael Ignatieff contends that human rights dogma is the new profession of faith of secular humanism, and the institutions that are the keepers of this doctrine are more concerned with affirmation of faith than in getting results.[55] In this sense, the claim that liberal secularisms occupy the same terrain as religions applies not only to worldviews but also to some international institutions.

In short, although the liberal international relations canon downplays religion and tends to take its own secularism for granted, religion may have played a formative role in liberal ideas, and religion may share some of the functional characteristics of liberal, secular, multilateral institutions.

Religion can be seen as integral to structures and processes at the core of the main intellectual traditions and research programs in international relations theory, though religion has rarely been the subject of explicit attention in any of them. Terrorism justified in the name of religion has brought this topic to the attention of the community of scholars studying international politics. However, the reason to think harder about the role religion should occupy in international studies is not mainly to understand current problems better, but to gain a deeper insight into the core concepts used to study international issues of all types.

"Mainstreaming" religion in international relations theory does entail risks, however, in both directions. One risk is that religious matters can be flattened to a degree that robs them of their distinctive character in an effort to plug them into inhospitable theories. Sometimes scholars have done this quite consciously as an explicit theoretical assumption—for example, Robert Pape's argument that religion matters for his strategic theory of terrorism only in that suicide bombers find it easier to dehumanize targets of a different religion. Although Toft in this volume treats religion as a variable in her strategic theory of violence, she does not flatten it to this degree, since she engages with the content of religious ideas and organizational forms. At the other end of the spectrum, Nexon does not flatten religion at all in addressing the concerns of international relations theory.

He treats religion as retaining its sacred character even while showing that its discursive frame encompasses strategic calculations. Different researchers will make different choices regarding this issue as they try to mainstream religion into general international relations theories.

The opposite risk is that healthy theories that have usefully illuminated international processes without much reliance on religion will be adulterated by bringing in religion in ways that contradict their core assumptions. International relations theorists have long differed in their tastes for parsimonious purity versus eclecticism. In bringing religion into their work, they will have to make choices, which will be fine as long as those choices are conscious ones whose costs are explicitly considered. If it is true, as most of the contributors here believe, that religion plays a significant and increasing role in international politics, more scholars will want to find ways to integrate it into their conceptual frameworks.

The chapters in this book embody a variety of choices on these issues. All are written by scholars who have made recognized contributions to international relations theory. These authors include the leading lights among those who are integrating religion into the academic field of international politics in a methodologically self-aware way. Together, their work provides a rich menu of choices for thoughtful readers to draw upon in designing their own approaches to mainstreaming religion in international relations theory.

NOTES

1. Eva Bellin, "Faith in Politics: New Trends in the Study of Religion and Politics," *World Politics* 60, no. 2 (January 2008): 315–347; Kenneth D. Wald and Clyde Wilcox, "Getting Religion: Has Political Science Rediscovered the Faith Factor?" *American Political Science Review* 100, no. 4 (November 2006): 523–529.

2. Alexander Wendt, *Social Theory of International Politics* (Cambridge: Cambridge University Press, 1999); Daniel Philpott, *Revolutions in Sovereignty: How Ideas Shaped Modern International Relations* (Princeton: Princeton University Press, 2001).

3. Samuel P. Huntington, "The Clash of Civilizations?" *Foreign Affairs* 72, no. 3 (Summer 1993): 22–49. Jonathan Fox and Shmuel Sandler, *Bringing Religion Into International Relations* (New York: Palgrave, 2004): 1–2, 9–33, 166–172, discuss the resistance of traditional international relations paradigms to religion, arguing that religion should be taken into account, while admitting that "religion is not the main driving force behind international relations" (p. 7).

4. Elizabeth Shakman Hurd, *The Politics of Secularism in International Relations* (Princeton: Princeton University Press, 2008).

5. Daniel H. Nexon, *The Struggle for Power in Early Modern Europe: Religious Conflict, Dynastic Empires, and International Change* (Princeton: Princeton University Press, 2009), and chapter 6 of this book.

6. John Gerard Ruggie, "Continuity and Transformation in the World Polity," *World Politics* 34, no. 2 (January 1983): 261–285; Daniel Philpott, "The Challenge of September 11 to Secularism in International Relations," *World Politics* 55, no. 1 (October 2002): 66–95.

7. Monica Duffy Toft, chapter 5 of this book.

8. Philpott and Shah, chapter 2 of this book.

9. See especially Nexon, *The Struggle for Power in Early Modern Europe*, and chapter 2.

10. Fox and Sandler, *Bringing Religion*, 15. See also Elizabeth Shakman Hurd, chapter 3 of this book.

11. Stephen D. Krasner, "Power Politics, Institutions, and Transnational Relations," in *Bringing Transnational Relations Back In*, ed. Thomas Risse-Kappen, (Cambridge: Cambridge University Press, 1995), 257–279, at 279. See also Jeff Haynes, "Transnational Religious Actors and International Politics," *Third World Quarterly* 22, no. 2 (2001): 143–158, and Sidney Tarrow, *The New Transnational Activism* (Cambridge: Cambridge University Press, 2005).

12. Hendrik Spruyt, *The Sovereign State and Its Competitors* (Princeton: Princeton University Press, 1994).

13. Micheline R. Ishay, *The History of Human Rights* (Berkeley: University of California Press, 2004), chapter 2.

14. Anthony W. Marx, *Faith in Nation* (Oxford: Oxford University Press, 2003).

15. Kenneth N. Waltz, *Theory of International Politics* (New York: Addison-Wesley, 1979), 82.

16. Robert Jervis, "Cooperation Under the Security Dilemma," *World Politics*, 30, no. 2 (January 1978): 167–214.

17. Stephen M. Walt, *The Origins of Alliances* (Ithaca: Cornell University Press, 1987).

18. Randall Schweller, "Neorealism's Status Quo Bias: What Security Dilemma?" *Security Studies* 5, no. 3 (Spring 1996): 90–121.

19. Stephen Van Evera, *Causes of War: Power and the Roots of Conflict* (Ithaca: Cornell University Press, 1999); Jack Snyder, *Myths of Empire: Domestic Politics and International Ambition* (Ithaca: Cornell University Press, 1991).

20. Thomas J. Christensen, *Useful Adversaries: Grand Strategy, Domestic Mobilization, and Sino-American Conflict, 1947–1958* (Princeton: Princeton University Press, 1996); Colin Dueck, *Reluctant Crusaders: Power, Culture, and Change in American Grand Strategy* (Princeton: Princeton University Press, 2006).

21. Markus Fischer, "Feudal Europe, 800–1300: Communal Discourse and Conflictual Practices," *International Organization* 46, no. 2 (spring 1992): 427–466; Rodney Hall and Friedrich Kratochwil, "Medieval Tales: Neorealist 'Science' and the Abuse

of History," and Fischer, "On Context, Facts, and Norms," *International Organization* 47, no. 3 (summer 1993): 479–500.

22. Robert Gilpin, *War and Change in World Politics* (Cambridge: Cambridge University Press, 1981); Barry Posen, "The Security Dilemma and Ethnic Conflict, *Survival* 35, no. 1 (Spring 1993): 27–47.

23. Victoria Tin-bor Hui, *War and State Formation in Ancient China and Early Modern Europe* (New York: Cambridge University Press, 2005).

24. Edward N. Luttwak, *The Grand Strategy of the Roman Empire from the First Century A.D. to the Third* (Baltimore: Johns Hopkins University Press, 1976); Alastair Iain Johnston, *Cultural Realism: Strategic Culture and Grand Strategy in Chinese History* (Princeton: Princeton University Press, 1995).

25. Michael Mann, *The Sources of Social Power*, vol. 1 (Cambridge: Cambridge University Press, 1986), chapters 9–10; Rodney Stark, *The Rise of Christianity* (Princeton: Princeton University Press, 1996).

26. See Spruyt, *The Sovereign State and Its Competitors*; Daniel Philpott, *Revolutions in Sovereignty* (Princeton: Princeton University Press, 2001); and chapter 6 in this book.

27. Nexon, chapter 6 of this book.

28. Toft, chapter 5 of this book.

29. Richard Lowenthal, *World Communism: The Disintegration of a Secular Faith* (New York: Oxford University Press, 1964).

30. Also relevant is the very Durkheimian book by Ernest Gellner, *Nations and Nationalism* (Ithaca: Cornell University Press, 1984), with its central distinction between Agraria and Industria.

31. Hurd, chapter 3 of this book.

32. Marx, *Fate of Nations*.

33. Gellner, *Nations and Nationalism*, 56.

34. John J. Mearsheimer, "Back to the Future: Instability in Europe after the Cold War," *International Security* 15, no. 1 (summer 1990): 21, 25.

35. Hurd, chapter 3 of this book.

36. Mark Juergensmeyer, *Global Rebellion: Religious Challenges to the Secular State, from Christian Militias to al Qaeda* (Berkeley: University of California Press, 2008).

37. Samuel P. Huntington, *The Third Wave: Democratization in the Late Twentieth Century* (Norman: University of Oklahoma Press, 1991).

38. Michael Hechter, "Alien Rule and Its Discontents" (paper presented at the annual meeting of the American Sociological Association, Montreal, 2006).

39. Robert A. Pape, *Dying to Win: The Strategic Logic of Suicide Terrorism* (New York: Random House, 2006).

40. Alexander B. Downes, *Targeting Civilians in War* (Ithaca: Cornell University Press, 2008).

41. Benjamin Miller, *States, Nations, and the Great Powers: The Sources of Regional War and Peace* (Cambridge: Cambridge University Press, 2007).

42. Margaret E. Keck and Kathryn Sikkink, *Activists Beyond Borders*, (Ithaca: Cornell University Press, 1998), 63.

43. Martha Finnemore, *The Purpose of Intervention* (Ithaca: Cornell University Press, 2003); Gary J. Bass, *Freedom's Battle: The Origins of Humanitarian Intervention* (New York: Alfred A. Knopf, 2008).

44. Neta Crawford, *Argument and Change in World Politics: Ethics, Decolonization, and Humanitarian Intervention* (Cambridge: Cambridge University Press, 2002), 138–149, 174–5, 180, 198–99.

45. Alastair Iain Johnston, *Cultural Realism*; David C. Kang, *China Rising: Peace, Power, and Order in East Asia* (New York: Columbia University Press, 2007).

46. See also Aaron P. Bosenecker and Leslie Vinjamuri, "Religious and Secular Actors, the 'Doers' of Transitional Justice" (paper presented at the annual meeting of the International Studies Association, New York, NY, February 15–18, 2009).

47. Michael W. Doyle, "Kant, Liberal Legacies, and Foreign Affairs," pts. 1 and 2, *Philosophy and Public Affairs* 12, no. 3 (Summer 1983): 205–223; 4 (Fall 1983): 323-353.

48. Chaim D. Kaufmann and Robert A. Pape, "Explaining Costly International Moral Action: Britain's Sixty-Year Campaign Against the Atlantic Slave Trade," *International Organization* 53, no. 4 (Fall 1999): 631–668.

49. Staffan Lindberg, *Democracy and Elections in Africa* (Baltimore: Johns Hopkins University Press, 2006).

50. For background on such assumptions and a critique, see Philip S. Gorski, "Historicizing the Secularization Debate: Church, State, and Society in Late Medieval Modern Europe, ca. 1300 to 1700," *American Sociological Review* 65, no. 1 (February 2000): 138–167.

51. Shmuel Eisenstadt, "Multiple Modernities," *Daedalus* 129, no. 1 (Winter 2000): 1–29; Peter J. Katzenstein, "Multiple Modernities as Limits to Secular Europeanization?" in *Religion in an Expanding Europe*, ed. Timothy A. Byrnes and Peter J. Katzenstein, (Cambridge: Cambridge University Press, 2006), 9–10.

52. Andrew Moravcsik, "Taking Preferences Seriously: A Liberal Theory of International Politics," *International Organization* 51, no. 4 (Autumn 1997): 513–554, at 526.

53. Robert Keohane, *After Hegemony: Cooperation and Discord in the World Political Economy* (Princeton: Princeton University Press, 1984).

54. Michael Barnett and Martha Finnemore, *Rules for the World: International Organizations in Global Politics* (Ithaca: Cornell University Press, 2004): 22–34.

55. Michael Ignatieff, *Human Rights as Politics and Idolatry* (Princeton: Princeton University Press, 2001). See also Stephen Hopgood, "Sinners in the Hands of an Angry ICC" (paper presented at the annual meeting of the International Studies Association, New York, NY, February 15–18, 2009).

2. THE FALL AND RISE OF RELIGION IN INTERNATIONAL RELATIONS

History and Theory

TIMOTHY SAMUEL SHAH AND DANIEL PHILPOTT

Religion has returned to global politics with ferocity and international relations theory has little to say about it. This is because the theory, like the phenomenon of international relations itself, has been secular from its very origins in the seventeenth century. This secularism served perfectly well for the
ensuing three centuries, during which global politics itself became progres-
sively more secular, culminating in the late 1960s. In 1968, the great sociologist Peter Berger spoke for intellectuals across the West when he told the *New
York Times* that "by the 21st century, religious believers are likely to be found
only in small sects, huddled together to resist a worldwide secular culture."[1]
But this will no longer do. Since that time, religion has surged in its political influence in every region of the globe and within virtually every religious
tradition, fueling democracy movements, terrorism, peace agreements, civil
war, reconciliation initiatives, economic development programs, transforma-
tions of domestic regimes, and laws that promote its cultural ends. In an act
of uncommon scholarly humility, Berger renounced his previous stance in
1999, pronouncing the world to be as "furiously religious as it ever was."[2] If
international relations theory, or comparative politics for that matter, is going
to understand religion, it will have to discard its erstwhile secularism and develop concepts that describe and theorize religious actors and religious ends
as precisely that: religious.

This chapter develops these claims in four sections. The first section explains how international relations took shape through a secularizing set of historical events—the transition from medieval Europe to the modern system of sovereign states that was consolidated around the Peace of Westphalia in 1648—as well as how the secular character of these events became ensconced in traditions of international relations thought. Next, we argue that secularization—not in the sense of a general decline in popular religious belief, but rather in the sense of a decline in religion's influence on politics—deepened over the next three centuries, first in Europe, then subsequently in politics around the globe. But then a sharp reversal occurred, and over the past four decades, religion's influence on politics has grown, abruptly challenging the secular character of both global politics and international relations theory. The third section charts this reversal. We end with a fourth section that explores how the assumptions of international relations theory must be revised if it is to describe and explain a global political reality in which religion is once again pervasive.

WHAT DOES IT MEAN TO BE SECULAR?

The secularism of international relations theory inhibits its ability to understand the ongoing resurgence of religion in global politics. But what exactly does it mean to be secular? No answer can be straightforward. Over the centuries the term *secular* has garnered a great variety of meanings, some denoting hostility toward religion, others remaining descriptively neutral, others emanating from religion itself. We propose that nine concepts of the secular help to map its possible range of meanings and, in turn, to distinguish in what sense international relations has been secular in practice and in thought. The first four are positive or neutral towards religion; the next five are negative.

The first and oldest concept of the secular dates back to medieval Europe, where it pertained simply to affairs outside the realm of the monastic. In a second sense, secular can refer to an idea or expression formulated so as to make specific reference to religion. The command "do not steal," for instance, is expressed in secular terms, but as one of the Ten Commandments, it is clearly not hostile to religion.

A third sense of the secular, much more apropos to the argument here, refers to the *differentiation* of religion from other spheres of social life—politics, economics, culture—but in a manner that does not necessarily spell the decline of the public influence of religion. Religion-friendly differentiation, it might be called. In the realm of politics, differentiation involves a mutual autonomy between religious bodies and political institutions in their foundational, constitutional authority.[3] In differentiated political orders, government respects religious freedom and refrains from involving itself in religious affairs, either favorably or unfavorably, while religious bodies eschew standing prerogatives to hold public office or influence policy. Differentiation corresponds to a low level of "government involvement in religion," the concept with which political scientist Jonathan Fox categorizes relationships between religion and state across the globe.[4] The United States, Fox shows, manifests the world's highest degree of separation, its government interfering with religion the least and acting so as to favor one religion over another the least, as prescribed by the First Amendment of the U.S. Constitution. Government involvement is generally lowest and differentiation highest in liberal democracies, though these vary considerably from state to state. Several liberal democracies either establish a single religious body as official—Great Britain, Denmark, Finland, Norway, Poland, and until recently Sweden—or lend strong public support to one or more religious bodies, as do Germany and Israel. But even these are highly differentiated in comparison to nondemocracies. Differentiation can also be found in the Islamic world, though far less commonly. Muslim-majority states Mali, Senegal, and Indonesia are now categorized as "free" by Freedom House, indicating a liberal democratic regime and a broad separation of religion and state. Mali and Senegal in particular rate low on measures of "government involvement in religion."[5] Over the past decade, religious organizations in Turkey have enjoyed increasing independence from state control, though this more differentiated relationship still lies precariously under the Damocletian sword of the Turkish military, which ever threatens to raze it. Islamic factions in Egypt, Malaysia, Jordan, and elsewhere also advocate for differentiated politics.

Opposite differentiation is what may be called *integration*—the intertwining of religion and state. It may take a relatively consensual form, where a state and a religious body support one another, as in medieval Europe, colonial Latin America, or contemporary Saudi Arabia and Iran. Or, it may take a hostile form, where a state seeks to integrate a religious body into its own authority through suppression, coercion, and often harsh persecution, as in Communist Russia, Bulgaria, and Romania or in revolutionary Mexico. In either case, religion enjoys little autonomy.[6]

Crucial for this third concept of the secular is that differentiation need not entail the decline of religion's political efficacy. Religion can influence politics quite strongly even when it is not established, legally favored, or otherwise constitutionally enshrined. The United States is illustrative. From a position of constitutional separation, religious bodies and interest groups have exerted strong public influence on politics through persuasion, lobbying, and the building of electoral coalitions. This possibility—that religion could remain politically efficacious from a differentiated institutional standpoint—has been proposed by a long line of philosophers of modernity, including nineteenth century theorists of civil society like Tocqueville and Hegel, the great scholar of religion Ernst Troeltsch in the early twentieth century, and contemporary sociologists of religion. It is the central insight of sociologist José Casanova's *Public Religion in the Modern World*, which argues that religion continues to play an influential "public" role in modern western liberal democracies. It also corresponds, at least generally, to what Elizabeth Shakman Hurd calls "Judeo-Christian secularism." Today, several Islamic theorists also espouse a form of differentiation between mosque and state that is friendly to Islam and its political influence.[7]

A fourth concept of the secular refers not to the decline of religion but rather to a social context that is particular to the modern world—namely, one in which faith is one of a wide array of socially available options rather than an established, unquestioned pillar in the architecture of the universe. Philosopher Charles Taylor has recently revived this concept in his book *A Secular Age*, though it has antecedents in the thought of sociologist Peter Berger and others.[8]

The subsequent five concepts of the secular in one way or another suggest a negative outcome for religion. The first four of these involve *secularization*, a process of religious decline. They represent what is known as "secularization theory," the claim that as the juggernaut of modernity advances through science, economic progress, free inquiry, technological progress, political liberalization, democratization, and biblical criticism, religion will recede and eventually disappear. Originating with Hobbes, Spinoza, Hume, and other philosophers of the Enlightenment, the theory gained ground in the nineteenth century in the thinking of Marx, Darwin, Nietzsche, and Feuerbach, and in the twentieth century in the thought of Durkheim, Weber, Dewey, Freud, and others, was widely held in the social sciences, philosophy, and other humanities in the West in the 1950s and 1960s, and still enjoys strong support today. Sometimes the thesis is sweeping: Religion, in all of its manifestations, is on the way out. But it has also been advanced in more limited, precise ways, corresponding to the following four concepts of the secular.

In the first of these concepts, and the fifth in our overall sequence, secularization occurs when large numbers of individuals cease to adhere to religious beliefs. The sixth sense of the secular is a decline in religious practice and community, a decline that can take place independently of a decline in belief, as asserted by sociologist Grace Davie, who has described a European trend of "belief without belonging."[9]

The seventh concept of the secular, also one of secularization, is like concept 3 in that it both asserts differentiation and plays a crucial role in the present argument. But here, differentiation is desuetude. Religion is becoming differentiated from other social spheres, it holds, though not in a way that reconfigures and preserves its influence, but instead as part and parcel of its general decline. Religion's loss of constitutional prerogatives and governmental support in the political sphere, then, is merely a way station to its eventual extinction.

In the eighth concept of the secular, religion loses its political influence due to the intentional efforts of regimes to suppress it rather than spontaneous decline. Here, secularization occurs through the onset of the hostile form of integrationism described above. This type of secularization need not correspond to the decline of religious belief or practice at all, but is the product of the intentional efforts of regimes to marginalize it. It is found in most Communist regimes, to be sure. A version also inheres in the French Revolution and its liberal republican legacy in European politics, emblematized in France's 1905 Law on the Separation of the Churches and State, which seeks not to eradicate religion but to

---

Box 2.1 Concepts of the Secular

Positive or neutral

1. *Secular* means pertaining to the world outside the monastic sphere.
2. *Secular* means a concept or use of language that makes no specific reference to religion or revelation but is not necessarily hostile.
3. *Secular* means some kind of differentiation or separation of religion from other spheres of society (political, economic, cultural, etc.) but not necessarily the decline of religion's influence.
4. *Secular* means a social context in which religious faith is one of many options available for choice rather than an unproblematic feature of the universe.

Negative

5. *Secularization* is a decline in the religious beliefs that individuals hold.
6. *Secularization* is a decline in religious practice and community.
7. *Secularization* is a differentiation of religion from other spheres of society (political, economic, cultural, etc.) in a way that entails, and is part and parcel of, a long-term decline in the influence of religion.
8. *Secularization* involves a decline of religious influence on politics, not due to a general long-term decline in religion, but rather because of the intentional efforts of regimes to suppress it. It does not necessarily involve a decline in religious belief or practice.
9. *Secularism* is an ideology or set of beliefs that advocates for the marginalization of religion from other spheres of life.

subject it to sharp state controls. Such a secularism was then transplanted onto Muslim soil in the Republic of Turkey, founded by Kemal Ataturk in 1924, and replicated in Arab nationalist regimes following World War II.

Finally, the ninth concept of the secular is different from all the others insofar as it is not a description of a process or state of affairs at all. It is rather secul*arism*, an ideology or set of normative beliefs that advocates the sequestration of religion from other spheres of life. Secularism usually accepts the descriptive claim that religion is declining, that differentiation is desuetude—but adds that it is a good thing. It is the set of moral beliefs held by the regimes described by concept 8. Secularism of this sort is what Hurd calls "laicism."

Box 2.1 summarizes the nine concepts of the secular.

THE SECULARIZATION OF INTERNATIONAL RELATIONS

International relations theory is secular in good part because it reflects the profoundly secularizing historical transformation that established modern international relations itself. It was not a transformation that involved a popular decline in religious belief or practice, the secularization encapsulated in concept 5. Rather, it involved a change in the authority structure of European politics: a trajectory entailing the secularization noted in concept 7—a continent-wide differentiation of religious and political authority that resulted in the decline of religious influence—and, within sovereign states, secularization of the sort described by concept 8, a subordination of religion to state authority.[10]

The events that established modern international relations in Europe during the seventeenth century consolidated a centuries-long metamorphosis away from an authority structure that was far less differentiated: that of Europe during the High Middle Ages, roughly from the eleventh to the thirteenth centuries. In this realm, up and down the church's hierarchy, ecclesiasts exercised prerogatives that were, from a modern perspective, temporal. Bishops held vast tracts of land, levied revenues, sometimes brandished the sword, helped to elect the Holy Roman Emperor, and often served as regents, chancellors, and advisers to kings, princes, dukes, and counts. The pope, though primarily the spiritual leader of the Catholic Church, also settled political disputes, sent large armies to fight crusades, and governed the papal states in central Italy.

Meanwhile, the Holy Roman Emperor, kings, princes, and nobles exercised notable authority over the affairs of the Church. Although the balance of authority had shifted sharply in the pope's favor in the Investiture Controversy of the eleventh century, the emperor and monarchs continued to exercise a hand in the appointment of bishops, the central unit of authority in the church, and to wield the sword to enforce religious orthodoxy.

Largely absent from this political patchwork was the attribute of authority that would become foundational to the modern states system: sovereignty, or supreme authority within a territory. The pope and the emperor each checked one another's prerogatives sufficiently to prevent the other's supremacy. In the Latin West, spiritual and temporal authority were never fused into one person. Reflecting the legacy of the fourth-century pope Gelasius's doctrine of the two swords and even more so Jesus' own injunction to "render to Caesar what is Caesar's and to God what is God's," some differentiation of powers persisted even in this most integrated of times. Neither were most kings and princes sovereign. In their territories resided vassals who often owed fealty as much to authorities outside their superior's territory as to their superior. In his influential article on the formation of the sovereign state system, international relations theorist John Gerard Ruggie called this crisscrossing web of obligations "heteronomy," to be distinguished from the segmented authority of the modern sovereign state system.[11]

Conversely, all of these obligations manifested yet another quality that the modern state system later eroded: civilizational unity. Though no one of them dominated the continent, authorities at all levels in medieval Europe commonly viewed themselves as part of a *Respublica Christiana*, a realm characterized by mutual moral ideals and a common spiritual membership.

Over the next three and a half centuries, this combination of unity in moral obligation and membership and fragmentation in authority would gradually, piece by piece, be replaced by sovereign states and their diametrically opposite combination of fragmentation in moral obligation and membership combined with segmentation and internal centralization in political authority. As early as the beginning of the fourteenth century, monarchs took advantage of the fragmentation between pope and emperor to assert their own authority. By the early sixteenth century, England, France, Spain, and Sweden all looked very much like sovereign states, while a small sovereign states system had existed for over a century in Italy. But Europe was still distant from a system of sovereign states. By 1519, Charles V had become King of Spain and Holy Roman Emperor, giving him authority over a united Spain, the Netherlands, and the central European territories of the Holy Roman Empire, along with the responsibility to enforce Catholic orthodoxy in all of these lands—a responsibility that would soon become crucial. Yet his authority was less than sovereign authority, at least within the empire, where it was shared with other officials. Meanwhile, the Italian states system imploded in 1527, swallowed up by other European powers.

What then accelerated Europe's historical momentum towards sovereign statehood was the Protestant Reformation, which began in 1517. Its political theology—i.e., the doctrines through which basic theological claims are translated into political ends—prescribed the seizure of the church's remaining temporal powers and the end of the emperor's right to enforce the church's spiritual powers. All of these powers would be taken up by the prince, making him effectively sovereign. Predictably, this attack on the very authority and legitimacy of the church and the empire would result in a counterattack by the emperor, giving Protestant churches all the more incentive to place their authority in the hands of the prince.

Wars along confessional lines ensued and were settled initially in the Peace of Augsburg in 1555. Based on the principle *cuius regio, euis religio*, the settlement allowed Catholic and Protestant princes each to enforce their own orthodoxy throughout their entire territory, effectively consolidating their sovereignty. But Augsburg proved unstable and contested, leaving behind claims and counterclaims that eventually exploded into the Thirty Years' War of 1618 to 1648.

A small literature now exists debating whether the Peace of Westphalia, the settlement that ended the Thirty Years' War, deserves to be regarded as the origin of modern international relations.[12] Our own view is that whatever precise historical realities changed through and after the settlement, Westphalia symbolized the consolidation of the long historical transformation from the authority structure of medieval Europe to that of the modern states system in the middle of the seventeenth century. The Westphalian synthesis, as this new authority structure can be called, consists of five strands, each of which describes a different aspect of political authority—and, we contend, a different dimension of secularization.

The first strand was the victory of the sovereign state and the corresponding curtailment of the transnational authority of the Holy Roman Empire and, by extension, the pope. Though the treaties that make up the Peace of Westphalia nowhere pronounce a sovereign states system, and while the Holy Roman Empire continued to exist until 1806, state sovereignty triumphed in 1648 in several respects. Again, several European states had already looked sovereign for a century or more. But in 1648, the Swiss Confederation and the United Provinces achieved official independence, the latter from Spain. And against the empire, German states recovered what they claimed were their "ancient rights" and acquired the right to form external alliances. In the diplomatic traffic of the time one hears frequent mention of state autonomy, the equality of states, an equilibrium of states, and even a concept of collective security—all intelligible only in the context of a nascent sovereign states system.[13]

True, princes in the empire did not receive complete authority to enforce their faith in their territories as they had won at Augsburg but rather agreed to tolerate specified proportions of Catholics, Lutherans, and Calvinists in particular regions and to refrain from seeking to convert other princes' subjects. But this was little different from an international agreement among sovereigns, much in the way that states today agree to regulate pollution or commerce within their borders. Though the institutions of the empire sometimes fostered cooperation between German states, with small exceptions these institutions interfered little with the substantive supreme authority of princes. Most of all, the empire would exercise no authority over states' governance of religion, the key area in which it sought to curtail sovereign powers prior to the peace.

On a continental scale, the sovereign state's victory and the empire's defeat advanced secularization in the sense of concept 7, a differentiation of religious and political authority that involved the decline of religion's political influence. In the Holy Roman Emperor and his allies, transnational Catholicism had found not only an advocate, but one who was willing to go to war to preserve its spiritual and ecclesial unity. As late as 1629, the Holy Roman Emperor Ferdinand II had issued an Edict of Restitution that rolled back the Protestant Reformation to its borders established in 1555 at the Peace of Augsburg, a date since which the Reformation had made substantial gains. Since the enforcement of religious orthodoxy by a temporal authority is a strong expression of integrationism, the defeat of the empire at Westphalia was a great stride toward secularization as differentiation. It was just for this reason that Pope Innocent X condemned the treaties as "null, void, invalid, iniquitous, unjust, damnable, reprobate, inane, empty of meaning and effect for all time."[14]

Effecting a continent-wide differentiation was also *the second strand of the Westphalian synthesis, a vast diminuendo in interventions to alter the governance of religion within the territory of states.* It was not a total silencing. The Netherlands' invasion of England in 1688, for instance, was in part motivated by religion. But such episodes were whimpers compared to the deafening roar of transnational religious wars between 1517 and 1648, culminating in the Thirty Years' War of 1618 to 1648, which killed one third to one quarter of the population of Germany, a scale of slaughter not to be seen again in this region until the twentieth century. In his major study of the history of war, political scientist Kalevi J. Holsti argues that religion caused only three wars between 1648 and 1713, all of these between Europeans and Muslims who were outside the sovereign states system.[15] By the eighteenth century, nonintervention had become a widely accepted norm in the international system, extolled by philosophers like Emeric de Vattel. Since the enforcement of religion across borders—and efforts to protect the practice of religion—had been such a central part of European politics for so long, the abatement of these efforts was a large stride towards secularization, understood as differentiation.

The third strand of the Westphalian synthesis involved secularization within states rather than transnationally, and a somewhat different kind of secularization, that of concept 8, involving the subordination of the church to the state. What obtained was not the far stronger political subordination of religion characteristic of the French Revolution and nineteenth century republicanism, or the even harsher repression characteristic of twentieth century dictatorships, but rather what came to be known as *Erastianism*, the strong governance of church affairs by the state, a stronger governance than had been seen in Europe since before the High Middle Ages.[16] Although each country had its own story of flux and contestation and its own unique arrangements, Erastianism was the general pattern. The major reform movements—German Lutheranism, Swedish Lutheranism, Scottish Presbyterianism, the Anglican Church, John Calvin's Geneva, and at times Dutch Calvinism—became national churches, crucial dimensions of whose authority, including their selection of top leaders, came under the control of the state. Writes Reformation historian Euan Cameron, "[U]ltimately, the Lutheran churches became very largely departments of state in their respective territories."[17] The French Catholic Church, too, was increasingly subject to the power of the king, a trend that Alexis de Tocqueville would later come to rue in his *Old Regime and the French Revolution*.[18] Almost nowhere in the continent did there exist a principled—as opposed to pragmatic—practice of religious freedom for individuals. Indeed the First Amendment of the U.S. Constitution, guaranteeing the free exercise of religion and proscribing a nationally established religion, stands as a sharp exception to the Erastian trend of the sixteenth through eighteenth centuries. Over the ensuing three and a half centuries a wide variety of religion-state relationships would arise under the carapace of the sovereign states: differentiated and integrationist, consensual and conflictual, taking the form of liberal democracy, theocracy, Arab nationalist regimes that sharply controlled religion, and dictatorships, both Communist and fascist, that sought to eliminate religion altogether.

The fourth strand complements the third, and involves the sharply reduced temporal powers of religious authorities, especially Catholic bishops. Though the Papal States and the temporal privileges of ecclesiasts persisted elsewhere, the practices of holding office, raising revenues, and ruling large tracts of land among bishops had diminished sharply since the onset of the Reformation in 1517. Thus, differentiation of authority on the continent was reinforced.

Finally, the rise of nationalism as a locus of popular identity and loyalty amounts to a fifth strand of the Westphalian synthesis. Recent scholarship places the origins of nationalism in Britain, France, Spain, Germany, Sweden, and elsewhere in the sixteenth and seventeenth centuries or even earlier, and makes the case for the central role of religion in shaping these origins, thus replacing an earlier wave of scholarship that argued for the origins of nationalism in nineteenth century industrialization.[19] Early modern religion, then, served to direct people to place "faith in nation," to borrow the title of Anthony Marx's book on the subject. Since nations seek self-government, often through an independent state, such faith also directed loyalties away from the transnational authority of the Catholic Church and thus reinforced differentiation.

Hurd has argued that secularism is "one of the most important organizing principles of modern politics."[20] We concur and argue that the formation of the modern sovereign states system was a secularizing set of events. We have told the story of this formation as one driven in good part by the ideas of the Protestant Reformation and the conflict that they sparked. This is not to ignore the strong impetus of changes in economics, technology, and the balance of power, all of which also favored the sovereign state over transnational authority structures, as a wide body of scholarship has claimed.[21] Material trends reinforced the secular after Westphalia, too. The rise of a commercial republic in the Netherlands, for instance, increased the social and political influence of wealthy and religiously liberal Dutch merchants in cities such as Amsterdam. In his recent study of the origins of religious liberty, political scientist Anthony Gill shows that the concern of the American colonies for creating a common market was one of the chief factors that led them to look past the demands of Puritans and Anglicans for the suppression of religious dissent and eventually to incorporate nonestab-lishment and religious liberty—i.e., differentiation—into the First Amendment of the U.S. Constitution.[22] Material factors and ideas conspired, then, to bring about a secularized state system.

SECULARISM AT THE ORIGINS OF MODERN INTERNATIONAL RELATIONS THEORY

Between the late fifteenth and late eighteenth centuries, as the sovereign states system evolved into being and began to function, philosophers sought to de-scribe it, explain it, and prescribe norms of conduct for it, and in so doing wrote the classic works and set forth the foundational commitments of realism and lib-eralism, the two great enduring traditions of international thought. What con-temporary international relations theorists have vastly underappreciated about these traditions and their origins is their secular character.

What does it mean for international relations thought to be secular? Two things. First, it means that its articulators describe the world along the lines of concept 7 of the secular, namely, as if the differentiation and decline of reli-gion's political influence have occurred. They write as if states, and indeed any other actors on the stage of international politics, pursue ends such as power, security, wealth, conquest, wars of defense, the protection of human rights, and the like, but do not pursue specifically religious ends and are not influenced by religious actors. Second, there is a normative dimension to their secularism, as in concept 9. By and large, the original modern philosophers of realism and liberalism did not just describe the secular character of international politics; they celebrated it. They advocated the Erastian subordination of religion to the state (concept 8), and some of them even hoped for the general decline of religious belief and practice (concepts 5 and 6), at least in its traditional forms. Both of these senses of the secular can be seen in the affirmation of the state, the description of states' actions and pursuits, as well as the normative views put forth by the founding fathers of realism and liberalism.

At the core of realism, from Machiavelli to Mearsheimer, is the notion of the state as a distinct political body with a distinct end, or "raison d'état," as Cardinal Richelieu famously put it. Machiavelli described the city states of Renaissance Italy as effectively sovereign and their politics as effectively free from ecclesiastical control. Even the Papal States engaged in war and diplomacy just like everyone else. Hobbes envisioned a sovereign Leviathan interacting with other sovereign states with no common superior.

Realists have also been unified by their conception of what the end of states is—namely, security, which can only be achieved through relative power, namely, military power, which includes armed forces as well as the population, wealth, technology, natural resources, and structures for taxation and recruitment needed to sustain them. For some realists, like Hobbes, it is the anarchical character of the international system—a condition of "self-help," as Kenneth Waltz would later describe it—that necessitates the drive for security and power. Machiavelli—and later, Hans Morgenthau—by contrast, are what Michael Doyle calls "fundamentalists," viewing the will to power as stemming from human nature and pervading politics at all levels.[23] Reasoning from either view or a combination of both, realists have always viewed the competition for relative power as ubiquitous and ends defined by religion or other ideals as either pursued insincerely or destined to fail when pursued sincerely.

For realists as for so many others, description closely corresponds with prescription. Machiavelli regarded both the church and Christian morality as effeminate and enfeebling of a prosperous, powerful, and well-ordered republic. Though his writings do not contain direct philosophical or theological arguments against Christian theology or natural law, he was, as philosopher Jacques Maritain argued in a 1942 essay, the first philosopher in the Western tradition to counsel princes "not to be good" if circumstances required it.[24] Writing during a time of religious war, Hobbes prescribed that the state take an overriding interest in stability and security and that the church be kept out of politics altogether. Even churchman Richelieu counseled French kings to follow the secularized morality of raison d'état and to act in a way that mostly eschewed the wishes of the Catholic Church.

In the writings of John Locke, Adam Smith, Immanuel Kant, and other contemporaries of the Enlightenment can be found the foundational ideas of what would prove the chief enduring competitor to realism in international relations thought, the liberal tradition. Uniting liberals is the rational confidence in the possibility that states can transcend their endless competition for power and cooperate in the pursuit of security, peace, and prosperity, at least under certain conditions: liberal republican (and later, democratic) regimes, free trade, and the presence of international law and institutions.

But the early liberals incorporated the early realists' fundamental secularism. They, too, saw states as the primary actors and religious actors as all but impotent in international politics. Though they thought that states could pursue their ends cooperatively, they conceived those ends as little other than peace, security, and prosperity, and not, say, altering the religion of their neighboring state. Thinkers like Adam Smith, writing at a time when Britain was growing aggressively as a commercial republic, placed particular stress on the pursuit of economic openness and the conditions for growing wealth.[25]

Normatively, liberals advanced secularization, too. A leitmotif in Enlightenment thought is the reconceptualization of Christianity and Judaism as deistic systems of rational ethics, stripped of supernatural revelation and miracles. Emblematic was Thomas Jefferson's bible, in which he redacted the New Testament so as to retain ethical teachings about reciprocal love and the like, but deleted all references to healings, resurrection, or anything miraculous. Enlightenment thinkers had little patience for religious institutions or hierarchies, either. Thinkers such as Grotius and Locke did not want to destroy Christianity, but they did seek to empower governments and citizens to keep the power of Christian churches and ministers in check. As with realists like Hobbes, a primary motivation behind liberals' Erastianism was a concern for stability. The previous century's religious wars, they thought, had taught that unleashed religious enthusiasm could only undermine order and liberty.

The secularism of early modern international relations theory was not total. Philosophers like the sixteenth-century Spanish Scholastics Francisco de Vitoria and Francisco Suarez, sixteenth-century Italian Protestant Alberico Gentili, and seventeenth-century Dutch philosopher Hugo Grotius reasoned about international relations consciously and explicitly from theological foundations. Among their common arguments was that states could under some circumstances intervene in other states to counteract the cruelty of a prince or some other egregious injustice—an early version of humanitarian intervention. Though Grotius was famous for arguing that the common laws of nature grounding international law would have some validity "even if there is no God or if He has no concern for the affairs of men," he fell far short of being a full-blown secularist. He believed that Christian statesmen should aspire to frame their policies in accordance with the laws of the Gospel and considered it a terrible scandal that they so conspicuously failed to do so. And he believed that some shared notion of divinity was an essential bedrock of society, including international society. However, he espoused a wide and tolerant notion of Christianity that was incompatible with all forms of interconfessional warfare and persecution.[26]

THE DEEPENING OF SECULARIZATION IN THE WEST, 1789–1917

From the late eighteenth century to the late twentieth century, political secularism continued its dramatic global expansion—both intellectually and politically, in theory and in practice. Here, we mean primarily concept 8, the subordination of religion to the state. The continental differentiation of religion and state consolidated at Westphalia, of course, was not to be reversed. Within international relations theory during this period, the most important long-term trends were the booming growth of liberalism in the Anglo-American context, through the ideas of thinkers like Jeremy Bentham, John Stuart Mill, and Woodrow Wilson, and the revival of realism during the 1930s and even more so in post–World War II America.[27] But neither of these trends revised the basic assumptions laid out by the early modern founders of these traditions, especially with respect to religion. Rather, the form of secularization that continued to build with great momentum during this period was the doctrine, reflected in thought and practice, that the state should actively subordinate religious authority to political authority, religious institutions to political institutions, and religious claims to political claims, all in the interest of promoting the well-being of society as a whole. Though much of this secularization occurred within states, perhaps making it seem like the subject of comparative politics or "political development," it was very much a transnational phenomenon, propelled by the diffusion of ideas and international networks.

As radically as the early modern political secularism of Grotius, Bodin, Hobbes, and Locke broke from medieval integrationism, and as much as it sought to reduce the influence of churches as political players, it seldom mounted a direct or open assault on religion per se and, indeed, almost always expressed itself in prima facie biblical and orthodox terms. The decisive break with this pattern came intellectually with Rousseau's *Social Contract* in 1762 and politically with the French Revolution, launched in 1789.

For the first time, Rousseau and his Jacobin acolytes openly identified the church and Christianity as implacably hostile to any free and flourishing republic.[28] Where a strong and flourishing republic required a Spartan-style love of country above all things, the church taught that heaven was the Christian's best and truest country. Where a unified republic required a love and devotion for all of one's fellow citizens, the church taught *extra ecclesia nulla salus* ("outside the church there is no salvation") and thus created a spiritual and social chasm between Christian citizens and non-Christian citizens. Where a free republic elevated liberty of mind and spirit as the highest principle, the church elevated submission and humble obedience to God and his servants as the foundations of the Christian life. A church that remained beyond the control of the republican state and free to propagate its teachings without hindrance was therefore not merely a latent source of political instability but an active opponent of its core principles and purposes.[29]

The sense of a Manichaean conflict between church and republic meant that a policy of church-state separation was not sufficient. Instead, the republican state had to adopt nothing less than a policy of radical subordination and indeed transformation vis-à-vis the church. This campaign of *Déchristianisation* consisted in a whole range of exotic innovations, including a new calendar based on the cycles of nature rather than the cycles of Christian salvation history as well as a new set of religious rituals revolving around a Cult of the Supreme Being.[30] But the policy also eliminated the church's right to perform marriages, its control over education, and its ownership of vast hectares of property. Even more seriously, the new regime brought the church much more strongly under its supervisory control. While even under the old regime the Gallican understanding between crown and pope involved a strong state role in the appointment of bishops and priests, the new regime took this further by requiring oaths of loyalty to the revolutionary republic and, in effect, ideological reeducation. Church personnel as well as ordinary Catholics who resisted these measures were subjected to violence on a massive scale, most notoriously in the Vendée.[31] It is therefore hardly inappropriate to see the Revolution as providing the template for subsequent and often violent programs of radical political secularism, including those carried out by revolutionaries in twentieth-century Russia, Mexico, Spain, Italy, Cambodia, Tunisia, and China.

Of course, the clock turned back on some of these measures as the forces of reaction strove mightily to kill the revolutionary "baby in the cradle," which they succeeded in doing with the advent of Napoleon and the eventual restoration of the monarchy. But the revolutionary flag was raised high enough and long enough that radicals throughout Europe and its settler societies in the

Americas rallied around it. And the radical-secularist template of the French Revolution inspired them to mobilize politically against the church as their enemy number one. Catholic countries throughout Europe and the Americas, thereafter, saw the rise of wave after wave of anticlerical movements and parties in the nineteenth and twentieth centuries.

The Revolution bequeathed a loose though real transnational family of republican and anticlerical movements. Sometimes these movements emerged with the help of French bayonets; in other cases they were spawned by the sheer demonstration effect of the French Revolution's success in overthrowing the ancien régime, as well as by the dissemination of its leading ideas. The writings of Thomas Paine, who lived in France in the early months of the Revolution (1789–90), had this kind of impact in the English-speaking world. The United Irish Movement and its violent 1798 insurrection, for example, were directly inspired by the French revolutionary example and ideas.[32] This diffusion and its consequences were by no means limited to Catholic countries. For the revolutionary Dutch Patriots, who were in exile in France in 1789, "the outbreak of the French Revolution, and universal ideology to which it gave rise, was an inspiring development."[33] In the case of the Netherlands, French bayonets and the contagious ideological fervor that infected the Patriots combined to bring much of the program of the French Revolution — including its radical secularism — to the Low Countries in the form of the Batavian Republic in 1795. A major priority of the Batavian Revolution, in fact, was to abolish the Dutch Reformed Church's special political ties and privileges.[34]

One revolutionary development in church-state relations that proved both especially portable and especially explosive was in education. In fits and starts and despite massive resistance, French republicans and liberals repeatedly pushed for a compulsory, state-supervised educational system designed to mold French youth into republican *citoyens*. During the Third Republic, its main features — lay-controlled teacher training in every department; universal and obligatory schooling; and state inspection of all schools, including church schools — were implemented as a top priority of the radical wing of the republican majority.[35] If the Catholic Church wished to continue to organize its own system of schools, it would have to do so at its own expense and in the face of ongoing criticism and suspicion on the part of republicans such as Jules Ferry, minister of public instruction during the early years of the Third Republic, who condemned them as "schools of counterrevolution, where one learns to detest and curse all of the ideas which are the honor and the purpose of modern France."[36] It is not for nothing that historian Theodore Zeldin observed that in France "the major [political] battle of the [nineteenth] century was between the priest and the schoolmaster."[37] Similar battles, in which churches strongly resisted state-directed "common school" programs, were fought throughout the nineteenth and into the twentieth centuries in the Netherlands, Belgium, the United States, Germany, and other countries.[38]

The sense of a widespread and intractable transnational conflict between the partisans of the church (especially but not only the Catholic Church) and the partisans of liberal political progress deepened considerably in the second half of the nineteenth century. A key turning point was 1864. What had sometimes been an inchoate anticlerical attitude or tendency crystallized into a coherent political program in numerous countries after the publication that year of Pope Pius IX's "Syllabus of Errors." The Syllabus condemned the doctrine that the pope "can and ought to reconcile himself with progress, with liberalism, and with modern civilization."[39] Pius IX didn't define his terms very clearly, and much of his animus against "modern civilization" no doubt sprang from the fact that a modern state—Italy—was in the process of stripping him of lands the papacy had controlled for a thousand years. Still, the widespread perception is what mattered for politics: "Europe saw the Pope condemn liberalism—whatever that was, the Pope condemned it."[40]

This pervasive perception almost immediately precipitated a host of organized political campaigns designed to subject the church to even greater state control and regulation. In Germany, Bismarck directed the Parliament to limit the power of the Catholic Church in the Kulturkampf of the 1870s. In Belgium, the Liberal Party in the late 1870s implemented a program to greatly restrict the Catholic Church's role in education. The 1871 Paris Commune included the desecration of churches. In 1870s America, the Blaine Amendments, designed to prevent states from financially aiding "sectarian" (i.e., Catholic) schools, won legislative approval in dozens of states and only narrowly failed to pass the U.S. Congress.[41] Later, in France, Combes, Briand, and other radical republicans pushed through the 1905 Law on the Separation of the Churches and State. While the law was less sweeping in its consequences than its framers intended, it nonetheless made a subordinationist political secularism (concept 8) an official, enduring, and nonnegotiable feature of France's political system and political culture—one that remains essentially intact to this day.[42]

1864 was significant for another reason: it was the year of the first meeting of the Communist International. And there is little doubt that "Marxism was the most powerful philosophy of secularization in the nineteenth century."[43] In its beginnings, Communism was not an atheist philosophy: in the 1840s, Friedrich Engels, much to his puzzlement and frustration, met Christian Communists everywhere he went—in Germany, France, and England. Saint-Simon had advocated a kind of Christian socialism, and Ferdinand Lassalle, who was a more influential Communist theoretician than Marx until about 1870, expressly combined Christianity and Communism. But after Lassalle's death in 1864 and the publication of Das Kapital in 1867, Communism as a philosophy and as a transnational political movement increasingly incorporated a radical form of political secularism. At best, "religion is a man's private concern," as the 1875 Gotha Program put it; at worst, it was incompatible with a unified working-class movement. Either way, religion as an institution and an allegiance had to be systematically subordinated to political movements that sought the liberation of the proletariat from capitalist oppression. Particularly at a moment when the pope seemed to be losing his transnational moral authority by declaring war on "progress," Communism spoke with a growing transnational moral authority—one which increasingly operated as an adversary rather than an ally of religion.

A host of other intellectual and political movements of the late eighteenth and nineteenth centuries that were otherwise mutually contradictory—Hegelian historicism, Bismarckian realism, Comtean positivism, Millian liberalism, American federalism, Benthamite utilitarianism, Spencerian progressivism, and Kantian rationalism—mostly agreed with Communists and radical republicans on a set of propositions that taken together yielded powerful ideological support for a program of political secularism: that a great new age of reason, freedom, and progress was arriving, or would soon arrive; that this new age would be the final (and almost always the third and last in these conceptions) and culminating era of human history, a kind of secular eschaton or millenium[44]; that God, or providence, or some divine or quasi-divine superintending force, almost always understood in ways markedly different from orthodox Christian conceptions of God, was orchestrating world history in some essentially irresistible fashion so as to usher in this new and final age; and that an essential if not primary agent in the realization of this new age was the modern state. Perhaps the most elegant expression of this view is embedded in the Great Seal of the United States: *Annuit coeptis, novus ordo seclorum* ("He [God] approves these beginnings, a new order of the ages"). A close second is Hegel's remark: "The state is the march of God in history."[45]

This whole package of ideas justifies a view of the state that is in one sense not necessarily secular, because it puts the state in the service of a world-historical mission imposed on it by a higher and often religious agency. But in another sense it is radically secular (in the sense of concept 8), because it grants the state a supreme and overriding authority over sacred institutions and authorities that in the past may have enjoyed comparable or even supreme powers and privileges. In other words, churches and other specifically religious, confessional, and "sectarian" institutions were *under a kind of religious obligation* to accept a subordinate role vis-à-vis the state so that history could reach its intended destination.

These ideas about historical progress and the secular state also helped to generate robust concepts of nationalism and internationalism, which, in turn, further contributed to the advance of political secularism in the nineteenth and twentieth centuries. Arguably the greatest and most influential nationalist of the nineteenth century was Giuseppe Mazzini. Leader of the Young Italy movement and briefly dictator of the Roman Republic in 1849, Mazzini repudiated traditional Catholicism in favor of a religion of "universal humanity." He rejected the Fall and original sin, but believed that God was leading mankind ineluctably toward the "angelification" of the individual and the establishment of God's kingdom on earth. But God's kingdom, he believed, would and should consist in the destruction of the papacy and its replacement by a secular council of the nations, headquartered in Rome. This council would represent the authentic nations of the world—that is, those that possessed the irrefutable marks of nationality, including natural frontiers, distinct languages, and distinct cultures.[46] Similar, quasi-religious elevations of the nation and nationalism achieved currency in France in the nineteenth century thanks to Jules Michelet and Ernest Renan.[47]

Echoing to some extent earlier thinkers like Giambattista Vico and Johann Gottfried Herder, Mazzini also believed that every nation had a distinct vocation or mission, and that the ultimate purpose of nations is to serve humanity and the international order as a whole. "For us the starting-point is Country; the object or aim is Collective Humanity."[48] Mazzini's views thus recalled the republican internationalism of Kant and anticipated the liberal internationalism of Wilson. Both of these latter views, like Mazzini's, held that the progress of international politics towards greater peace was in some mysterious respect the will of providence. However, both Kant and Wilson were also like Mazzini in holding that the essential mechanism whereby a just and peaceful international society would be established had nothing to do with religious exhortations to peace based on the Gospels—the sort that were common in the writings of Erasmus, Grotius, and writers on just war theory throughout the eighteenth century. Nor did it have anything to do with restoring the authority of the papacy or establishing a universal Christian council or creating some other religious agency to adjudicate conflicts between Christian peoples—such as Grotius, among others, dreamed of. Rather, the key to bringing about a just and peaceful international society lay almost exclusively in an entirely secular political mechanism—namely, the global spread of republican government along with its corollary, national self-determination. And this process was occurring inexorably—as Kant, for one, seemed to take pleasure in pointing out—not because politicians and peoples were scrupulously conforming their behavior to the rigors of the Christian religion but entirely because "nature guarantees perpetual peace by the actual mechanism of human inclinations."[49] Secular international goals were being achieved by secular means.

THE DIFFUSION OF POLITICAL SECULARISM
BEYOND THE WEST, 1917–1967

The political secularism that was radicalized and diffused throughout much of the West in the century after the French Revolution of 1789 was in many ways further radicalized and even more widely diffused in the half century after the Russian Revolution of 1917.[50] States bent on containing the social and political influence of institutionalized religion in many instances adopted a yet more militant program—that of eliminating the social and political influence of religion altogether, in some cases by destroying, subjugating, or eviscerating religious institutions and centers of religious authority. Meanwhile, states outside the West that had not yet been exposed to secularism in theory or practice became experiments in radical political secularization. In this period, again, secularism diffused through transnational networks.

Nineteen seventeen can be taken as the rough beginning of this era of ultra-radical political secularism. "Nineteen hundred and seventeen was a busy year for governments turning their faces from God," writes political scientist Anthony Gill. "Not only did the constitutional council in Mexico effectively outlaw the Roman Catholic Church and other religious denominations but also a group of even more radical state builders [i.e., the Bolsheviks] seized power in a country halfway around the world."[51] Combined with the already firmly established radicalism of French laicism and the subsequent radicalism of the Kemalist Revolution of the early 1920s, these revolutions succeeded in planting radical secularist experiments in the heart of the Catholic, Orthodox, and Muslim worlds within the first three decades of the twentieth century.

Revolutionary political activism of the Left and the Right was indeed the most consequential force for radical political secularization in the twentieth century. Often inspired by the French Revolution, leftist revolutions like those in China and Cuba and nationalist revolutions like those in Turkey and Egypt created systems that, at least for a time, greatly increased the power of governments around the world to regulate, contain, and suppress religious organizations. Nazi totalitarianism, spread by military occupation to some twenty countries, coercively deprived religious bodies of their independence and social influence and, of course, sought to entirely eradicate one religion in particular.

Thanks to such revolutionary and totalitarian movements, that part of the Russian Orthodox Church that was not wiped out became an organ of the Soviet state; the Catholic Church in Mexico was criminalized and deprived of its property and its right to engage in political activity; the Ottoman Caliphate and sharia law were abolished in Turkey, much to the outrage of Muslims around the world, particularly in British India; the Lamaist theocracy in Tibet was systematically destroyed and the Dalai Lama ultimately forced into exile by Chinese Communists between 1957 and 1959;[52] perhaps the largest grass-roots religious organization in the Muslim world, the Muslim Brotherhood, was decimated and driven underground by Egyptian authorities in the 1950s and 1960s; and the Nazis refused to permit the independence of religious bodies in preaching, education, and publication in Nazi-controlled countries, arresting or murdering thousands of religious leaders who resisted the National Socialist policy of subordinating religious institutions to the state.

These revolutionary forms of political secularism and their aggressive assaults on religion might seem like outliers. However, at the approximate mid-point in the twentieth century, in 1945, M. Searle Bates found in his exhaustive analysis of religion-state relations worldwide that "recent intensifications of nationalism have fused with the increasing power and functions of the State to imperil and even to crush, in some lands, a liberty of religion formerly achieved." The result, he found, was that "[r]eligious liberty is today denied, deformed, or restricted for all or for part of the people in most of the countries of the world."[53] In fact, by our rough calculation, at least 50 percent of the world's population lived under secularist political regimes—understood as regimes that systematically restricted the right and capacity of religious organizations to influence society and politics, in the sense of concepts 8 and 9—at some point between 1917 and 1967.

As Bates notes, the surging nationalism associated with decolonization was a major force for secularism. The nationalisms of Atatürk in Turkey, Senanayake in Sri Lanka, Nehru in India, Nasser in Egypt, Nkrumah in Ghana, Sukarno in Indonesia, and Kenyatta in Kenya all generally appealed to notions of national or civilizational greatness in which religion was but one subordinate element. Often, their concepts of national identity deliberately bracketed or subordinated substantive religious contributions in the hope of unifying diverse ethnic and religious groups in the context of anticolonial struggles and postcolonial nation building.[54] Sometimes, nationalists in this period *used religious appeals precisely to marginalize the social or political influence of traditional religion*, as when Bourguiba of Tunisia, after publicly raising a glass of lemonade to his lips during Ramadan, proclaimed, "You 'are permitted' to drink during Ramadan, for the 'holy war,' that is, the effort to unite Islam, is first and foremost the battle of production. Conserve your strength so that you may work hard."[55] Because these leaders had slain all manner of colonial dragons and in some cases a domestic dragon or two, they enjoyed a charismatic authority that enabled them to secure a modicum of legitimacy—for a time, anyway—for their sometimes audacious experiments in secular nationalism. Of course, to speak of these leaders as a group is not to imply that the secularist political agendas of, say, Nehru and Atatürk, or Bourguiba and Sukarno, were identical in all respects. Though Nehru, for example, secured a temporary ban against the Hindu nationalist Rashtriya Swayamsevak Sangh (RSS) in the exceptional circumstances following Mahatma Gandhi's assassination in 1948, and though he personally bemoaned the influence of religion on Indian society,[56] he never undertook a wholesale Kemalist-style effort to drive organized religion out of Indian public life. At the same time, though their tone and tactics differed, virtually every member of the first generation of postcolonial leaders articulated the hope that religious leaders and organizations would assume a smaller political role and exercise less political influence in their societies. They acted on this hope in different ways and with varying degrees of aggression, but it was a hope they all shared nonetheless.

This remarkable group of secular nationalists in fact constituted a powerful transnational network. Among its members, there was profound mutual ideological borrowing and influence as well as tangible mutual support and coordination. In his youth, Nasser read Nkrumah and Gandhi; Nehru backed Nasser in the Suez Crisis and Nkrumah in his bid to make the Gold Coast independent; they all learned socialism from Marx and state-centered industrialization and economic planning from the Soviets, as well as from each other; they drew inspiration from Mazzini; and they stunned the world when they gathered dozens of world leaders to form (what seemed at the time) a united front at Bandung.

These trends towards political secularism were closely related to the dominant dynamics of international politics. The calamity of World War I served to discredit throne-and-altar alliances between religion (especially Christianity, but also Islam in the Ottoman Empire) and the nation-state. The postmillenialist religious utopianism that helped to fuel liberal internationalism collapsed in the face of the failure of the League of Nations and the rise of violent totalitarianisms in the 1920s and 1930s, causing even religious thinkers to repudiate faith-based, idealistic or moralistic approaches to international politics in favor of essentially secular doctrines like realism. Even the theologian Reinhold Niebuhr—whom Martin Wight aptly termed a "Christian Machiavellian"—articulated skepticism that the deeds and policies of states could be understood as religiously motivated. In a world suffused with power, any pursuit of a religious or otherwise transcendent ideal would come to ironic ruin.[57] Normatively, he counseled statespersons to choose the lesser of two evils.

Furthermore, dominant global conflicts in this period tended to organize international politics into rival blocs defined in essentially secular terms: Republicans versus Nationalists in the Spanish Civil War; the Allies versus the Axis in World War II; the United States and the Western bloc versus the Soviet Union and the Eastern bloc in the Cold War; European colonial powers versus anticolonial movements such as the Indian National Congress and the Egyptian Free

Officers, as well as anticolonial ideologies such as pan-Arabism or pan-African-
ism. Even those who tried to remain aloof from these conflicts often did so in
the name of an alternative form of secular transnationalism, such as the Non-
Aligned Movement launched by Nehru, Nasser, Nkrumah, Sukarno, and Tito at
the Bandung Conference in 1955.

The "Bandung Generation" of Third-World statesmen was hardly alone,
however, in thinking that an essential ingredient of modern progress was the
secularization of politics. Sometimes called the rationalization of authority,
sometimes characterized as the absence of "praetorianism,"[58] the capacity of
states to build up their own sources of authority and resist undue influence
by religious and other actors was considered a hallmark of modern political
development by an entire generation of postwar American social scientists
and public intellectuals, including Gabriel Almond, Sidney Verba, Walt
Whitman Rostow, David Apter, Daniel Lerner, Samuel Huntington, Arthur
Schlesinger Jr., Rupert Emerson, and Walter Lippmann.[59] Influenced by
such ideas, American policymakers placed their bets on aggressively modernizing and secularizing leaders like the Shah of Iran and Ngo Din Diem of
Vietnam.[60] Circa 1960, perhaps the only thing the U.S. State Department,
the faculty of the Harvard Government Department, the Communist International, and the leaders of the Bandung Conference agreed on is that a
society can be successful only insofar as its government and its citizenry keep
religion from exercising a substantive influence on its politics. No secularity,
no modernity.

THE REVERSAL OF POLITICAL SECULARISM
THROUGHOUT THE WORLD,
1967 TO THE PRESENT

By the late 1960s, everyone (a term we don't use lightly) believed that the widespread aspiration for political secularism—for a politics and public life free of
substantive religious influences—was rapidly becoming reality in virtually all
parts of the world.[61] Writing about politics in Nasser's Egypt, Nkrumah's Ghana,
Bourguiba's Tunisia, and Sihanouk's Cambodia, Jean Lacouture observed in
1970 that "religion is doing such a good job of strengthening political authority
. . . that it is paving the way for its own deterioration."[62] Richard Mitchell, a sensitive analyst of religious politics in the Middle East, predicted in 1968 that "the
essentially secular reform nationalism now in vogue in the Arab world will continue to operate to end the earlier appeal of [the Muslim Brotherhood]."[63] Most

sweepingly, it was in this same year that Peter Berger made his strong forecast about the fizzling out of religion. Secularization, it seemed, was not so much a speculative academic theory as an imminent global reality.

Despite political secularism's apparently unstoppable advances in the course of the twentieth century, it began to experience serious setbacks in the 1960s. These setbacks rapidly multiplied after 1967.

First, many of the most important agents of political secularism declined or disappeared. Nehru died in 1964, opening up space in the world's largest democracy for a more religious politics[64]; a series of coups thrust Sukarno from power in 1965, culminating in the liquidation of Indonesia's Communist Party (PKI) and the gradual rise of a more religion-based politics; Nkrumah was overthrown in a coup in 1966, thus ending the ideological hegemony of "Nkrumahism" and paving the way for Ghana's churches to assert a more independent political influence[65]; and Nasser's armies were crushed by Israel in 1967, marking the beginning of the end of secular pan-Arabism, and clearing the way for Nasser's rival, King Faisal of Saudi Arabia, to create a new transnational movement defined by religion, the Organization of the Islamic Conference (OIC), which met for the first time in 1969.[66] At least as importantly, Nasser's defeat in 1967 and death in 1970 cleared the way for a variety of actors to forge—with growing success over time—a transnational, pan-Islamic consciousness. At the same time, Communism, which had been a preeminent agent of global political secularization for a hundred years, was increasingly on the moral and strategic defensive thanks to the Sino-Soviet split, the Soviet invasion of Czechoslovakia in 1968, the publication of Solzhenitsyn's *Gulag Archipelago* in 1973, and the Soviet invasion of Afghanistan in 1979. A movement that seemed to be in the vanguard of modern progress in the 1870s looked more like a declining and ideologically exhausted empire in the 1970s.

Second, many religious movements formerly sidelined or discredited by the global rise of political secularism began making a comeback in the 1960s and 1970s. The Roman Catholic Church received a fresh burst of social and political self-confidence through the Second Vatican Council (1962–65), and then through the dynamic papacy of John Paul II (1978–2005), which led the Church to affirm democracy and religious freedom and operate as an autonomous actor in civil society. Gone were the days of defensive concordats with individual governments or close alliances with fascist regimes like those of Franco in Spain or Salazar in Portugal.[67] Hindu nationalism, the object of systematic attack and marginalization by the secular Congress Party (it was forbidden to be simultaneously a Congress member and a member of "communal" groups like the RSS), played an increasingly assertive and influential role in politics, with its political wing, the Bharatiya Jana Sangh, winning 10 percent of the national vote in the 1967 general elections and helping to form the Janata coalition that resoundingly defeated Indira Gandhi's Congress in 1977.[68] The formation of an Islamic Republic in Iran in 1979 inspired Muslim movements around the world, Sunni and Shia alike, to believe that it was possible to Islamize politics and society.[69]

In general, one can discern a powerful qualitative shift in the orientation of religious organizations around the world in the second half of the twentieth century: in every major religious tradition, leaders and key movements abandoned an exclusive focus on spiritual or cultural activity, and took up political activity as an integral component of their religious mission. The Muslim Brotherhood dropped the apoliticism of its founder, Hasan al-Banna, in favor of direct political engagement; RSS members in India began organizing political parties and other politically active organizations; the Catholic Church promoted far more robust clerical and lay activism in defense of human rights; conservative Protestants in the United States abandoned their long fundamentalist self-isolation and distaste for politics, lasting from the 1925 Scopes trial to the late 1940s, in favor of organized and sustained social and political activism through such bodies as the National Association of Evangelicals and World Vision;[70] and influential Buddhist leaders such as Walpola Rahula in Ceylon called for an end to quiescence on the part of monks and lay Buddhists and instead for a robust engagement with politics.[71]

But why did religious organizations demonstrate a growing desire and power to shape international politics after the late 1960s? Certainly, "retail" explanations—the death or overthrow of charismatic secular leaders, the declining legitimacy of Communism, the failure of secular states and ideologies to deliver rapid development—are part of the story. However, broader "wholesale" explanations are required to clarify why religious actors made a political comeback across the international system, in such a wide variety of regions and religious traditions, and among both developed and developing countries.

The first such explanation is that some of the dominant political and social trends of the nineteenth and twentieth centuries were not nearly as formidable in their opposition to religion as analysts anticipated. Modernization was expected to weaken the hold of religion on society as people became more free, rational, and cosmopolitan. Programs of political secularization were intended to cut religion off from financial and symbolic support it received from the state, whereupon the social power of religious institutions, it was assumed, would weaken or collapse. However, such programs of institutional separation or differentiation between state and religion, though often imposed on religion by aggressive secularists, did not necessarily end up weakening religion. Religious actors may have enjoyed fewer privileges, but they soon realized they had more freedom to maneuver.[72] And the urbanization, economic development, and growth of literacy brought about by modernization often created a petite bourgeoisie with the inclination and resources to give religious actors support and loyalty the state had ceased to provide. In other words, modernization and secularization (in the sense of concept 3, institutional differentiation) often combined to increase the autonomy and capacity of religious organizations to formulate their own political agendas and mobilize their own resources and followers.[73]

The second "wholesale" explanation is that global democratization greatly increased the opportunity of religious actors to compete freely for political influence. At least some charismatic Third-World leaders, such as Nasser, Bourguiba, Nkrumah, and Atatürk, were effective secularizers because they were latter-day Rousseauian lawgivers: they sat at the apex of authoritarian or only partially democratic systems, and they could impose their secularist decrees in the name of the "general will" without having to secure any genuine mandate from the people in competitive elections. With the number of "free" and "partly free" countries jumping from 93 in 1975 to 147 in 2005,[74] religious groups and organizations around the world have enjoyed a greater opportunity to influence the political process by forming lobbies, fielding candidates, organizing political parties, and inviting politicians of all kinds to try to win their support. In countries that combine some modernization with little or no democratization, religious and other organizations experience dissonant dynamics. They may enjoy an increased capacity to formulate their own agenda and mobilize resources, but have little or no opportunity to promote that agenda in the formal political process, a mixture of conditions that is likely to generate violent militancy when combined with an integralist political theology. It is therefore not surprising that regions of the world that have experienced some modernization, little democratization, and the widespread diffusion of militant political theologies—the Arab Middle East and North Africa, above all—have produced radical religious movements such as Al Qaeda and Hizballah.[75]

A third explanation is that globalization increased the capacity of religious actors to project influence, mobilize resources, and attract followers across national boundaries, greatly enhancing their overall political position vis-à-vis nation-states. It was widely assumed that globalization would create a single global village, wiping away or at least blurring differences of religion, culture, and ethnicity.[76] But however much globalization has caused people to appreciate their common humanity, it has also caused some people to appreciate their religious particularity—how *different* their religion is from the religion (or lack of religion) espoused by the people they see on TV or the Internet. Moreover, the closing of otherwise vast distances of space and time has enabled particular groups of co-religionists not only to feel like spiritual brothers and sisters even across national boundaries but to act, react, and organize as coherent political agents.

Millions of Christians around the world, for example, circulate bulletins via email and the Internet detailing how their fellow believers are persecuted in far-flung, obscure locales like Orissa in eastern India, Kaduna in Nigeria, and Sulawesi in Indonesia. And they act in remarkably coordinated fashion, forming transnational advocacy networks and coalitions that pressure governments and international organizations to stop the assaults on their faith.[77] In 2005 Muslims around the world rapidly learned, via cable television and the Internet, how Muhammad had been depicted and dishonored in cartoons published in Denmark, and soon Muslim governments, the OIC, and tens of thousands of ordinary Muslims were lodging vehement protests as well as organizing efforts in international bodies to proscribe religious "defamation."[78] The expansion and intensification of global immigration, communication, and transportation has made it possible for more and more religious communities to establish effective transnational networks and organizations. In short, not only do religious actors think globally, they also *act* globally. And thanks to the accelerating processes of globalization, they can increasingly muster resources, mobilize constituencies, and apply pressure on governments and international organizations in ways that other non-state actors—and even some states—can only dream of.

The foregoing broad-brush portrait of the rise and decline of political secularism inevitably omits and distorts important events and trends. The period we describe as one long and dramatic ascent for political secularism, 1789 to 1967, also saw the rise of some politically important religious movements, such as Christian Democracy in Western Europe and the Civil Rights movement in the United States, which succeeded at least to some extent in resisting the general trend. Likewise, the period we describe as the reversal of political secularism, 1967 to the present, has seen some forms of political secularism remain fairly resilient, such as French laicism or the Chinese government's powerful combination of Communism, capitalism, and Han nationalism. And our entire narrative would have to be crafted differently for the United States, which has remained persistently religious, though even here a sweeping "secular revolution" occurred in elite culture and politics in the late nineteenth and early twentieth centuries.[79] Overall, we are confident that a basic qualitative shift in international politics has occurred: during most of the period between 1789 and 1967, political secularism put religious actors and ideologies on the defensive in much of the world; during most of the period between 1967 and the present, the situation has been reversed, with politically engaged religious actors of all kinds, in every part of the world, putting secular regimes and ideologies on the defensive, no doubt most spectacularly on September 11, 2001.

INCORPORATING RELIGION INTO
INTERNATIONAL RELATIONS THEORY

Given the previous state of secularization, the resurgence of religion in global politics amounts to an accumulation of anomalies that now calls for a Kuhnian paradigm shift in international relations theory. Indeed, if international relations theory is to take into account religion's distinctive political role—and thus understand global politics better—it must undertake a revision more radical than merely incorporating religion into its existing assumptions. The central focus of classical and neorealism on the state and its ends of power and security leave little room for religion.[80] The same goes for neoliberalism, the rationalist strand of the liberal tradition, which posits the state as a unitary actor, though it also stresses the efficacy of international institutions, and usually posits the ends of states as power, security, or wealth-maximization.[81] Classical liberalism acknowledges the influence of a variety of state ends and domestic actors as well as international institutions, perhaps allowing religion to function as one of the domestic actors that shapes states' policies. But religion's scope and influence is far broader than this theoretical space will allow. The centrality of secularism in liberal thought also hinders a robust incorporation of religion. International relations scholars have often posited Marxism (or socialism) as a third competitor, though far less so after 1989.[82] But because of its axiomatic treatment of religion as an "opiate" of the masses and as an impotent strand of the bourgeois superstructure, this tradition will prove of little help. More welcome to religion ought to be a theory that has overtaken Marxism as a third force in recent years and that centrally stresses identity: constructivism. As Jack Snyder points out in his introduction to this volume, however, religion has not played a strong role in this tradition as of yet. One inhibiting factor may be the theoretical commitment of constructivism's founding father, political scientist Alexander Wendt, to viewing the state as a unitary actor and the primary actor in international politics.[83] It is possible, of course, that a state might adopt religious ends as its own; some states do. But, as we are about to argue, recognizing religion as an actor that is not easily subsumed into the state is one of two major revisions that international relations theory ought to undertake. The other is a recognition of the distinctive ends and worldviews that religious actors hold.

In both their demography and their claims to legitimacy, religious communities spill over the boundaries of states. Most closely adhering to state boundaries are Hinduism and Judaism, though even they have large diasporas. Christianity and Islam, the world's largest religions, claim 2.1 and 1.5 billion people, respectively. Every major world religion is far older than the modern state and is based on a legitimacy claim far more encompassing than the state. Not just their populations but also their authority structures straddle states. This is perhaps most true for the Catholic Church, the most centralized of the major religions, but also holds for the Muslim Brotherhood, the World Council of Churches, the network of Orthodox Churches, the World Hindu Council (VHP), and many others. World Vision, an evangelical relief and development agency, operates in some one hundred countries and sports a budget of $1 billion, larger than the GNP of forty-nine countries. Even when religious actors influence primarily the politics of a single state, they are often supported by co-religionists from the outside. Consider "the Catholic Wave," the disproportionately strong role of the Catholic Church and of majority Catholic countries in the "third wave of democracy."[84] Crucial to the oppositional stances of national churches in Brazil, Chile, Malawi, Spain, Poland, the Philippines, and elsewhere was the Second Vatican Council. In cases like Poland, Rome assisted a national church quite directly—i.e., through Pope John Paul II. Al Qaeda, itself a non-state actor, purports to act on behalf of the entire *umma*, or body of Muslims, seeks to establish the rule of a transnational caliph, not a state, and claims to assist particular aggrieved Muslims within states across the world. Behind the passage of the International Religious Freedom Act by the U.S. Congress in 1998 was the crucial role of evangelicals acting on behalf of fellow evangelicals across the globe. Just as religious actors do not easily fit into the boundaries of states, neither do they fit easily into the boundaries of "international relations" or "comparative politics," the disciplinary subfields that Westphalia created. Far better at capturing their nature is what political scientist Susanne Rudolph called "transnational civil society."[85]

If religious organizations do not fit easily into existing international relations theories, neither do their ends. Unlike states, international organizations, the European Union, NGOs with political purposes, or any of the domestic actors that are organized to influence politics—parties, labor unions, lobbies, legislatures, courts, and the like—religious communities are not rooted fundamentally in political ends but rather in beliefs and practices oriented around claims about the ultimate ground of existence. How they orient themselves toward politics depends in part upon how they then translate these basic claims into doctrines of the political order—what we have called political theology. These doctrines will be consistent with the organization of the states system and the ends of states to greater and lesser degrees, depending on how this translation takes place. Sometimes a religious actor's political theology will challenge the international system radically: witness Al Qaeda. In other cases, probably the vast majority, a political theology will "work within the system" insofar as it accepts the basic parameters of the state and the states system but advocates particular kinds of policies or regime structures that may or may not coincide with the status quo. The U.S. Catholic bishops condemn the Iraq War as unjust; the BJP in India pushes for a stronger public recognition of a Hindu homeland; the Russian Orthodox

Church urges Russia to clamp down on foreign Protestant missionaries; more sweepingly, the Justice and Development Party in Turkey challenges the secular character of Turkey's constitution; the Islamic government of Sudan declares a harsh form of sharia as the law of the land; and the Tamil Tigers fight for a Sri Lanka in which they are not discriminated against by a Buddhist government. Flanking this middle ground at the other end of the spectrum are religious actors whose ends are indistinguishable from secular ones. German liberal Protestant theologian Adolph Harnack, fully co-opted by Prussian nationalism, wrote speeches for Kaiser Wilhem II justifying Germany's attack on Belgium in 1914. But even when religious ends work within or wholly converge with those of the state, this is only true because of how they have been derived from claims about matters that are far more ultimate than the state or the states system.

As these examples show, political theology leads religious actors to an enormous variety of political ends, including support for democratization, terrorism, civil war, peace agreements, political reconciliation, economic development, religious freedom, theocracy, the persecution of minorities, human rights, environmental justice, and many others. It is not our claim that ideas alone are what drive the politics of religions. Their differentiation from the state, their size, their internal organization, the intensity of their adherents' beliefs, their demographic and economic characteristics, their historical relationship to the state and temporal authorities, and many other factors will make a difference. Our plea, rather, is that international relations theory ought to recognize far more than its current traditions do the distinct character of religious ends and how they translate into politics, as well as the distinct character of religious actors.

Neither of these pleas amounts to a research program. But they do challenge the assumptions of the most influential traditions in international relations thought and call for new premises on which research on religion's influence in global politics might be based. New assumptions are needed because the most enduring traditions have been highly secularized from their inception and because the resurgence of religion in global politics makes this secularism no longer viable.

NOTES

The authors are indebted to Monica Duffy Toft, whose extensive scholarly collaboration on related projects on religion and global politics contributed importantly to the ideas contained in this chapter. The fruits of this collaboration appear in Monica Duffy Toft, Daniel Philpott, and Timothy Samuel Shah, *God's Century: Resurgent*

Religion in Global Politics (New York: Norton, 2011). The authors also thank Peter Berger and Peter Katzenstein for their helpful comments.

1. Peter L. Berger, "A Bleak Outlook is Seen for Religion," *New York Times*, February 25, 1968, 3.

2. Peter L. Berger, "The Desecularization of the World: An Overview," in *The Desecularization of the World: Resurgent Religion and World Politics*, ed. Peter L. Berger (Washington, D.C.: Eerdmans/Ethics and Public Policy Center, 1999), 2.

3. For an articulation and elaboration of this definition, see Daniel Philpott, "Explaining the Political Ambivalence of Religion," *American Political Science Review* 103, no. 3 (2007): 506–07.

4. Jonathan Fox, *A World Survey of Religion and the State* (Cambridge: Cambridge University Press, 2007).

5. Jonathan Fox, *A World Survey of Religion and the State* (Cambridge: Cambridge University Press, 2007), 250–251.

6. Philpott, "Ambivalence of Religion," 506–07.

7. Abdullahi Ahmed An-Na'im, *Islam and the Secular State: Negotiation the Future of Shari'a* (Cambridge, MA: Harvard University Press, 2008), Abdullahi Ahmed An-Na'im, *Toward an Islamic Reformation: Civil Liberties, Human Rights, and International Law* (Syracuse, NY: Syracuse University Press, 1990), Abdulaziz Abdulhussein Sachedina, *The Islamic Roots of Democratic Pluralism* (New York: Oxford University Press, 2001), Abdolkarim Soroush, *Reason, Freedom, and Democracy in Islam: Essential Writings of Abdolkarim Soroush* (New York: Oxford University Press, 2002).

8. See, for instance, Peter Berger, *The Sacred Canopy: Elements of a Sociological Theory of Religion* (New York: Random House, 1967).

9. Grace Davie, "Believing without Belonging: Is This the Future of Religion in Britain?" *Social Compass* 37 (1990).

10. Much of the following account of the transition from medieval Europe to the modern system of sovereign states and the role of religion in this transition is adapted from Daniel Philpott, *Revolutions in Sovereignty: How Ideas Shaped Modern International Relations* (Princeton: Princeton University Press, 2001), 75–149.

11. John Gerard Ruggie, "Continuity and Transformation in the World Polity: Toward a Neorealist Synthesis," in *Neorealism and Its Critics*, ed. Robert O. Keohane (New York: Columbia University Press, 1986).

12. Stephen D. Krasner, "Westphalia and All That," in *Ideas and Foreign Policy: Beliefs, Institutions, and Political Change*, ed. Judith Goldstein and Robert O. Keohane (Ithaca: Cornell University Press, 1993); Daniel Nexon, *The Struggle for Power in Early Modern Europe: Religious Conflict, Dynastic Empires, and International Change* (Princeton: Princeton University Press, 2009); Andreas Osiander, "Sovereignty, International Relations, and the Westphalian Myth," *International Organization* 55, no. 2 (2001); Philpott, *Revolutions in Sovereignty*; Benjamin Straumann, "The Peace of Westphalia (1648) as a Secular Constitution," *Constellations* 15, no. 2 (June 2008); Benno Teschke, *The Myth of 1648: Class, Geopolitics, and the Making of Modern International Relations* (London: Verso, 2003).

13. Andreas Osiander, *The States System of Europe, 1640–1990* (Oxford: Clarendon Press, 1994), 27, 41, 77–89.

14. Quoted in David Maland, *Europe in the Seventeenth Century* (London: Macmillan, 1966), 16.

15. Kalevi Holsti, *Peace and War: Armed Conflicts and International Order, 1648–1989* (Cambridge: Cambridge University Press, 1991), 46–59.

16. Erastianism is named for Thomas Erastus, a Swiss doctor and theologian in the school of reformer Ulrich Zwingli. He held that the state possessed a right and a duty to carry out punishments for ecclesiastical offenses, as well as, of course, for civil ones. Erastianism became known as a wider doctrine of the supremacy of the secular state through the writings of Richard Hooker in the seventeenth century, particularly his *Of the lawes of ecclesiasticall politie* (1593–1662) and his speeches in the Westminster Assembly of 1643.

17. Euan Cameron, *The European Reformation* (Oxford: Oxford University Press, 1991), 153.

18. Alexis de Tocqueville, *The Old Regime and the French Revolution* (Garden City, N.Y.: Doubleday, 1955).

19. For the most recent scholarship, see Linda Colley, *Britons: Forging the Nation* (New Haven, CT: Yale University Press, 1992); Adrian Hastings, *The Construction of Nationhood: Ethnicity, Religion, and Nationalism* (Cambridge: Cambridge University Press, 1997); Anthony W. Marx, *Faith in Nation: Exclusionary Origins of Nationalism* (New York: Oxford University Press, 2003); Anthony D. Smith, *Chosen Peoples : Sacred Sources of National Identity* (Oxford: Oxford University Press, 2003). Representing the previous wave are Benedict Anderson, *Imagined Communities* (London: Verso, 1983); Ernest Gellner, *Nations and Nationalism* (Ithaca: Cornell University Press, 1983); E. J. Hobsbawm, *Nations and Nationalism Since 1780: Programme, Myth, Reality* (Cambridge: Cambridge University Press, 1992).

20. Elizabeth Shakman Hurd, *The Politics of Secularism in International Relations* (Princeton: Princeton University Press, 2008), 23.

21. Philpott, *Revolutions in Sovereignty*, 137–47.

22. Anthony Gill, *The Political Origins of Religious Liberty* (Cambridge: Cambridge University Press, 2008), 60–113. Gill's work is an important, rigorous one in the growing body of scholarship in political science and religion. Our own view of the origins of religious liberty, though, stresses the causal role of ideas more strongly. See Timothy Samuel Shah, "The Accumulation of Many Laws," review of *The Political Origins of Religious Liberty*, by Anthony Gill, *Review of Politics* 71, no. 2 (Spring 2009): 327.

23. I have benefitted greatly from Michael Doyle's taxonomy of realists in *Ways of War and Peace* (New York: Norton, 1997). He categorizes Hobbes and Waltz as "structural" realists and Machiavelli and Morgenthau as "fundamentalists." On Hobbes, see also a section of an essay by Stanley Hoffmann, "Rousseau on War and Peace," in *Janus and Minerva: Essays in the Theory and Practice of International Politics* (Boulder, CO: Westview Press, 1987), 25–36.

24. Jacques Maritain, "The End of Machiavellianism," in *The Crisis of Modern Times. Perspectives from the Review of Politics, 1939–1962*, ed. A. James McAdams (Notre Dame, IN: University of Notre Dame Press, 2007).

25. Doyle, *Ways of War and Peace*, 230–50.

26. For the role of theology in Grotius's conception of international law, see Hugo Grotius, *De Jure Belli ac Pacis Libri Tres (On the Law of War and Peace, Three Books)*, trans. Francis W. Kelsey, vol. 2, *The Classics of International Law*, ed. James Brown Scott (Oxford: Clarendon Press, 1925), especially the Prolegomena and Book 2, chapter 20; for his Erastian views and broad Christian theology, see Hugo Grotius, *Ordinum Hollandiae Ac Westfrisiae Pietas*, ed. and trans. Edwin Rabbie, Studies in the History of Christian Thought, ed. Heiko Oberman (Leiden: Brill, 1995).

27. On liberalism in international relations theory, see Doyle, *Ways of War and Peace*; Andrew Moravcsik, "Taking Preferences Seriously: A Liberal Theory of International Politics," *International Organization* 51, no. 4 (1997); Michael Joseph Smith, *Liberalism and International Reform* (Cambridge: Cambridge University Press, 1992); Arnold Wolfers and Laurence Martin, *The Anglo-American Tradition: Readings from Thomas More to Woodrow Wilson* (New Haven, CT: Yale University Press, 1956).

28. Lynn Avery Hunt, *Politics, Culture, and Class in the French Revolution*, Studies on the History of Society and Culture (Berkeley: University of California Press, 1984).

29. Jean-Jacques Rousseau, *On the Social Contract: With Geneva Manuscript and Political Economy* (New York: St. Martin's Press, 1978).

30. Hunt, *Politics, Culture, and Class*; Simon Schama, *Citizens: A Chronicle of the French Revolution* (New York: Knopf, 1989).

31. Michael Burleigh, Earthly Powers: *The Clash of Religion and Politics in Europe, from the French Revolution to the Great War* (New York: HarperCollins, 2005).

32. Conor Cruise O'Brien, *Ancestral Voices: Religion and Nationalism in Ireland* (Chicago: University of Chicago Press, 1995), 14ff.

33. Jonathan Israel, *The Dutch Republic: Its Rise, Greatness, and Fall, 1477–1806*, in *Oxford History of Early Modern Europe*, ed. R. J. W. Evans (Oxford: Clarendon Press, 1995), 1115.

34. Israel, *The Dutch Republic*, 1125.

35. Charles Leslie Glenn Jr., *The Myth of the Common School* (Amherst, MA: The University of Massachusetts Press, 1987), 240.

36. Quoted in Glenn, *Myth of the Common School*, 241.

37. Theodore Zeldin, *France, 1848–1945*, vol 2, *Politics and Anger*, Oxford History of Modern Europe (Oxford: Clarendon Press, 1973), xiii.

38. Glenn, *The Myth of the Common School*; Stathis N. Kalyvas, *The Rise of Christian Democracy in Europe*, The Wilder House Series in Politics, History, and Culture (Ithaca: Cornell University Press, 1996); Christian Smith, ed., *The Secular Revolution: Power, Interests, and Conflict in the Secularization of American Public Life* (Berkeley: University of California Press, 2003).

39. Owen Chadwick, *The Secularization of the European Mind in the Nineteenth Century : The Gifford Lectures in the University of Edinburgh for 1973–1974*, Gifford Lectures (Cambridge: Cambridge University Press, 1975), 111.

40. Chadwick, *The Secularization of the European Mind*, 111–112.

41. Philip Hamburger, *Separation of Church and State* (Cambridge, MA: Harvard University Press, 2002); John T. McGreevy, *Catholicism and American Freedom: A History*, 1st ed. (New York: Norton, 2003).

42. Zeldin, *France, 1848–1945*.

43. Chadwick, *The Secularization of the European Mind*, 66.

44. O'Brien, *Ancestral Voices*, 16.

45. G. W. F. Hegel, *Elements of the Philosophy of Right* (Cambridge: Cambridge University Press, 1991).

46. Martin Wight, *Four Seminal Thinkers in International Theory: Machiavelli, Grotius, Kant, and Mazzini* (Oxford: Oxford University Press, 2005), 89–115.

47. Hans Kohn, *Prophets and Peoples: Studies in Nineteenth Century Nationalism* (New York: Collier, 1961), 46–75.

48. Quoted in Martin Wight, *Four Seminal Thinkers*, 101.

49. Immanuel Kant, "Perpetual Peace: A Philosophical Sketch," in *Kant's Political Writings*, ed. Hans Reiss (Cambridge: Cambridge University Press, 1970), 114.

50. The material in the next two sections relies on Timothy Samuel Shah's forthcoming, *Secularism Is Dead: The Global Rise and Fall of Godless Government* (Stanford, CA: Hoover Institution Press).

51. Anthony Gill, *The Political Origins of Religious Liberty*, Cambridge Studies in Social Theory, Religion, and Politics (Cambridge: Cambridge University Press, 2008), 168.

52. Donald Eugene Smith, *Religion and Political Development, an Analytic Study*, The Little, Brown Series in Comparative Politics (Boston: Little, Brown, 1970), 122–123.

53. M. Searle Bates, *Religious Liberty: An Inquiry* (New York: Harper, 1945), 1.

54. See, for example, Jawaharlal Nehru, *The Discovery of India* (Calcutta: Signet Press, 1946).

55. Jean Lacouture, *The Demigods: Charismatic Leadership in the Third World*, 1st ed. (New York: Knopf, 1970), 179.

56. On Nehru's antipathy to religion, see, for example, Shashi Tharoor, *Nehru: The Invention of India* (New York: Arcade Publishing, 2003).

57. Reinhold Niebuhr, *Christian Realism and Political Problems* (New York: Scribner, 1953), and *The Irony of American History* (New York: Scribner, 1952).

58. Samuel P. Huntington, *Political Order in Changing Societies* (New Haven, CT: Yale University Press, 1968).

59. See, for example, Daniel Lerner, *The Passing of Traditional Society: Modernizing the Middle East* (Glencoe, IL: Free Press, 1958); and Gabriel Abraham Almond and Sidney Verba, *The Civic Culture: Political Attitudes and Democracy in Five Nations* (Princeton: Princeton University Press, 1963).

60. Michael E. Latham, *Modernization as Ideology: American Social Science and "Nation Building" in the Kennedy Era* (Chapel Hill, NC: University of North Carolina Press, 2000).

61. Many of the arguments in this section were developed in collaboration with Monica Duffy Toft and originally appeared in Timothy Samuel Shah and Monica Duffy Toft, "Why God Is Winning," *Foreign Policy*, July/August 2006, 38 and in more

extended form in Timothy Samuel Shah and Monica Duffy Toft, "God is Winning: Religion in Global Politics," in *Blind Spot: When Journalists Don't Get Religion*, ed. Paul Marshall, Lela Gilbert, and Roberta Green (Oxford: Oxford University Press, 2009), 11–30.

62. Jean Lacouture, *The Demigods*, 40.

63. Richard P. Mitchell, *The Society of the Muslim Brothers* (New York: Oxford University Press, 1993), xxiii–xxiv.

64. Thomas Blom Hansen, *The Saffron Wave: Democracy and Hindu Nationalism in Modern India* (Princeton: Princeton University Press, 1999); Christophe Jaffrelot, *The Hindu Nationalist Movement in India* (New York: Columbia University Press, 1996).

65. Kwesi A. Dickson, "The Church and the Quest for Democracy in Ghana," in *The Christian Churches and the Democratisation of Africa*, ed. Paul Gifford (Leiden: Brill, 1995), 261–275.

66. Noor Ahmad Baba, *Organisation of Islamic Conference: Theory and Practice of Pan-Islamic Cooperation* (Dhaka, Bangladesh: University Press Limited, 1994), 52–70.

67. Daniel Philpott, 'The Catholic Wave,' *Journal of Democracy* 15, no. 2 (2004): 32–46. On the importance of the pope's leadership during the last phase of the Cold War, see John Lewis Gaddis, *The Cold War: A New History* (New York: Penguin Press, 2005).

68. Bruce Desmond Graham, *Hindu Nationalism and Indian Politics: The Origins and Development of the Bharatiya Jana Sangh*, Cambridge South Asian Studies 47 (Cambridge: Cambridge University Press, 1990).

69. Mark Juergensmeyer, *The New Cold War? Religious Nationalism Confronts the Secular State* (Berkley: University of California Press, 1993).

70. Joel A. Carpenter, *Revive Us Again: The Reawakening of American Fundamentalism* (New York: Oxford University Press, 1997).

71. Walpola Rahula, *The Heritage of the Bhikkhu: A Short History of the Bhikkhu in Educational, Cultural, Social, and Political Life* (New York: Grove Press, 1974).

72. Ivan Vallier, "The Roman Catholic Church: A Transnational Actor," *International Organization* 25, no. 3 (1971): 479–502.

73. Rodney Stark and Roger Finke, *Acts of Faith: Explaining the Human Side of Religion* (Berkeley: University of California Press, 2000); Christian Smith and Michael Emerson, *American Evangelicalism: Embattled and Thriving* (Chicago: University of Chicago Press, 1998).

74. Aili Piano, Arch Puddington, and Mark Y. Rosenberg, *Freedom in the World 2006: The Annual Survey of Political Rights & Civil Liberties* (New York: Freedom House, 2006).

75. This is roughly the argument of Mohammed M. Hafez, *Why Muslims Rebel: Repression and Resistance in the Islamic World* (Boulder, CO: Lynne Rienner, 2003).

76. Peter Singer, *One World: The Ethics of Globalization* (New Haven, CT: Yale University Press, 2002). The strengths and limits of this view are explored in Benjamin R. Barber, *Jihad vs. McWorld* (New York: Ballantine Books, 1996).

77. Allen D. Hertzke, *Freeing God's Children: The Unlikely Alliance for Global Human Rights* (Lanham, MD: Rowman & Littlefield, 2004).

78. Hassan M. Fattah, "At Mecca Meeting, Cartoon Outrage Crystallized," *New York Times*, February 9, 2006.

79. Christian Smith, ed., *The Secular Revolution: Power, Interests, and Conflict in the Secularization of American Public Life* (Berkeley: University of California Press, 2003).

80. Robert O. Keohane, "Realism, Neorealism, and the Study of World Politics," in *Neorealism and Its Critics* (see note 11).

81. See David Baldwin, "Neoliberalism, Neorealism, and World Politics," in *Neorealism and Neoliberalism: The Contemporary Debate*, ed. David Baldwin (New York: Columbia University Press, 1993); and Robert O. Keohane, *After Hegemony: Cooperation and Discord in the World Political Economy* (Princeton: Princeton University Press, 1984).

82. See, for instance, the excellent analysis of Doyle in *Ways of War and Peace*.

83. Alexander Wendt, *Social Theory of International Politics* (Cambridge: Cambridge University Press, 1999). See also the essays in a seminal constructivist volume, Peter J. Katzenstein, ed., *The Culture of National Security: Norms and Identity in World Politics* (New York: Columbia University Press, 1996), none of which deals with religion. Katzenstein himself, though, has since become one of the field's leading advocates of the study of religion. He, along with political scientist Timothy A. Byrnes, later edited an important volume on religion's role in European politics, Timothy A. Byrnes and Peter J. Katzenstein, eds., *Religion in an Expanding Europe* (Cambridge: Cambridge University Press, 2006). Constructivism's quality of being theoretically open to religion but containing only a nascent track record of scholarship on religion might also be attributed to the English School. For a effort to bring religion in, see Scott Thomas, *The Global Resurgence of Religion and the Transformation of International Relations: The Struggle for the Soul of the Twenty-First Century* (New York: Palgrave Macmillan, 2004).

84. Samuel P. Huntington, *The Third Wave: Democratization in the Late Twentieth Century* (Norman, OK: University of Oklahoma Press, 1991).

85. Susanne Hoeber Rudolph, "Introduction: Religion, States, and Transnational Civil Society," in *Transnational Religion and Fading States*, ed. Susanne Hoeber Rudolph and James Piscatori (Boulder, CO: Westview Press, 1997).

3. SECULARISM AND
INTERNATIONAL RELATIONS THEORY

ELIZABETH SHAKMAN HURD

Contemporary international relations theory takes the Euro-American definition of religion and its separation from politics as the starting point for social
scientific inquiry. I adopt a different starting point. Secularism refers to a series
of political settlements that define, regulate, and manage religion in modern
politics, including international politics. This chapter draws attention to the
politics surrounding these settlements. It examines two trajectories of secularism, understood as sets of practices that embody what it means to be "secular"
in particular times and places. The first is laicism, in which religion is portrayed
as an impediment to modernization and development. The second is Christian
or Judeo-Christian secularism, in which religion is portrayed as a source of unity
and identity within cultures and civilizations, and conflict between them. In
examining the history and politics of these forms of secularism, I develop four
take-away points for scholars of international relations (IR):

- International relations theorists need to pay closer attention to how foundational cultural and normative categories such as the secular and the religious
  operate politically in international affairs. Varieties of secularism are not reducible to material power or resources but play a constitutive role in creating agents and in contributing to the international normative structures in
  which these agents interact.

- Varieties of secularism developed at the domestic and regional levels are influential at the global level. These secularisms reflect shared interests, identities, and understandings about religion and politics, and constitute part of the social and cultural foundation of international relations. They contribute to the construction of national and supranational interests and identities, serve as strategies for the management of religious diversity and religious pluralism, contribute to the creation of inclusionary and exclusionary group identities, and influence international conflict and cooperation.
- The social, historical, and philosophical particularities and contingencies of various forms of secularism suggest that realist, liberal, and constructivist theories of international relations, international law, and international order that consider religion to a private sphere need to be reevaluated.
- Until recently, a consensus has separated a Judeo-Christian-derived notion of the "sacred" from an allegedly universal "secular" reason. This consensus has defined the terms through which religion and politics are conceptualized in the field of international relations. Yet as other formulations of the sacred and secular make themselves heard, this consensus is showing signs of strain. How these strains are addressed is critical to world politics. Claims to universality grounded either in the claim to have overcome religio-cultural particularities altogether, as in laicism, or to have located the key to democratic moral and political order in a particular religio-cultural heritage, as in Judeo-Christian secularism, are problematic.

To develop these points I draw on the rich conceptual vocabularies of Charles Taylor, José Casanova, William Connolly, and Talal Asad, bringing their arguments to bear upon international politics. Taylor offered the original impetus for my approach to multiple secularisms in "Modes of Secularism," which describes an "independent political ethic" variety of secularism and a "common ground" strategy of secularism that turn out to be "ancestral to rather different understandings of secularism today."[1] Casanova also laid the groundwork for the multiple secularisms argument in referencing two paths for managing the public/private distinction: liberal and civic/republican. Like Taylor and myself, he is cautiously critical of both of these traditions, "the liberal perspective because it insists on the need to confine religion to a private sphere, fearing that public religions must necessarily threaten individual freedoms and secular differentiated structures; the civic-republican perspective because . . . like the liberal perspective it also conceives of public or civil religions in premodern terms as coextensive with the political or societal community."[2] From an international relations standpoint, Casanova's emphasis on three ethnocentric prejudices in Euro-American theories of secularization is particularly important. He cites a bias for Protestant subjective forms of religion, a bias for "liberal" conceptions of politics and the public sphere, and a bias for the sovereign nation-state as the systemic unit of analysis. Connolly also draws attention to the cultural particularities of modern varieties of secularism, observing that the secularism of Rawls and Habermas draws cultural sustenance from the "private faiths" of those who embody the European traditions from which Christian secularism emerged.[3] Asad explores the construction of modern categories of the secular and the religious, unpacking the assumptions that govern Western forms of secularism including the specific concepts of religion, ethics, and politics that they presuppose.[4]

This chapter builds on these contributions to examine the history and politics of two secularist traditions that have been influential in international politics. Laicism is a discursive formation that attempts to distill a particular understanding of religion and ban it from politics. The secular spheres are emancipated and expanded, as Casanova argues, "at the expense of a much-diminished and confined religious sphere."[5] Judeo-Christian secularism is a matrix of discourse and practice that claims the secular as a unique Western achievement. These varieties of secularism are neither mutually exclusive, nor are they the only forms of secularism in existence. There is no strong or necessary dividing line between them; an individual or institution may draw on resources from both simultaneously. They are not free-floating discourses but are disciplined into individuals and collectivities. As a result, the study of secularism, like the study of nationalism, requires an examination of particular historical contexts and particular social and political practices. It is the study of how these discourses are deployed and with what effects.

These varieties of secularism are influential within and between countries that inherited, borrowed, had imposed upon them, or somehow ended up living with (or in tension with) the secular and religious traditions of historical Latin Christendom, including Europe and its settler colonies, Turkey, Iran, and India. Practitioners, theorists, and ordinary people inculturated into these forms of secularism rely upon, reproduce, and contest these organizing frames to make sense of events involving religion and politics, including international politics. Secularisms pre-structure discourse involving politics and religion, in the sense described by Hayden White.[6] In the language of international relations theory, they are productive forms of power that work "through diffuse constitutive relations" to contribute to the "situated social capacities of actors."[7] They are vehicles through which shared interests and identities involving religion and politics that developed at the domestic, regional, and transnational levels become influential globally.

The argument carries a number of implications for international relations theory. First it marks a significant departure from the cognitivist "trap" criticized by Krasner and other critics of constructivism. As Krasner argues, "Norms, though not irrelevant, do not have the weight that constructivism has attributed to them."[8] I agree. Norms alone do not carry the weight often ascribed to them in constructivist analyses.[9] Norms cannot be analyzed outside of the structures of power and embodied social practices in which they take shape and are expressed. This is the case not only for traditions of secularism but also for formations of nationalism, varieties of capitalism, and other powerful organizing principles and practices of modern collective life. My approach accommodates the "weightiness" of secular authority, expressed not only through beliefs but also habits of speech, sensibilities, practices, and ways of being in the world. Though perhaps a different way of dealing with the "inevitable lightness of norms" than Krasner envisioned, this approach opens possibilities for constructivist theorizing that accounts for the influence of norms without reducing them to individual thoughts and beliefs.

Second, charting the influence of different forms of secularism and their complex and co-constitutive relation with the category of religion poses a fundamental challenge to the clash of civilizations narrative in which religion is portrayed as a fixed source of communal identity that generates conflict in world politics. Tracing the history and politics of the categories of the secular and religious shows that to identify something as *religion* and assign to it a permanent and fixed role in politics is itself a political move. In my understanding of the social construction of secularism,[10] elements of religion escape attempts to define and confine it to particular roles, spaces, or moments in politics. It is not possible to stabilize the category of religion and lock in its relationship to politics.

Third, most international relations scholarship operates on the assumption that secular nationalism and national identity have transcended religion and religious identity. My argument provides evidence to the contrary. Secularist traditions and the religious commitments that are refracted and rephrased through them are implicated in and even partially constitutive of national identity. Religion has contributed to the creation of what Peter van der Veer describes as "public spheres of political interaction central to the formation of national identities."[11] Secularisms play a significant role in creating and contributing to inclusionary and exclusionary group identities, whereby certain religious actors are brought in as fit for political participation in politics while others are excluded. As such, secularisms may be observed to be cultural-national projects of normalizing various religions and particular religious actors as either fit or unfit to participate in politics.

Finally, a more nuanced account of the interplay between religion and politics presents an alternative to realist, liberal, and constructivist theories in which religion is simply considered a private affair. According to conventional accounts, religion was "privatized" in 1648 at the Peace of Westphalia as a solution to sectarian violence in Europe. Yet this claim to delimit the terms and boundaries of modern politics by defining religion as its private counterpart is a politicized move that must be historically contextualized. Secularism is a form of authorized knowledge that creates and perpetuates particular claims about the limits of modern politics; claims which have become established settlements operating below the threshold of public international discourse. These settlements lie at the core of modern assumptions about and practices of state sovereignty.

The next section takes a brief look at the ancestral historical and philosophical context from which these forms of secularism emerged, as reflected in the writings of Immanuel Kant. This excursion, charting the debts owed by modern forms of secularism to Kantian philosophy and ultimately to Christian tradition, lays the groundwork for the subsequent discussion of Euro-American varieties of secularism and international politics.

KANT AS A FORERUNNER OF SECULARISM

Though well known in the field of international relations for his contributions to theories of cosmopolitanism and the democratic peace, Kant was also an important forerunner of modern forms of secularism.[12] In fact, the legacy of Kant's rational religion may someday be judged to outweigh his other contributions. Kantian universal moral philosophy sought to address the adversarial effects of religious sectarianism in Europe. To do so, it laid a template for a generic form of Protestant Christianity that was intended to supersede sectarian faith. This template served as an important precursor of and resource for later articulations of secularism. To understand it is to catch a glimpse of the philosophical and religious context out of which modern European and American secularisms emerged. It is also to gain a sense of how historical, religious, and philosophical legacies continue to resonate in the modern politics of secularism.

To overcome sectarianism Kant proposed elevating universal philosophy, or rational religion, to the position previously reserved for Christian theology.[13] Rational religion was a generic form of Christianity that would replace and render publicly inert sectarian faith. The key to Kantian rational religion is that it is anchored in a metaphysic of the supersensible that is presupposed by any agent of morality.[14] As Connolly argues, "Kant anchors rational religion in the law of morality rather than anchoring morality in ecclesiastical faith."[15] This allows Kant to retain the command model of morality from Augustinian Christianity while shifting the proximate point of command from the Christian God to the individual moral subject.[16] By shifting the point of command to the individual moral subject, however, Kant also ensures that "authoritative moral philosophy and rational religion are now only as secure as the source of morality upon which they draw"—individual apodictic recognition.[17] In this way, Kant's rational religion, although it seeks to displace Christian ecclesiastical theology, actually retains at least four traces of it:

> First, it places singular conceptions of reason and command morality above question. Second, it sets up (Kantian) philosophy as the highest potential authority in adjudicating questions in these two domains and in guiding the people toward eventual enlightenment. Third, it defines the greatest danger to public morality as sectarianism within Christianity. Fourth, in the process of defrocking ecclesiastical theology and crowning philosophy as judge in the last instance, it also delegitimates a place for several non-Kantian, nontheistic perspectives in public life.[18]

Kant was a forerunner of secularism rather than a secularist himself.[19] Yet the forms of secularism that evolved out of the Kantian settlement consisted of "a series of attempts to secure these four effects without open recourse to the Kantian metaphysic of the supersensible. Secularism, in its dominant Western forms, *is* this Kantian fourfold without [a] metaphysical portfolio."[20]

This Kantian influence is discernible in both forms of secularism discussed in this chapter. Laicism represents itself as an authoritative public morality based on a singular conception of reason. It rejects theology in public life as dangerous sectarianism and harbors an antipathy toward nontheistic and non-Kantian philosophies, as well as philosophies of public order derived from Islamic tradition. Laicism attempts to contain ecclesiastical intrusions into public life.[21] Its overarching objective is to provide "an authoritative and self-sufficient public space equipped to regulate and limit 'religious' disputes in public life."[22] To achieve this "Kantian effect," it constantly reinscribes the boundary between public and private, secular and religious, mundane and metaphysical; boundaries that are often legitimated through reference to the dictates of logic, science, reason, or nature.[23] Connolly has described this as "the secular variant of Christianity."[24]

In this secularized Christian moral order, which arguably has powerfully influenced certain dimensions of the modern international order, the spheres of social control are divided between the realm of the Judeo-Christian sacred, on the one hand, and the realm of secular morality, international law, and international order on the other. A consensus separating the Judeo-Christian sacred from universal secular and scientific reason defines the terms through which the sacred and the secular are conceptualized in international relations. The idea that a single logical, natural universal moral order is slowly replacing religion has been influential in Kantian-inspired theories of international relations;

the work of David Held, Martha Nussbaum, and Francis Fukuyama all reflect this assumption.[25]

Like laicism, Judeo-Christian secularism also aspires to serve as an authoritative public morality based on a singular conception of reason. It marginalizes nontheistic and non-Kantian philosophies, including Islamic ones, and seeks to regulate particular kinds of religious intrusions in public discourse. The difference is that whereas laicism claims to have superseded religion and religious origins, Judeo-Christian secularism elevates and expands upon a different aspect of Kant's moral philosophy: his insistence that among all the available ecclesiastical creeds, Protestant Christianity comes closest to "universal rational religion."[26] Judeo-Christian secularism positions itself more warmly toward the metaphysical portfolio rejected by laicism, drawing upon different elements of Kantian philosophy to sustain a distinctive narrative of modern secularism, in which Christianity, and later Judeo-Christianity (with all of the tensions inherent in that hyphen), is depicted as the moral foundation of modern Euro-American secular democracy. The Judeo-Christian origins of modern secularism are held up and valued in this story; claims to secular order are emboldened and not scuttled through reference to them. Unlike laicism, which considers secularism universal, or at least universalizable, Euro-American secularism is portrayed here as culturally embedded, fixed, and largely unproblematic.

One of the arguments this chapter makes is that both of these narratives pose distinct problems from the perspective of the pluralization of world politics. Claims to universality grounded either in the laicist claim to have overcome religio-cultural particularity altogether, or in the Judeo-Christian secularist claim to have located the key to secular, scientific, and/or moral order in a single religio-cultural heritage are both problematic because they privilege and normalize a particular European experience of religion and politics at the expense of other histories and traditions of negotiating relations between political and religious authority.

References to Christian secularism call attention to the complex relations between Christianity (and beginning in the mid-twentieth century, the moral tradition referred to as Judeo-Christianity) and secularism, a subject of heated debate among philosophers, theologians and historians.[27] Theologian John Milbank argues that "all the most important governing assumptions of [secular social] theory are bound up with the modification or the rejection of orthodox Christian positions. These fundamental intellectual shifts are . . . no more rationally 'justifiable' than the Christian positions themselves."[28] Milbank concludes that only Christian theology offers a viable alternative to both secular reason and "nihilism." Christian theologian Arend Theodor van Leeuwen, according to Mark Juergensmeyer, argued that "the idea of a secular basis for politics is not only culturally European but specifically Christian."[29] For van Leeuwen, "secular culture was . . . Christianity's gift to the world."[30] While Juergensmeyer argues that van Leeuwen's thesis about the Christian origins of modern secularism "is increasingly regarded as true, especially in Third World countries," he criticizes it for implying that secularism was *uniquely* Christian, and argues that other civilizations do have distinctions between priestly and secular authority.[31] Juergensmeyer does not suggest, as does van Leeuwen, that Christianity is the *unique* foundation of secular democracy. Instead, he is sympathetic toward the argument that particular forms of secularism are historically specific formations. Juergensmeyer therefore supports van Leeuwen's argument, as do I, that "the particular form of secular society that has evolved in the modern West is a direct extension of its past, including its religious past, and is not some supracultural entity that came into being only after a radical juncture in history."[32]

In reaching these conclusions, however, Juergensmeyer wrestles with and ultimately leaves unresolved a tension in the study of secularism that motivates my own work. On the one hand, he acknowledges the complex yet much-interrupted relation between Christian history and doctrine and modern Christian, Judeo-Christian, and post-Christian secularisms. On the other hand, unlike van Leeuwen, he wants to leave open the possibility that alternative forms of secularism can and have emerged in non-Christian settings. Yet in the same moment that Juergensmeyer gestures toward the need to disaggregate secularism and examine its historical trajectories and variable relations to religion, he describes religion and secular nationalism as opposing "ideologies of order" and concludes that, "there can ultimately be no convergence between religious and secular political ideologies."[33] I disagree. Rather than closing down inquiry by positing the religious and the secular as mutually exclusive ideologies of order, we need to take a closer look at how particular trajectories of secularism have been constructed in relation to religion and what this has meant for international politics.

THE INTERNATIONAL POLITICS OF LAICISM

In *The Secular City*, Harvey Cox writes that "it will do no good to cling to our religions and metaphysical versions of Christianity in the hope that one day religion or metaphysics will once again be back. They are disappearing forever and that means we can now let go and immerse ourselves in the new world of the secular city."[34] Hardt and Negri's *Empire* describes the evanescent quality of religion, suggesting that "every metaphysical tradition is now completely worn out."[35] This view is also influential in the academy, where, as Esposito

observes, "religious faith was at best supposed to be a private matter. The degree of one's intellectual sophistication and objectivity in academia was often
equated with a secular liberalism and relativism that seemed antithetical to religion. . . . Neither development theory nor international relations considered
religion a significant variable for political analysis."[36] In this view, "the mixing
of religion and politics is regarded as necessarily abnormal (departing from the
norm), irrational, dangerous and extremist."[37]

Laicism is a powerful tradition of the secular city, world "empire," and Western academy that presumes that metaphysical traditions have been exhausted
and transcended. It is one of the founding principles of modern political thought
and one of the pillars of the modern separation of church and state. There are
many manifestations of laicism, including the exclusion of religion from the
spheres of power and authority in modern societies (structural differentiation),
the privatization of religion, and decline in church membership and individual religious belief. Laicism is a powerful organizing principle of state politics
influential in France, the former Soviet Union, Turkey, and China. Derived
from the Jacobin tradition of laïcisme, it is described by Partha Chatterjee as "a
coercive process in which the legal powers of the state, the disciplinary powers
of family and school, and the persuasive powers of government and media have
been used to produce the secular citizen who agrees to keep religion in the private domain."[38] Laicism, like other forms of secularism, is a form of discipline.

Others have described this tradition. Casanova suggests that the privatization
of religion is "mandated ideologically by liberal categories of thought which
permeate not only political ideologies and constitutional theories but the entire
structure of modern Western thought."[39] According to Taylor, the overarching
objective of the "independent political ethic" mode of secularism, similar to
laicism and pursued by Grotius and others, is to identify features of the human
condition that allow the deduction of exceptionless norms about peace and
political obedience, making religion irrelevant to politics.[40] As Grotius famously
argued, "etsi Deus non daretur . . . even if God didn't exist, these norms would
be binding on us."[41] The result is that "the state upholds no religion, pursues no
religious goals, and religiously defined goods have no place in the catalogue of
ends it promotes."[42] Van der Veer and Lehmann observe that "it is a fundamental assumption of the discourse of modernity that religion in modern societies
loses its social creativity and is forced to choose between a sterile conservation
of its premodern characteristics and a self-effacing assimilation to the secularized world."[43] Richard King describes laicism as the attempt to define and then
exclude (whatever laicists identify as) religion:

> The Enlightenment preoccupation with defining the "essence" of phenomena such
> as "religion" or "mysticism" serves precisely to exclude such phenomena from the

realms of politics, law and science, etc.—that is, from the spheres of power and authority in modern Western societies. Privatized religion becomes both clearly defined and securely contained by excluding it from the public realm of politics.[44]

International relations theory operates on the assumption that religion was excluded from spheres of power and authority in modern societies in the course of creating the modern state. Realist and liberal approaches reflect the assumption that religion has been confined to the private sphere or has diminished altogether.[45] As Katzenstein observes, "Because they are expressions of rationalist thought deeply antithetical to religion, the silence of realist and liberal theories of international relations on the role of religion in European and world politics is thus not surprising."[46] Thomas refers to the assumption that religion has been privatized as "the Westphalian presumption."[47] It is now increasingly clear that a more complicated story is waiting to be told.

Most of the literature on religion, the Protestant Reformation, and the Westphalian settlement (which ended the Thirty Years' War of 1618 to 1648) describes the decline of religion in European public life. Skinner observes that after Luther, "the idea of the Pope and Emperor as parallel and universal powers disappears, and the independent jurisdictions of the *sacerdotium* are handed over to the secular authorities."[48] Pizzorno refers to this transition as the "Gregorian moment," describing it as the most emblematic episode of what he calls "absolute politics" in Western history, which "lies at the root of the transfer, as it were, of the collective responsibility for ultimate ends from a collectivity having the boundaries of Christianity, and including all believers tied by this particular bond of faith, to separate collectivities defined by the territorial boundaries of one state and including all the individuals identified by their living within those boundaries."[49] Philpott emphasizes in this volume the significance of the Protestant Reformation and processes of secularization that emerged from it to challenge the temporal powers and decrease the public role of the church, while contributing to the emergence of a proto-sovereign states system.[50] Krasner has suggested that "the idea of sovereignty was used to legitimate the right of the sovereign to collect taxes, and thereby strengthen the position of the state, and to deny such right to the church, and thereby weaken the position of the papacy."[51] He concludes that Westphalia "delegitimized the already waning transnational role of the Catholic Church and validated the idea that international relations should be driven by balance-of-power considerations rather than the ideals of Christendom."[52] Finally, Cavanaugh argues that the conflicts of the sixteenth and seventeenth centuries inverted the dominance of ecclesiastical over civil authorities through the creation of the modern state, preparing the way for the eventual elimination of the church from the public sphere.[53]

Westphalian republicanism was organized around a modern conception of social and political order in which individual subjects assemble a society under a single sovereign authority. By challenging the arbitrary rights of kings in the name of the common good,[54] the new republicanism did delegitimize and transform preexisting hierarchic forms of order, as most conventional accounts have it. Yet the new republicanism also reinforced a particular kind of distinction between natural and supernatural order that came out of, and remained indebted to, a broader Christian framework.[55] Early republican order was characterized by a strong idea of providence and a pervasive sense that men were enacting a master plan that was providentially preordained. Taylor has suggested that the idea of moral order underlying this arrangement would in fact be unrecognizable to non-Westerners due to its emphasis on a providential plan to be realized by humans.[56] That early republicanism was situated within this broader Christian context fits with Krasner's observation, also noted by Shah and Philpott in chapter 2 of this book, that in the Treaty of Osnabrück (one of two treaties that made up the Peace of Westphalia along with the Treaty of Münster), religious toleration was limited to Lutherans, Calvinists, and Catholics.[57] Westphalia, as Nexon concludes, contributed to a "territorialization of religion" leading toward the "formation of polities in which territory, state, and confession were closely linked."[58]

The set of strategies and practices for managing religion and politics that I am referring to as "laicism" emerged gradually and fitfully, and not without rivals, out of this Christian-influenced Westphalian moral and political order. Although laicism presents itself as a universalizable discourse that emerged from the Westphalian settlement as a solution to the wars of religion, Connolly's description of it as "a specific fashioning of spiritual life . . . carved out of Christendom" comes much closer to the mark.[59] Joshua Mitchell takes this argument a step further, observing that even "the idea of the sovereign self, the autonomous consenting self, emerged out of Christianity . . . [and] paying attention to the religious roots of consent in the West alert[s] us to the fact, that it is in fact a provincial development, not necessarily universalizable."[60] From the perspective of international relations, it is clear that the influence of Christianity upon the original Westphalian "secular" settlement makes it difficult to subsume modern international order into realist and liberal frameworks that operate on the assumption that religion has been privatized. The traditions of secularism that form the subject of this chapter contribute to the constitution of particular forms of state sovereignty that purport to be universal in part by *defining* the limits of state-centered politics with "religion" on the outside.

Modernization theory, the policy expression of the commitment to build a modern Westphalian state, exemplifies the power of these laicist commitments. It is characterized by the assumption that "managing the public realm is a science which is essentially universal and that religion, to the extent it is opposed to the Baconian world-image of science, is an open or potential threat to any polity."[61] As Falk argues, the exclusion of religion from the spheres of power and authority "was intended to facilitate governmental efficiency as well as to provide the basis for a unified politics of the state in the face of religious pluralism, and a background of devastating sectarian warfare. Ostensibly, in the modern world religious identity was declared irrelevant to the rational enterprise of administering the political life of society."[62] In viewing religion as an impediment to the scientific management of the domestic and international public realms, modernization theory reflects laicist assumptions. Modern state builders were to confine religion to the private realm to ensure the proper demarcation of public and private, religious and secular. This paradigm was considered to be universal, or at least universalizable. As T. N. Madan wrote in one of the earliest and most influential articles on the subject, "The idea of secularism, a gift of Christianity, has been built into Western social theories' paradigms of modernization, and since these paradigms are believed to have universal applicability, the elements, which converged historically—that is in a unique manner—to constitute modern life in Europe in the sixteenth and the following three centuries, have come to be presented as the requirements of modernization elsewhere."[63]

Laicist assumptions sit quietly beneath the surface of structuralist and materialist approaches to international relations that approach religion as epiphenomenal to more fundamental material interests. Neorealism assumes that states have fixed and innate interests and that state behavior is constrained by international structure defined by factors such as the distribution of power, technology, and geography. Historical materialism, following Marx, dismisses religion as "a mode of consciousness which is other than consciousness of reality, external to the relations of production, producing no knowledge, but expressing at once the anguish of the oppressed and a spurious consolation."[64] These materialist approaches to state interests neglect the constitutive and productive role of social norms and embodied practices. Secularism cannot be reduced to material power or resources, but plays a constitutive role in creating agents and contributing to the normative structures in which they interact. Even constructivists have paid little attention to the politics of secularism. Focusing on the interaction of preexisting state units to explain how international norms influence state interests, identity, and behavior,[65] the literature on the social construction of the state system has ignored the secular and religious, or treated religion as private by prior assumption.[66]

The most significant implication for international relations of these differing attempts to expel religion from politics or treat it as privatized is that they demand "not only the sharing of the (independent political) ethic but also of its foundation—in this case, one supposedly independent of religion."[67] Laicism defines religion by designating that which is not religious, or the secular.[68] In doing so, it demarcates the legitimate limits of politics. Laicist settlements are a form of politics that, as Pizzorno argues with reference to absolute politics, "set[s] the boundaries between itself and other activities. To define what is within or without the scope of politics, one needs laws, or abolition of laws, hence political decisions, political activities, and discourse."[69] My point is that setting the terms for what constitutes legitimate politics and legitimate religion is a culturally and historically variable determination. As David Scott argues, "part of the problem to be sketched and investigated therefore has precisely to do with the instability of what gets identified and counted by authorized knowledges as 'religion': how, by whom, and under what conditions of power. In other words, the determining conditions and effects of what gets categorized as 'religion' are historically and culturally variable."[70]

European and American secularisms are forms of discipline that emerged out of Latin Christendom. They rely upon and reproduce particular definitions and assumptions about the secular and the religious. These traditions are not universal and they are constantly shifting. Consider, as an illustration of the fluidity of these categories, the derivation of the English term "religion" from the Latin *religio*.[71] In the pre-Christian era Cicero provided an etymology of the term linking it to the Latin verb *relegere*: to "retrace" or "reread."[72] In pre-Christian times *religio* referred to retracing the ritual of one's ancestors. As King observes, "This understanding of the term seems to have gained provenance in the 'pagan' Roman empire and made *religio* virtually synonymous with *traditio*." The Roman idea of *religio* tolerated a variety of different traditions, since the exclusion of one tradition in order for another to be practiced was not required.[73] Early Christians were referred to as atheists because they did not belong to a recognizable *traditio* and did not acknowledge the gods of others.[74] Yet as Christians increased their power among the Romans, they transformed the meaning of *religio* by severing its association with ancestral traditions:

> It became increasingly important within early Christian discourses to drive a wedge between the traditional association of *religio* with *traditio*. This occurred through a transformation of the notion of *religio*. Thus in the third century CE we find the Christian writer Lactantius explicitly rejecting Cicero's etymology, arguing instead that *religio* derives from *re-ligare*, meaning to bind together or link.[75]

So as Christianity became more powerful, *religio* came to be associated with "a worship of the true and a superstition of the false."[76] For Christians, and many Westerners in general, religion came to denote a bond of piety between *one true* God and man. Cavanaugh dates this modern concept of religion to the late fifteenth century and the writings of Marsilio Ficino, whose 1474 *De Christiana Religione* represents religion as a universal human impulse. In the sixteenth and seventeenth centuries, "religion moves from a virtue to a set of propositions . . . at the same time [as] the plural 'religions' arises, an impossibility under the medieval usage."[77]

The reformulation of *religio* by European theorists offers a set of clues to understanding religion and contemporary international politics because it established "the monotheistic exclusivism of Christianity as the normative paradigm for understanding what a religion is."[78] The reification of the category of religion by European political theorists as only referring to (Christian) belief or a set of propositions influenced European social order, European colonial projects, and relations with other civilizations, as well as, later, European forms of secularism. In the 1790s Kant, for example, could not fathom the idea of more than one valid religion:

> *Differences in religion*: an odd expression! Just as if one spoke of different *moralities*. No doubt there can be different kinds of historical *faiths*, though these do not pertain to religion, but only to the history of the means used to promote it, and these are the province of learned investigation; the same holds of different religious *books* (Zendavest, the Vedas, Koran, and so on). But there is only a single *religion*, valid for all men in all times. Those [faiths and books] can thus be nothing more than the accidental vehicles of religion and can only thereby be different in different times and places.[79]

Writing in the same decade, Joseph Endelin de Joinville, the surveyor general in the administration of Frederic North, first governor of British possessions in Ceylon, affirmed that "religion" could refer only to a Christian belief system:

> An uncreated world, and mortal souls, are ideas to be held only in an infant state of society, and as society advances such ideas must vanish. A *fortiori*, they cannot be established in opposition to a religion already prevailing in a country, the fundamental articles of which are the creation of the world, and the immortality of the soul. Ideas in opposition to all religion cannot gain ground, at least cannot make head, when there is already an established faith.[80]

Crucially, and for reasons having to do with the problems associated with the management of religious pluralism within Europe, European political theorists emphasized the idea of religion as a set of beliefs rather than the more embodied Ciceronian understanding of *religio* and *traditio*.[81] As King concludes, "Modern discussions of the meaning and denotation of the term *religio* tend to follow Lactantius's etymology, thereby constructing a Christianized model of religion that strongly emphasized *theistic belief* (whether mono-, poly-, heno-, or pantheistic in nature), exclusivity, and a fundamental dualism between the human world and the transcendent world of the divine to which one 'binds' (*religare*) oneself."[82]

The forms of secularism discussed here inherited a definition of religion that is indebted in specific ways to the European experience of managing religious diversity in a Christian-majority Europe. In modern, religiously diverse societies, attempts to manage the terms through which this received understanding of religion is defined (and then confined) lead to conflict between laicists, policing the boundary of what they define as the public sphere, and their rivals, who view this policing as an extension of religion in the name of an alternative (laicist) set of metaphysical assumptions.[83] As Taylor explains:

> What to one side is a more strict and consistent application of the principles of neutrality is seen by the other side as partisanship. What this other side sees as legitimate public expressions of religious belonging will often be castigated by the first as the exaltation of some peoples' beliefs over others. This problem is compounded when society diversifies to contain substantial numbers of non-Judaeo-Christian religions. If even some Christians find the "post-Christian" independent ethic partisan, how much harder will Muslims find it to swallow it.[84]

In holding fast to a particular definition of religion and then excluding it from politics, laicism defines both politics and religion in a particular fashion. Laicism marks out the domain of the secular and associates it with public authority, common sense, rational argument, justice, tolerance, and the public interest.[85] It identifies the religious as that which it is not, and associates religion with a personal God and beliefs about that God.[86] Laicism, then, is not simply the absence of religious or theological discourse. It is more complex than a clean laicism-religion oppositional binary would suggest, enacting a particular kind of theological discourse in its own right. It "theologizes" the religions that it oversees, by which I mean it discourses and reasons theologically, or speculates in theology.[87]

Connolly writes that for many secularists, religion is "treated as a universal term, as if 'it' could always be distilled from a variety of cultures in a variety of times rather than representing a specific fashioning of spiritual life engendered by the secular public space carved out of Christendom."[88] Milbank, arguing from within a Christian ontology, refers to the "critical non-avoidability of the theological and metaphysical," and observes that differing approximations of this appear in the work of Alasdair MacIntyre, Gillian Rose, René Girard, Guy Lardreau, and Christian Jambet.[89] Stephen White argues from his weak ontological position that "the supposedly neutral, 'freestanding' nonontological standpoint is, in fact, a perspective constitutively infused with an ontological desire to hold an authoritative center in the flux of political life . . . the desire for a definitive center is what needs to be diffused."[90] From different positions, these thinkers concur that although laicism purports to stand outside and above the contested territory of religion and politics, it does not. It is located on a spectrum of theological politics.

In its strongest formulations, laicism leads to the normalization of various religions and religious actors as either fit or unfit for participation in democratic politics. As Taylor observes with regard to global politics, "Defined and pursued out of the context of Western unbelief, [laicism] understandably comes across as the imposition of one metaphysical view over others, and an alien one at that."[91] In legislating the terms through which the secular and the religious are defined and experienced, laicism rules out particular kinds of linkages between religion (as laicism defines it) and spheres of power and authority such as law, science, and politics within states. In defining the limits of state-centered politics with religion on the outside, it serves as a template for the management of religious pluralism within states and the conduct of state sovereignty between them.

In defining the starting point in relation to which the religious is constructed, laicism contributes to the production of the categories that it presupposes. It is most powerful when this process remains invisible or unseen, representing itself as the natural order that emerges when there is no ideology present.[92] Laicism presents itself as public, neutral, and value-free, while religion, religious actors, and religious institutions are posited as private, affective, and value-laden. Religion is denominated as the domain of the violent, the irrational, and the undemocratic. Thus Cavanaugh argues that, "liberal theorists . . . assume that public faith has a dangerous tendency to violence,"[93] and Appleby refers to the "conventional wisdom that religious fervor—unrestrained religious commitment—inevitably expresses itself in violence and intolerance."[94] Laicism is the "conventional wisdom" adopted by Cavanaugh's liberal theorists. The secular public sphere is construed as the domain of reason, objectivity, deliberation, and justice, and the religious private sphere the domain of subjectivity, transcendence, effeminacy, and affect. Laicism guards against (what it defines as) religion in the public sphere; religious presence is seen as unnatural, infectious, undemocratic, and theocratic.[95] To adapt Bonnie Honig's insight about virtue theorists, laicists "distance themselves from the remainders of their politics and that distance enables them to adopt a not terribly democratic intolerance and derision for the other to whom their democratic institutions are supposed to be (indeed claim to be) reaching out."[96] These religious subjects, as Roxanne Euben has shown, become repositories for laicist anxieties about relations between politics, religion, and violence.[97]

THE INTERNATIONAL POLITICS OF
JUDEO-CHRISTIAN SECULARISM

Judeo-Christian secularism developed in the mid-twentieth century, primarily though not exclusively in the United States, and is distinguished by the partial displacement of the dominant narrative of Protestant hegemony and the representation of certain moral and political values as held in common by Christianity and Judaism and connected to particular Western traditions of law and governance. While laicism seeks to confine religion to the private sphere, this second invented secularist tradition connects contemporary Euro-American secular formations to an historical legacy of Western Christian and (beginning in the mid-twentieth century and then only selectively) Judeo-Christian values, cultural and religious beliefs, historical practices, legal traditions, governing institutions, and forms of identification. The common claim of Judeo-Christian secularism of all varieties, and the key to understanding it as a form of authority, is that Western political order is grounded in a set of core values originating in Judeo-Christian traditions that cannot (or should not) be diluted or denied.

Let me be clear. In referring to Judeo-Christian tradition, I do not mean to suggest that there is agreement between or within Jewish or Christian traditions about what this term means, or even whether it should be used at all. There isn't. Rather, of interest to me is that the term has become a signifier of a particular and extraordinarily powerful argument: that there is such a thing as a "Judeo-Christian" religious and moral tradition, and that it serves as the fount and foundation of modern political values such as liberty, equality, and secularism. Many individuals are socialized or disciplined into this worldview and rely upon it implicitly to organize the world through the lens provided by its assumptions. The narrative of Judeo-Christian secularism, which tells a story that connects a broad and diverse set of religious traditions to Western models of secular governance, has been particularly influential in the American political imagination. In attempting to come to terms with the cultural and political significance of this variety of secularism, I am not suggesting that Judeo-Christian values *actually* form the basis of Western institutions or styles of governance such as secular democracy, but rather that the *conviction* among adherents to this narrative that these moral values ground Western practices of secular democracy is in itself powerful enough to warrant critical scrutiny. I am not suggesting that the concept of a Judeo-Christian tradition is or is not a valid one; this is not for me to decide.[98] I am suggesting that a specific kind of civic republican tradition emphasizing the connections between moral values allegedly held in common by Judaism and Christianity (the Old Testament, the Ten Commandments, etc.) and particular styles and traditions of governance including but not limited to liberty, equality, and the separation of church and state has become quite powerful and therefore merits scholarly attention. This tradition is real *because* it is imagined; I am not asserting that it is imagined because it is real. To make the latter kind of claim, as President Obama once remarked in reference to the question of when life begins, would be above my pay grade.

An example of this narrative is the religious populism of Richard John Neuhaus.[99] He argues that universally valid traditional Catholic moral arguments should replace secular public godlessness as the basis of American identity, community, and foreign policy. Americans in his view are a Christian people, and Catholic natural law should serve as a universal moral-religious foundation for American public life.[100] Drawing on the arguments of John Courtney Murray, Neuhaus argues that Catholicism is not the enemy of liberalism but "its true source and indispensable foundation."[101] For Neuhaus and others who represent different variations of this tradition, religion (understood as Catholicism, Christianity, and/or Judeo-Christianity, depending upon whom you ask) is the elemental defining feature and moral basis of Western civilization. Ted Jelen has described this position with reference to Peter Berger's concept of a sacred canopy: "In the United States, a 'Judeo-Christian' tradition is thought to provide a moral basis for political life—what some analysts have described as a 'sacred canopy' beneath which political affairs can be conducted. Religion is thought to perform a 'priestly' function of legitimating political authority."[102] Christian and/or Judeo-Christian-derived forms of secular order, in this view, are among the core values of Western civilization and help constitute the common ground upon which Western democracy rests. Religion plays an important constitutive role not outside but *within* secular politics, serving what Jelen describes as "the basis of an ethical consensus without which popular government could not operate."[103] This narrative draws on what Casanova describes as a "celebratory Protestant reading of modernity, going from Hegel's *Early Theological Writings* through the Weber-Troeltsch axis to Talcott Parson's interpretation of modern societies as the institutionalization of Christian principles."[104]

In the laicist narrative, the Christian identity of the West has been superseded, radically transformed, and for all practical purposes rendered irrelevant. A modern, rational West was reinvented and rejuvenated by democratic tendencies inherited from its Greek and Roman predecessors. The Judeo-Christian secularist story does not share the assumption that after the Protestant Reformation and the Enlightenment, linkages between Western politics and public forms of Christianity were definitively severed. It works out of a different set of assumptions about the relationship between Christianity and modern political identities and institutions. Rather than eschewing religion, it draws upon and rephrases earlier European arrangements in which church and state each represented a different aspect of the same divine authority, as Gedicks describes:

Prior to the Reformation . . . the concepts "religious" and "secular" did not exist as
descriptions of fundamentally different aspects of society. Although there clearly was
tension and conflict in the relation between church and state during this time, the
state was not considered to be nonreligious. Both church and state were part of the
Christian foundation upon which medieval society was built.[105]

The Reformation led to the distillation of two separate spheres of influence:
the spiritual, led by the church, and the temporal, overseen by the state. Luther
and Calvin revived and strengthened Augustine's concepts of the "city of God"
and the "city of men," which described two aspects of the sovereign authority
of God as embodied in the church and the state. However, they also made this
split more fundamental by claiming that "God had instituted two kingdoms
on earth, one spiritual to be ruled by the church, and the other temporal to be
ruled by a civil sovereign."[106]

In the United States, the sense of a larger Christian context within which
both church and state were embedded set the terms of public discourse until
quite recently, and at certain times and places it still does.[107] Following the
influx of immigrants to the United States in the late nineteenth and early twentieth centuries, however, it became politically expedient to couch political programs in increasingly nonsectarian terms to ensure success at the polls.[108] While
Protestant discourse took a back seat to a more generic civic religion, a de facto
Protestant establishment continued to set the ground rules: "Protestantism still
affected public business, but implicitly, more as the source and background of
political movements than as the movements themselves."[109]

The civic republican imagination of the Protestant majority in early America formed the basis of a particular understanding and practice of religion and
democratic politics. The Protestant influence in early America was evident in
Legislative prayer, state acknowledgment of Easter, Christmas, Thanksgiving,
and the Christian Sabbath, and the outlawing of blasphemy and punishment of
atheism.[110] Protestants "opposed a particular Protestant denomination to Protestantism in general, which later they did not equate with an establishment. The
notion of prayer and worship based on the Bible accepted by all Protestants did
not amount to a general establishment, but constituted an essential foundation
of civilization."[111] To be secular, in this line of reasoning, meant not to privilege
one Protestant denomination over another. The "common ground" of Protestant
civilization was taken for granted, with dissenting Christians and others excluded
from it. It is worth noting that a similar situation prevailed contemporaneously in
England. In his analysis of nineteenth-century debates between British evangelicals and their utilitarian rivals, Van der Veer finds that, despite their differences,
both sides agreed that "civil society and the forms of knowledge on which it was
based were ultimately part and parcel of Christian civilization."[112]

This Protestant claim to a common ground, though slowly eroded by the increasing religious diversification of the American population and eventually modified to incorporate both Catholic and, after World War II, Jewish influences, has retained a cultural foothold in the modern imaginary. It is out of a celebratory reading and cautious amendment of this cultural inheritance that the Judeo-Christian secularist narrative emerged and continues to shape modern dispositions toward the secular and the place of religion within it. The tradition of Judeo-Christian secularism is the cultural heir of a de facto Protestant establishment. A narrative of Protestant hegemony has been transformed in the American imaginary into a slightly more liberalized pluralism, still drawing sustenance from a tradition in which particular religions (first Protestant Christianity, then Christianity more broadly, then Judaism) are linked to the possibility of civilization and cited as the source of first principles for governing institutions. Tocqueville described this famously in reference to the United States:

> In the United States it is not only mores that are controlled by religion, but its sway extends over reason. . . . So Christianity reigns without obstacles by universal consent. . . . Thus while the law allows the American people to do everything; there are things which religion prevents them from imagining and forbids them to become. . . . Religion, which never intervenes directly in the government of American society should therefore be considered as the first of their political institutions.[113]

Following in Tocqueville's footsteps, Bellah, Connolly, Juergensmeyer, Taylor, Van der Veer, Morone, and Pizzorno have chronicled the ways in which religious tradition resonates in and is rephrased through modern varieties of liberalism and secularism.[114] Morone paints a lively portrait of American history in which the nation develops "not from religious to secular but from revival to revival."[115] Connolly points to a tendency in canonical liberal thinkers, such as J. S. Mill, to extol Judeo-Christian tradition as the moral basis of civilizational unity and identity. For Mill, Connolly suggests, it is "through Jewish and Christian culture above all that a territorial people acquires the civilizational conditions of possibility for representative government."[116] Van der Veer identifies a long tradition of combining liberalism and evangelical moralism in Anglo-American political thought, describing British Liberal leader William Gladstone's (1809–98) writings as invoking a "liberal view of progress . . . but added to this is the notion that progress is the Christian improvement of society and that in such progress we see the hand of God."[117] Charles Taylor describes a "common ground" mode of secularism, in which members of a political community agree upon an ethic of peaceful coexistence and political order based on doctrines common to all Christian sects, or even to all theists.[118] He suggests that this represented a successful compromise in Europe for warring sects because "political injunctions that flowed from this common core trumped the demands of a particular confessional allegiance."[119] The objective was not to expel religion from politics in the name of an independent ethic, as in laicism, but to prevent the state from backing one (Christian) confession over another by appealing to that which all held in common. This even-handedness between religious traditions was, according to Taylor, the basis of the original American separation of church and state,[120] indicating the role that varieties of secularism have played as strategies for the management of religious diversity and religious pluralism.

Judeo-Christian secularism differs from laicism in that it does not aspire or claim to exclude religion (understood as Christianity or Judaism or values they hold in common) from modern spheres of power and authority. It diverges from laicism with regard to the role of religious tradition in the establishment and maintenance of the secularist "separation" of church and state. While laicism works on the assumption that religion has receded out of modern spheres of authority and into the private realm or disappeared altogether, Judeo-Christian secularism is a variant of what Jelen calls religious "accommodationism," maintaining that "religion (singular) is ultimately good for democratic politics, because a *shared* adherence to a common religious tradition provides a set of publicly accessible assumptions within which democratic politics can be conducted."[121] The separation of church and state is envisioned and experienced as a unique Western achievement that emerged out of a shared adherence to a common set of European religious and political traditions. Christianity, as van Leeuwan argued, led to modern secularism.

In international relations, these assumptions are palpable in arguments portraying various religious traditions as sources of particular styles and institutions of governance, forms of civilizational identity, and clashes between so-called civilizations. Christianity, in some versions, Judeo-Christianity in others, has culminated in the unique Western achievement of the separation of church and state and the development of liberal democracy.[122] As Samuel Huntington argued, "Western Christianity, first Catholicism and then Protestantism, is historically the single most important characteristic of Western civilization."[123] This prevailing dualism between "God and Caesar, church and state, spiritual and temporal authority . . . contributed immeasurably to the development of freedom in the West" and shaped a number of "the factors which enabled the West to take the lead in modernizing itself and the world."[124] Religion is the bedrock of this cultural inheritance, differentiating between civilizations and between individuals: "In the modern world, religion is a central, perhaps *the* central, force that motivates and mobilizes people."[125]

Huntington's framework divides the world into those who share the Judeo-Christian common ground and those who do not. It is strikingly similar to the divisions proposed in the fourteenth century by an Italian jurist, Bartolus de Sassoferato, who divided the world into five classes: the "populus Romanus," or "almost all those who obey the Holy Mother Church," and four classes of "populus extranei": the Turks, the Jews, the Greeks, and the Saracens.[126] Bartolus's scheme parallels Huntington's seven or eight major civilizations: Western, Confucian, Japanese, Islamic, Hindu, Slavic-Orthodox, Latin American, and "possibly African." Anthony Pagden describes its effects:

> The effect of Bartolus's ethnic division is once again to limit "the world" to a distinct cultural, political, and in this case religious, community. And again it places boundaries between what may be counted as the domain of the fully human world, and those others—which because of their rejection of the hegemony of the Western Church now also included the Greeks—who have no place within the *civitas*, and so no certain claim upon the moral considerations of those who do.[127]

The assumption that a Judeo-Christian secular common ground ends abruptly at the edge of Western civilization leads to the defense of this ground against both internal and external enemies, resulting in what Connolly has called "civilizational wars of aggressive defense of Western uniqueness."[128] These can become aggressive as the common ground is challenged both internally and externally in a world made up not only of Christians and Jews but also Muslims, Hindus, Buddhists, atheists, agnostics, and Deleuzeans, among others. As Taylor observes, "With the widening band of religious and metaphysical commitments in society, the ground originally defined as common becomes that of one party among others."[129] At this juncture, either this (mythical) common ground is renegotiated or an aggressive defense of it is set in motion. Neuhaus opts for the latter, arguing that the godless are incapable of a "morally convincing account" of the nation, and concluding that "those who believe in the God of Abraham, Isaac, Jacob, and Jesus turn out to be the best citizens."[130]

This religio-secular triumphalism finds expression in international relations in the idea that Western powers have a monopoly over the proper relationship between religion and politics. As Keane argues:

> The principle of secularism, which "represents a realisation of crucial motifs of Christianity itself" (Bonhoffer), is arguably founded upon a sublimated version of the Christian belief that Christianity is "the religion of religions" (Schleiermacher), and that Christianity is entitled to decided for non-Christian others what they can think or say—or even whether they are capable of thinking and saying anything at all.[131]

This position normalizes particular religions and religious actors and marginalizes most non-Western and non-Judeo-Christian negotiations of religion and politics. If the dualism between spiritual and temporary authority is accepted as uniquely Western and Judeo-Christian, then non-Westerners who want to democratize have no alternative but to adopt Western forms of secularism. As Bernard Lewis puts it:

> Separation of church and state was derided in the past by Muslims when they said this is a Christian remedy for a Christian disease. It doesn't apply to us or to our world. Lately, I think some of them are beginning to reconsider that, and to concede that perhaps they may have caught a Christian disease and would therefore be well advised to try a Christian remedy.[132]

In this scenario non-Westerners who do not advocate for Western (Christian) forms of secularism are portrayed as children who refuse to acknowledge that they are sick and need to stay in. On the other hand, those who do advocate for separationism are subject to the charge that they are advancing pale imitations of a robust Western secular ideal, thereby departing from (and potentially betraying) indigenous tradition. This binary delegitimizes indigenous trajectories of secularization because they are associated with selling out to Western power and betraying local tradition rather than being seen as legitimate alternatives. The oppositional relationship between Euro-American secular politics and forms of political Islam, such that the latter is categorically assumed to be a threat to the former, is a direct consequence of this worldview.[133]

Honig describes two conflicting political impulses: the desire to decide undecidabilities, and the will to contest established institutions and identities.[134] She criticizes political theorists who limit their definition of politics to the "juridical, administrative or regulative tasks of stabilizing moral and political subjects, building consensus, maintaining agreements, or consolidating communities and identities."[135] Rather than theorizing politics, she argues, they displace it.[136]

Like their counterparts in political theory, scholars of international relations yearn for closure and consensus, at least regarding religion and politics. As Michael Barnett points out, "Actors struggle over the power and the right to impose a legitimate vision of the world because doing so helps to construct social reality as much as it expresses it."[137] For most political scientists this is a secular vision of the world and a secular social reality. Most of us, perhaps unconsciously, perhaps less so, think, work, struggle against, and live within variations of the two traditions of secularism described in this essay. These secular laws, institutions, and sensibilities do not merely reflect social reality; they construct it, providing "a set of parameters, focal points, or even points of contention around which political discourse revolves."[138] They are forms of discipline that facilitate closure and agreement around received cultural, political, and legal settlements of the relation between religion and politics. Secularism, it turns out, is a powerful "pattern of political rule."[139]

The politics of secularism falls just beyond the peripheral vision of the empiricist and rational-choice methods that have dominated mainstream American political science, and consequently, it has only recently been subject to sustained analysis in this discipline. Secularist settlements are sustained by a variety of assumptions: secularization as the most recent step in the worldly realization of Judeo-Christian morality, secularization as the natural evolution toward a universal morality that has transcended the need for metaphysical moorings, secularization as a commendable side-effect of democratization and economic and political modernization, and secularization as the triumphant globalization of a modern state system in which religion has been privatized once and for all, among others. Though often jostling with each other for supremacy, and sometimes colliding head-on, these powerful narratives and projects serve, for better or for worse, to manage religious diversity, imbue state interest and identity with meaning, secure an image of contemporary international order as modern, secular, and democratic, and normalize particular religions and religious actors as fit or unfit for participation in politics both within and above the level of the state.

The entanglements between these secularist formations and various religious traditions, real or imagined, and real because they are imagined, confirm Barnett's observation in this volume that secular and religious elements in international order are not as cleanly segregated as many international relations theorists may have assumed. As Bruno Latour concludes, "What sort of world is it that obliges us to take into account, at the same time and in the same breath, the nature of things, technologies, sciences, fictional beings, religions large and small, politics, jurisdictions, economies and unconsciousnesses? Our own, of course."[140]

NOTES

This chapter is based on "Varieties of Secularism," chapter 2 of my book *The Politics of Secularism in International Relations* (Princeton: Princeton University Press, 2008). Excerpts from the book are reprinted with permission of Princeton University Press.

1. Charles Taylor, "Modes of Secularism," in *Secularism and Its Critics*, ed. Rajeev Bhargava (Oxford: Oxford University Press, 1998), 33–36.

2. José Casanova, *Public Religions in the Modern World* (Chicago: University of Chicago Press, 1994), 216.

3. William E. Connolly, *Why I Am Not a Secularist* (Minneapolis: University of Minnesota, 1999), 73–96.

4. Talal Asad, *Formations of the Secular: Christianity, Islam, Modernity* (Stanford: Stanford University Press, 2003), 2.

5. José Casanova, "A Reply to Talal Asad," in *Powers of the Secular Modern: Talal Asad and His Interlocutors*, eds. David Scott and Charles Hirschkind (Stanford: Stanford University Press, 2006), 23.

6. Hayden White, *The Content of the Form* (Baltimore: Johns Hopkins University Press, 1989).

7. Michael Barnett and Raymond Duvall, "Power in International Politics," *International Organization* 59 (Winter 2005): 48.

8. Stephen D. Krasner, *Sovereignty: Organized Hypocrisy* (Princeton: Princeton University Press, 1999), 51.

9. "Social life is not simply a matter of systems of meaning . . . These anthropological tendencies which accord a critical priority to systems of human meaning . . . leave unposed the question of how different forms of discourse come to be materially produced and maintained as authoritative systems." Talal Asad, "Anthropology and the Analysis of Ideology," *Man* 14, no. 4 (1979): 618–19.

10. Elizabeth Shakman Hurd, *The Politics of Secularism in International Relations* (Princeton: Princeton University Press, 2008), chapter 1.

11. Peter van der Veer, "The Moral State: Religion, Nation, and Empire in Victorian Britain and British India," in *Nation and Religion: Perspectives on Europe and Asia*, eds. Peter van der Veer and Hartmut Lehmann (Princeton: Princeton University Press, 1999), 39.

12. Connolly, *Why I Am Not a Secularist*, 33.

13. Ibid., 30. See also Immanuel Kant, *The Conflict of the Faculties*, trans. Mary J. Gregor (Lincoln: University of Nebraska Press, 1992).

14. Connolly, *Why I Am Not a Secularist*, 30.

15. Ibid., 31.

16. Ibid.

17. Ibid.

18. Ibid., 32.

19. Ibid., 33.

20. Ibid., 32 (emphasis in original).

21. Ibid., 26.

22. Ibid., 5.

23. William E. Connolly, *The Ethos of Pluralization* (Minneapolis: University of Minnesota Press, 1995), 189.

24. Ibid., 181.

25. Immanuel Kant, *Perpetual Peace, and Other Essays on Politics, History, and Morals*, trans. Ted Humphrey (Indianapolis: Hackett, 1983); David Held, *Democracy and the Global Order: From the Modern State to Cosmopolitan Governance* (Stanford: Stanford University Press, 1995); Martha C. Nussbaum, *For Love of Country: Debating the Limits of Patriotism*, ed. Joshua Cohen (Boston: Beacon

Press, 1996); Francis Fukuyama, "The End of History?" *The National Interest* 16 (1989): 3–18.

26. William E. Connolly, "Europe: A Minor Tradition," in *Powers of the Secular Modern*, 80.

27. Carl Schmitt *Political Theology: Four Chapters on the Concept of Sovereignty*, trans. George Schwab (Cambridge, MA: MIT Press, 1985); Karl Löwith, *Meaning in History* (Chicago: University of Chicago Press, 1949); Hans Blumenberg, *The Legitimacy of the Modern Age*, trans. Robert M. Wallace (Cambridge, MA: MIT Press, 1986).

28. John Milbank, *Theology and Social Theory: Beyond Secular Reason* (Oxford: Blackwell, 1993), 1.

29. Mark Juergensmeyer, *The New Cold War? Religious Nationalism Confronts the Secular State* (Berkeley: University of California Press, 1993), 16; Arend Theodor van Leeuwen, *Christianity in World History: The Meeting of the Faiths of East and West*, trans. H.H. Hoskins (New York: Scribner's, 1964).

30. Juergensmeyer, *The New Cold War?* 17.

31. Ibid., 17–18.

32. Ibid., 18.

33. Ibid., 197.

34. Harvey Cox, *The Secular City* (New York: Macmillan, 1965), 4.

35. Michael Hardt and Antonio Negri, *Empire* (Cambridge, MA: Harvard University Press, 2000), cited in William E. Connolly, *Pluralism* (Durham, N.C.: Duke University Press, 2005), 150.

36. John L. Esposito, *The Islamic Threat: Myth or Reality?* 2nd ed. (New York: Oxford University Press, 1992), 200.

37. John L. Esposito, "Islam and Secularism in the Twenty-First Century," in *Islam and Secularism in the Middle East*, eds. John L. Esposito and Azzam Tamimi (New York: New York University Press, 2000), 9.

38. Partha Chatterjee, "The Politics of Secularization in Contemporary India," in *Powers of the Secular Modern*, 60.

39. Casanova, *Public Religions*, 215.

40. Taylor, "Modes of Secularism," in Bhargava, *Secularism and Its Critics*, 33.

41. Ibid., 33–34.

42. Ibid., 35.

43. Peter van der Veer and Hartmut Lehmann, introduction to *Nation and Religion: Perspectives on Europe and Asia*, ed. Peter van der Veer and Hartmut Lehmann (Princeton: Princeton University Press, 1999), 10.

44. Richard King, *Orientalism and Religion: Postcolonial Theory, India and "the Mystic East"* (London: Routledge, 1999), 11.

45. Scott Thomas argues that this applies equally to the English School in "Faith, History and Martin Wight: The Role of Religion in the Historical Sociology of the English School of International Relations," *International Affairs* 77, no. 4 (2001): 926.

46. Peter Katzenstein, "Multiple Modernities and Secular Europeanization?" in *Religion in an Expanding Europe*, ed. Peter Katzenstein and Timothy Byrnes (Cambridge: Cambridge University Press, 2006), 31.

47. Scott M. Thomas, *The Global Resurgence of Religion and the Transformation of International Relations* (New York: Palgrave Macmillan, 2005), 33.

48. Quentin Skinner, *The Foundations of Modern Political Thought*, vol. 2, *The Age of Reformation* (Cambridge: Cambridge University Press, 1978), 353.

49. Alessandro Pizzorno, "Politics Unbound," in *Changing Boundaries of the Political*, ed. Charles S. Maier (Cambridge: Cambridge University Press, 1987), 34.

50. See also Daniel Philpott, *Revolutions in Sovereignty: How Ideas Shaped Modern International Relations* (Princeton: Princeton University Press, 2001).

51. Stephen D. Krasner, "Westphalia and All That," in *Ideas and Foreign Policy: Beliefs, Institutions, and Political Change*, ed. Judith Goldstein and Robert Keohane (Ithaca: Cornell University Press, 1993), 238.

52. Stephen D. Krasner, "Sovereignty," *Foreign Policy*, January/February 2001, 21. On the alleged violation of state autonomy in the Westphalian settlement by provisions enforcing religious toleration that undermined the principle of *cuius regio, eius religio* see Krasner, *Sovereignty: Organized Hypocrisy*, 77–84.

53. William T. Cavanaugh, "A Fire Strong Enough to Consume the House: The Wars of Religion and the Rise of the State," *Modern Theology* 11, no. 4 (October 1995): 398–400.

54. Craig Calhoun, *Nationalism* (Minneapolis: University of Minnesota, 1997), 70.

55. This is not to ignore the deep divisions among Christians in Europe at the time. As Nexon observes, "when we view Europeanization as a long historical process, we inevitably confront the creation of Europe as a community through, first, the extrusion of religious difference and, second, the management of religious schism within a broader Latin Christian community" (Daniel Nexon, "Religion, European Identity, and Political Contention in Historical Perspective," in Katzenstein and Byrnes, *Religion in an Expanding Europe*, 260).

56. Charles Taylor, Seminar on Secularization, Northwestern University, Evanston, Illinois, Spring 2003. This argument is elaborated in *A Secular Age* (Cambridge, MA: Belknap Press of Harvard University Press, 2007).

57. Treaty of Osnabrück (1648), 240, 241, article VII, cited in Krasner, *Sovereignty*, 81.

58. Nexon, "Religion, European Identity, and Political Contention," 277.

59. Connolly, *Why I Am Not a Secularist*, 23.

60. Joshua Mitchell, remarks made during the Conference on Theology, Morality, and Public Life (University of Chicago Divinity School, Chicago, February 25–27, 2003).

61. Ashis Nandy, "The Politics of Secularism and the Recovery of Religious Tolerance," in Bhargava, *Secularism and Its Critics*, 129.

62. Richard Falk, "Religion and Politics: Verging on the Postmodern," *Alternatives* 13 (1988): 381.

63. T. N. Madan, "Secularism in Its Place," *Journal of Asian Studies* 46, no. 4 (November 1987): 754.

64. Talal Asad, *Genealogies of Religion: Discipline and Reasons of Power in Christianity and Islam* (Baltimore: Johns Hopkins University Press, 1993), 46.

65. Peter J. Katzenstein, ed., *The Culture of National Security: Norms and Authority in World Politics* (New York: Columbia University Press, 1996).

66. Thomas Biersteker and Cynthia Weber, eds., *State Sovereignty as a Social Construct* (Cambridge: Cambridge University Press, 1996).

67. Taylor, "Modes of Secularism," 38.

68. "In the discourse of modernity 'the secular' presents itself as the ground from which theological discourse was generated" (Asad, *Formations of the Secular*, 192).

69. Pizzorno, "Politics Unbound," in Maier, *Changing Boundaries of the Political*, 28.

70. David Scott, "Conversion and Demonism: Colonial Christian Discourse and Religion in Sri Lanka," *Comparative Studies in Society and History* 34, no. 2 (1992): 333.

71. King, *Orientalism and Religion*, 35–36.

72. Derrida argues that *relegere* is from *legere* (to "harvest" or "gather") and is a Ciceronian tradition continued by W. Otto, J.-B. Hollmann, and Benveniste. He notes also a second etymological source of the word *religio*: *religare*, from *ligare* (to "tie" or "bind"), and traces this tradition from Lactantius and Tertuliian to Kobbert, Ernout-Meillet, and Pauly Wissola. Jacques Derrida, "Faith and Knowledge: The Two Sources of 'Religion' at the Limits of Reason Alone," in *Religion*, ed. Jacques Derrida and Gianni Vattimo, trans. David Webb (Palo Alto, CA: Stanford University Press, 1998), 34–35.

73. King, *Orientalism and Religion*, 36. The only restriction on *religio* in the Roman context was that practices were not allowed to impinge upon acceptance of civic responsibilities.

74. Ibid.

75. Ibid.

76. Lactantius, *Institutiones Divinae* IV.28, trans. Sister M. F. McDonald, 1964, 318–320, cited in King, *Orientalism and Religion*, 36.

77. Cavanaugh, "A Fire Strong Enough to Consume the House," 404.

78. King, *Orientalism and Religion*, 37.

79. Immanuel Kant, "To Perpetual Peace: a Philosophical Sketch," in Humphrey, *Perpetual Peace, and Other Essays on Politics, History, and Morals*, 125.

80. Joseph Endelin de Joinville, "On the Religion and Manners of the People of Ceylon," *Asiatick Researches* 7 (1803): 397–444, cited in Scott, "Conversion and Demonism," 347.

81. King, *Orientalism and Religion*, 37. My thanks to Courtney Bender for her comments and suggestions.

82. Ibid., 37 (emphasis in original).

83. Taylor, "Modes of Secularism," 36.

84. Ibid., 36–37.

85. Connolly, *Why I Am Not a Secularist*, 21.

86. Ibid.

87. *Oxford English Dictionary Online*, s.v. "Theologize," http://ets.umdl.umich.edu/cgi/o/oed/oed-idx?q1=theologize&type=Lookup (accessed 05/30/2007).

88. Connolly, *Why I Am Not a Secularist*, 23.

89. Milbank, *Theology and Social Theory*, 3.

90. Stephen K. White, *Sustaining Affirmation: The Strengths of Weak Ontology in Political Theory* (Princeton: Princeton University Press, 2000), 140.

91. Taylor, "Modes of Secularism," 37.

92. Melani McAlister makes this argument with regard to gender in *Epic Encounters: Culture, Media, and U.S. Interests in the Middle East* (Berkeley: University of California Press, 2001), 232.

93. Cavanaugh, "A Fire Strong Enough to Consume the House," 409.

94. Scott Appleby, *The Ambivalence of the Sacred: Religion, Violence, and Reconciliation* (Lanham, MD: Rowman & Littlefield, 2000), 5.

95. See, for example, the biological references to Islamism as a contagion in French media coverage of the dispute surrounding a 2004 law prohibiting conspicuous religious symbols in public schools, discussed in John Bowen, *Why the French Don't Like Headscarves* (Princeton: Princeton University Press, 2006).

96. Bonnie Honig, *Political Theory and the Displacement of Politics* (Ithaca: Cornell University Press, 1993), 6.

97. Roxanne L. Euben, *Enemy in the Mirror: Islamic Fundamentalism and the Limits of Modern Rationalism* (Princeton: Princeton University Press, 1999).

98. For a discussion of "secular witnesses belonging to the Judeo-Christian tradition" and the attempt to come to terms with their response to suicide bombing that is suggestive of one way in which this categorization may be helpful, see Talal Asad, *On Suicide Bombing* (New York: Columbia University Press, 2007), 91.

99. For another variation see Rodney Stark, *The Victory of Reason: How Christianity Led to Freedom, Capitalism, and Western Success* (New York: Random House, 2005).

100. Damon Linker, "Without a Doubt: A Catholic Priest, a Pious President, and the Christianizing of America," *New Republic*, April 3, 2006. On Neuhaus's philosophy, see Richard John Neuhaus, *Catholic Matters: Confusion, Controversy, and the Splendor of Truth* (New York: Basic Books, 2006); *The Naked Public Square* (Grand Rapids, MI: Eerdmans, 1984); and *The Catholic Moment* (New York: HarperCollins, 1990). For two very different critiques, see Damon Linker, *The Theocons: Secular America Under Siege* (New York: Doubleday, 2006); and Cavanaugh, "A Fire Strong Enough to Consume the House," 410–412.

101. Linker, "Without a Doubt."

102. Ted Jelen, *To Serve God and Mammon: Church-State Relations in American Politics* (Boulder, CO: Westview Press, 2000), 11. On the sacred canopy, see Peter L. Berger, *The Sacred Canopy: Elements of a Sociological Theory of Religion* (New York: Doubleday, 1967); and Neuhaus, *The Naked Public Square*.

103. Jelen, *To Serve God and Mammon*, 34.

104. Casanova, "A Reply to Talal Asad," in Scott and Hirschkind, *Powers of the Secular Modern*, 21.

105. Frederick Mark Gedicks, "The Religious, the Secular, and the Antithetical," *Capital University Law Review* 20, no. 1 (1991): 116.

106. Ibid., 117–118.

107. Today in the United States, seven states still have provisions barring atheists from holding office, though technically these provisions are unenforceable according

to the supremacy clause of the Constitution. While the Supreme Court reaffirmed that federal law prohibits states from requiring any kind of religious test for officeholders in 1961, hostility toward atheists persists in many regions. See "In North Carolina, Lawsuit Is Threatened Over Councilman's Lack of Belief in God," *New York Times*, December 12, 2009, http://www.nytimes.com/2009/12/13/us/13northcarolina.html?_r=2.

108. Gedicks, "Religious, the Secular, and the Antithetical," 122.

109. Ibid.

110. Ibid., 123.

111. Thomas Curry, *The First Freedoms*, 123–4, cited in Gedicks, "Religious, the Secular, and the Antithetical," 123n30.

112. Peter van der Veer, "The Moral State: Religion, Nation, and Empire in Victorian Britain and British India," in Van der Veer and Lehmann, *Nation and Religion*, 28.

113. Alexis de Tocqueville, *Democracy in America*, trans. George Lawrence (New York: Harper and Row, 1969), 292.

114. See Robert Bellah's concept of American civil religion in *Beyond Belief: Essays on Religion in a Post-Traditional World* (Berkeley: University of California Press, 1991) and Juergensmeyer's argument on American nationalism as a blend of secular nationalism and the symbols of Christianity into a form of "civil religion" in *The New Cold War?* 28.

115. James A. Morone, *Hellfire Nation: The Politics of Sin in American History* (New Haven, CT: Yale University Press, 2003), 3.

116. Connolly, *Why I Am Not a Secularist*, 78.

117. Van der Veer, "The Moral State," 24.

118. Taylor, "Modes of Secularism."

119. Ibid., 33. Taylor cites Pufendorf and Locke as examples.

120. Ibid., 35.

121. Jelen, *To Serve God and Mammon*, 90.

122. Samuel P. Huntington, "Religious Persecution and Religious Relevance in Today's World," in *The Influence of Faith: Religious Groups and U.S. Foreign Policy*, ed. Elliot Abrams (New York: Rowman & Littlefield, 2001), 60.

123. Samuel P. Huntington, *The Clash of Civilizations and the Remaking of World Order* (New York: Simon & Schuster, 1996), 70.

124. Ibid., 70, 72.

125. Ibid., 63.

126. Anthony Pagden, *Lords of All the World: Ideologies of Empire in Spain, Britain and France, c. 1500–c. 1800* (New Haven, CT: Yale University Press, 1995), 28. *Saracen* is a Greek word that was synonymous with *Arab* in pre-Islamic times and referred to Arabic-speaking Muslims of indeterminate race in medieval times. After the twelfth century it became synonymous with *Muslim*, like the terms *Turk* and *Moor*. Mohja Kahf, *Western Representations of the Muslim Woman*, (Austin: University of Texas Press, 1999), 181n5.

127. Pagden, *Lords of All the World*, 28.

128. William E. Connolly, "The New Cult of Civilizational Superiority," *Theory and Event* 2, no. 4 (1998), http://muse.jhu.edu/login?uri=/journals/theory_and_event/v002/2.4connolly.html.

129. Taylor, "Modes of Secularism," 33.

130. Neuhaus, cited in Linker, "Without a Doubt."

131. John Keane, "Secularism?" in *Religion and Democracy*, ed. David Marquand and Ronald L. Nettler (Oxford: Blackwell, 2000), 14.

132. Bernard Lewis, "Islam and the West: A Conversation with Bernard Lewis" (Pew Forum on Religion and Public Life, Washington, D.C.: April 27, 2006), http://pewforum.org/events/index.php?EventID=107.

133. Elizabeth Shakman Hurd, "Political Islam and Foreign Policy in Europe and the United States," *Foreign Policy Analysis* 3, no. 4 (October 2007): 345–367.

134. Bonnie Honig, *Political Theory and the Displacement of Politics* (Ithaca: Cornell University Press, 1993), 201.

135. Ibid., 2.

136. Ibid.

137. Michael Williams, "Hobbes and International Relations: A Reconsideration," *International Organization* 50, no. 2 (Spring 1996): 213–37, cited in Michael Barnett, *Dialogues in Arab Politics: Negotiations in Regional Order* (New York: Columbia University Press, 1998), 250.

138. Bukovansky, *Legitimacy and Power Politics: The American and French Revolutions in International Political Culture* (Princeton: Princeton University Press, 2002), 25.

139. Talal Asad, "Responses," in Scott and Hirschkind, *Powers of the Secular Modern*, 219.

140. Bruno Latour, *We Have Never Been Modern*, trans. Catherine Porter (Cambridge, MA: Harvard University Press, 1993), 129.

4. ANOTHER GREAT AWAKENING?

International Relations Theory and Religion

MICHAEL BARNETT

Are international relations theorists about to awake from their long, secular slumber and discover that the world has had, continues to have, and always will have a religious dimension? There is clearly a growing interest in religion, much of it driven by its presumed association with various forms of collective violence. Yet so far international relations theorists have spent little time wondering how religion in global life might implicate their existing theories of international relations or how existing theories of international relations might help us better understand the shape, forms, and consequences of religion in world affairs.[1] Should international relations theorists atone for their sins of omission and engage the religious world? I confess that I was among the guilty—and I write as someone whose "first career" was the international relations of the Middle East. If the Middle East did not convince me to take religion seriously, then what did? An encounter with Alice's Cheshire cat during my recent research on the evolution of the international humanitarian order.

The international humanitarian order is generally understood to include the network of international and nongovernmental organizations and the constellation of rules, norms, and principles that are intended to reduce the suffering of distant strangers.[2] Most contemporary writing on the subject presumes it is secular and humanistic because it cites principles of humanity and not religion, refers to an international and not a religious community, and adheres to the principles of impartiality and not difference based on religious identity. Yet as

I began excavating the origins of this order, I began digging through layers of religious sedimentation. Religious agencies dominated the relief sector until after World War II. Missionaries and the religiously inclined helped to protect indigenous populations and, in doing so, articulated basic human rights. The International Committee of the Red Cross (ICRC) was established by a gentile Genevan society that firmly believed that the Christian moral order was under assault by modernizing forces and that voluntary medical societies comprised of (Christian) citizens would strengthen Christian society. And, at bedrock, I encountered the abolitionists, who were not only religious but represented a new brand of evangelicalism. I then played history's tape forward, tracing the evolution of these religiously inspired institutions, and discovered, to my great surprise, that the religious appeared to melt into a secular sky — rather like the Cheshire cat, leaving behind only a winsome smile. Ever since, I have traveled backward and forward, and then forward and backward, mesmerized by the shifting boundaries of the religious and the secular.

How are we to make sense of this relationship between religion and humanitarianism? One possibility is that this is some kind of confidence trick. Has religion, namely Christianity, discovered a stealth method for converting the world? Have religious organizations discovered that they can use humanitarian institutions to launder religious values? Is this why so many narratives of humanitarianism are sprinkled with Christian symbolism, with references to sacrifice, redemption, offering, atonement, and salvation? If we want to defend this possibility, then we must be prepared to imagine that all those non-Christian countries that helped to negotiate many of the founding conventions were not aware of how manipulated they were by their Christian interlocutors, and that those thousands of aid workers who work for secular agencies do not realize how they are part of God's plan. Another possibility is that values once associated with Christianity, including, charity, love, and compassion, are not specific to Christianity but are truly cross cultural. There is evidence that the international human rights conventions emerged from a relatively impressive dialogue, but the ICRC crafted its Code of Conduct in relative isolation, though it is now exploring whether other religions have comparable traditions.[3] A third possibility is that humanitarianism is another instance of secularization. The world has undergone secularization, and humanitarianism is not apart from but rather part of that world. Yet before we get carried away with this possibility, we must recognize that sociologists of religion no longer subscribe to the strong versions of this thesis.[4]

Humanitarianism's androgynous quality — its ability to defy the standard binary of religious and secular — challenges our understanding of the international order and how international relations theorists should study it. This chapter proceeds in two sections. The first considers the religious dimension of international order. International relations theorists resemble liberal political theorists to the extent that their categories of analysis separate the political from the religious.[5] Yet such categorizations are more deceptive than informative because the distinction rests on ever-shifting sands. This becomes particularly evident in the Europeanization of the world during the nineteenth century and the rise of international rules, laws, and rights designed to protect the vulnerable. Yet, following on my earlier observations regarding religion's game of peek-a-boo, there are reasons to question the purported demise of religion and rise of secularism in the twentieth century. I tease out some alterative possibilities, including how the discourse of secularism makes possible a sphere of religion and how the liberal international order, which seemingly rests on nonsectarian grounds, might nevertheless represent its own kind of religion. The second section explores the implications of these observations for how international relations scholars should study religion in world affairs. Specifically, I argue that while constructivism is not the answer, it does offer several important commandments (not quite ten, but enough to get us started). I conclude by offering that while there are good reasons to take religion seriously, it is not the only kind of faith that exists in world affairs.

RELIGION AND MODERN WORLD ORDER

Do we live in a religious world? Most international relations theorists would probably answer yes. Does the modern international order have a religious foundation? Most would probably say no. The resistance to acknowledging the international order's religious foundations comes from two, somewhat contradictory, directions. The first is fear. Modern international relations history tends to treat religion as a principal source of conflict, violence, and war, and secularism as the great antidote. The discipline's founding historical moment occurred when the wars of religion in Europe were pacified by the presumed separation of church and state and the creation of a secularized sovereignty and the principle of noninterference, targeted specifically at those actors, religious and otherwise, that used religion to justify their interventions in the affairs of another state. Today the mere mention of religion summons images of religious fanatics constructing communities isolated from the modern world and producing suicide bombers. It is now almost conventional wisdom that the Arab-Israeli conflict is potentially resolvable if it remains a "nationalist" conflict but potentially intractable if it becomes a religious war. There are times when religion affects the state's foreign policy, but, following the general view that religion is part of the irrational, it almost always causes the state to act in ways that are counter to its national interests. For instance, according to some realists religious communities can form interest groups to shape the state's foreign policy, but doing so invariably harms the state "objective national interest."[6] Although religious forces and figures have spawned many of the norms, legal principles, and ethics that are normatively valued, international relations theorists have placed religion on the international community's "most wanted" list.[7]

The second reason international relations theorists resist acknowledging the international order's religious basis is that although they treat religion as a source of mayhem, they somewhat paradoxically act as if it has little causal significance and thus can be safely ignored. Materialist theories such as hard-core realism and Marxism have little patience for religious claims on the grounds that they are epiphenomenal or superstructural; the international distribution of power and states, and the economic structure and classes, are all we need to know. Labeling a state *Islamic* or *Christian* does not do any meaningful explanatory work; a state is a state is a state. Marxists have argued that economic forces explain the rise and success of the antislavery movement.[8] Some observers claim that Iranian President Mahmoud Ahmadinejad is motivated by an eschatological branch of Islam; therefore, this "irrational" actor cannot be deterred through standard threats and punishments.[9] Realists counter that he is a "rational" actor using Islam to legitimate a foreign policy made dangerously reckless by a surfeit of oil money and America's misadventures abroad, and that ultimately he will be constrained by external reality.

Surprisingly, religion gets little respect from those theories of international relations that explicitly theorize the ideational elements of global affairs. Consider the English school. Its theorization of the multilayered ontology of international order and its historical scholarship on the European origins of international society should encourage attention to religion. However, discussions of the origins of modern international society conform to the "religion is the root of all evil" thesis, to the extent that the Peace of Westphalia and other treaties and conventions that put religion in its place are viewed as the great stabilizers.[10] English school scholars do consider how Christianity became fused with civilizing processes during the nineteenth century. However, religion seems to have disappeared with the London Missionary Society and been overtaken by other (secular) institutions of modern international society.[11] Religion also vanishes from their analytical frameworks. Moving from a Hobbesian to a Lockean to a Kantian world order does not require any consideration of religion. In fact, their theorization of a Kantian world order insinuates that peoples are unified by basic Enlightenment principles and forms of solidarity that have a rationalized basis. In short, even when English school scholars speculate about the possibility of forms of cosmopolitanism, it is always in a secular register.

There is potentially an interesting tale to tell regarding this omission.[12] The founding fathers of the English school, including Martin Wight and Hedley Bull, were quite cognizant of the power of religion in world affairs throughout international history. They were also quite aware of the secularizing trends in global society, particularly evident after World War I and apparently accelerating after World War II. They considered this historical evolution a positive development because it stabilized international order around rationalized principles that had a universal appeal.[13] Famously, the English school has difficulty separating normative from positive theory, and what they did next conformed to this predilection: they decided to omit religion from their discussions regarding the principles of modern international order, in part because they assumed that religion was inherently destabilizing, and in part because they allowed their normative conclusions to influence their theoretical framework. Since the pioneers of the English school decided to omit religion, its followers may have reflexively continued this tradition without fully recognizing the built-in bias.

Constructivism might be the best hope for integrating religion into international relations research—after all, it forcefully argues that ideas, norms, identity, and culture have a causal significance in world affairs. However, it too disappoints. It is not that religion does not get mentioned, per se. Rather, it is that religion becomes subsumed under concepts such as identity, norms, and values, which in turn are nearly always treated as secular phenomena. Religion becomes a modifier, describing the source of the identity, the norms, and the values. But it rarely gets center stage.[14] Religious activists are often feted for their strategic acumen in forging the international human rights regime, but the rights regime is almost always treated as a secular development—not religious. Individuals credited with founding some of the most important modern institutions of care are acknowledged to have been motivated by Christian principles, but these institutions are defined as secular, universal, and humanistic. In short, constructivist theory, particularly when examining the evolution of international norms, contains an implicit secularization thesis. Among the possibilities for this move, two are particularly important. One is that its framework, and the very language of identity and values, cannot accommodate religious experience.[15] The other is that the theory does not have religious blinders on but rather is implicitly suggesting how international norms and rules that once had a decidedly Christian flavor have become truly intercultural. In either case, constructivists seem to have felt little pressure to consider the religious in global affairs. To what extent does religion help explain how the "world hangs together"?[16]

Should international relations scholars make amends and find religion? The answer is hardly obvious and partly depends on what theorists are hoping to gain. One possibility is that they might gain a theistic theory of international relations. Such theories are present in fundamentalist, eschatological, and millenarian doctrines. Presumably, our theories of international relations are secular because they are premised on social science methods and not a divine plan that cannot be immediately known to us but instead depends on revelation or scripture. I say presumably because vestiges of the religious might be unknowingly part of our theories. The revival of classical realism has included a reexamination of the importance and influence of Reinhold Niebuhr, whose religious beliefs shaped his theory of world politics.[17] Rear Admiral Arthur Thayer Mahan's writings on American expansion and the importance of sea power in geopolitics were motivated by a belief that the United States had a divine mission and central role to play in the global expansion of Christianity.[18] Neoliberal institutionalism is built on a religious foundation: it sits atop welfare economics, and welfare economics in turn rests on evangelical social and economic thought.[19]

As Jack Snyder notes in the introduction to this volume, it will be much easier to persuade international relations theorists of the necessity of incorporating religion if its causal significance can be convincingly hypothesized or demonstrated. Following in this spirit and in the context of my earlier comments regarding how different international relations theories have tended to exclude religion from their calculations regarding the foundations of international order, this chapter selectively samples the history of humanitarianism to suggest some of the consequences of neglect. Specifically, my discussion of humanitarianism highlights two themes: the first concerns the unstable, fluid, and negotiated relationship between the religious and the secular in the global order; the second concerns how the religious operates at various moments in the causal chain, including as discourse that is productive of ways of knowing and making the world intelligible, as beliefs that are the source material for identity and interests, as ideology that can help justify material interests, and as constraints upon the profane.

A signature conclusion of much of the literature on European expansion is that a religiously defined humanitarianism helped to motivate and justify the conquest and colonization of the world. Certainly, European countries were motivated by power and profit, but there was also a strong element of purpose — religious purpose. This religious dimension was most closely connected to a civilizing mission as defined by Christian discourse.

Missionary activity was the central embodiment of the cultural and religious expansion of Europe.[20] Although missionary movements accompanied the spread of the West and were increasingly visible in outposts in the New World, missionary activity entered a new, vigorous, and more sustained chapter in the early nineteenth century. Evangelicalism was a major reason for this new energy. Now that it was possible for individuals to elect to escape eternal damnation, evangelicals believed that they had a mission to spread the gospel and give all nonbelievers the choice.[21] Adopting militaristic language like a "crusade against idolatry" and "war for salvation," missionaries spread out across the world, hoping to give individuals the opportunity to restore their right relationship with God.[22] Toward that end, missionaries preached and proselytized, and attempted to express their religious commitments through activities that were designed to instill moral sobriety, and to create a civilized society through religious institutions and the introduction of modern schools as well as advances in health, science, and technology.[23]

It is important to get beyond the standard view that missionaries and colonialism had a hand-in-glove relationship, but it must be acknowledged that their relationship was in some ways mutually beneficial. For many, the West and Christianity were synonymous. Colonialism gave missionaries a sense of confidence and the ability to move into once inhospitable lands. In fact, the failure to respond to these new opportunities could trigger in them feelings of guilt and remorse.[24] In particular, Britain's fortunes were treated as a sign of God's grace, giving the country and its evangelicals special responsibilities for helping the backward races.[25] Commerce and Christianity also developed a close association. For many evangelicals and missionaries, commerce was not an end in itself but rather a means to an end. For some it would help eliminate the slave trade, which many considered evil; for others it would allow individuals to pursue their own ambitions beyond the reach of cruel political forces; and for still others, drawing on the moral economics of Adam Smith and other theorists, commerce and morality were compatible.[26] Missionaries, foreign capitalists, and colonial administrators could share the urge to civilize the colonial peoples, to transform them and their societies so that they resembled European states. While the missionaries might not have had the explicit goal of helping further the interests of the administrators and foreign capitalists, many of their activities had the effect of helping to make the local population more susceptible to outside control.[27] In general, for many missionaries the debate was not about whether there should and could be a positive relationship between missionary work and colonialism, but rather whether there was a causal relationship between the two.[28]

Yet missionaries often collided with colonial administrators and foreign capitalists who pursued power and profits and not God.[29] Humanitarians and missionaries wanted to convert and civilize, and while colonial authorities were not necessarily opposed to such missions, they often privileged security and commercial interests. For instance, the British population's desire to stamp out the slave trade led to the ill-fated British expedition to the Sudan in 1882, opposed on strategic grounds by Prime Minister Gladstone.[30] Colonial administrators frequently had little interest in civilizing the population, especially if it might complicate colonial rule or cause political rebellion, and engaged in all kinds of exploitation that missionaries found gravely irreligious.

Missionaries and foreign capitalists also clashed at various moments. Missionaries looked suspiciously on foreign capitalists who seemed willing to do anything to make a profit, who hardly comported themselves along Christian principles, and who desired to transform individuals into consumers, promoting not righteousness but rather hedonism.[31] Missionaries frequently saw their job as not only converting the local population but also reminding their compatriots about the temptations of sin and what happens when individuals find salvation in material goods and not in the gospel.[32] Foreign capitalists, in turn, often viewed missionaries as meddlesome busybodies, ready to incite unrest among the population, an accusation previously leveled by slave owners.[33] For instance, during the nineteenth century British missionaries advocated the abolition of the Indian practice of suttee, or the self-immolation of widows. The East India Company's initial position was one of indifference to all dimensions of Indian society, an indifference that translated into a 1772 company policy of noninterference concerning religion and local institutions. Utilitarian rather than principled factors drove this policy: it held that any move that might be interpreted by the local population as proselytization could trigger a rebellion, hardly good for business. Before the governor-general would consider suspending this policy, then, he had to calculate that it would not gravely damage the company's financial and political health. Ultimately, he decided to take the risk because of a desire to convey to the British public the image of an enlightened rule, to show by example good governance and progress—and the superiority of Western civilization.[34]

Although humanitarianism was closely associated with world order as defined by the European powers, many missionaries and liberal humanitarians developed a multicultural sensibility resembling that of many human rights activists today. Although missionaries had a well-earned reputation for viewing derisively the habits and customs of the local populations and treating them as less than fully human, at times their encounters forced them to reevaluate their own identities, values, and understanding of self in relationship to the colonial "other."[35] An interesting development of the nineteenth century was the subtle but significant shift from the project of destroying other cultures and religions to trying to create the social conditions that would improve their well-being.[36] This development had various related sources, including growing critical self-reflection in response to the accusation that missionaries were paternalistic and imperialistic, and the growing influence of new interpretations of social gospel that highlighted equality, justice, and solidarity.[37] By the end of the nineteenth century, many American missionaries were treating charitable institutions such as clinics, orphanages, and schools less as magnets for possible converts and more as vehicles for saving societies.

The World Missionary Conference (WMC) held in Edinburgh, Scotland, in 1910, a highly self-conscious and scientific effort to consider how best to Christianize the world, reflects many of these world order issues.[38] In preparation for the meeting, the conference planners created several committees to place the missionary project on a more scientific and systematic footing. It is difficult to exaggerate their ambitions and accomplishments. The organizing committee wanted their discussions to be informed by empirical analysis and not guesswork; this "scientific" turn was a natural outgrowth of the development of the professional field of missiology—the application of scientific methods to assess missionary practices, a movement led by the American evangelist A. T. Pierson.[39] Accordingly, the committee surveyed hundreds of missionaries, who, in many respects, were the anthropologists of their day, having lived for years among the "natives" and observed their cultural and religious practices. The vast majority of the missionaries responded, and many with lengthy, detailed, and handwritten reports. The committee then summarized the findings in a set of reports that were designed to consider how to advance the missionary project.[40]

Many western political, economic, and religious elites did not see missionary activity as a separate and distinct feature of Western expansion, but rather as a critical element of it. Consequently, in attendance were some of the most important religious, political, and economic figures of the period. The presiding officer was Lord Balfour, who opened the conference with a warm statement from the King of England. The American delegation included Rear Admiral Alfred Thayer Mahan; William Jennings Bryan; John Mott, a winner of the Nobel Peace Prize and one of the best-known evangelical ministers of the period; and Seth Low, the former mayor of New York City and President of Columbia University. Theodore Roosevelt could not attend, but sent a very warm letter of congratulations and reflected on the conference's importance to the Western international order.

The conference members' concern with how to most effectively and efficiently promote the missionary movement led them to try and understand the conditions under which a society would be receptive to the message of the gospel. Toward that end, and following the fashion of the times, they created a hierarchy of societies, ranking them in terms of where they fell on a civilizational scale. Being closer to civilization was no guarantee that a society would be more receptive to the gospel; by their accounts, Japan was nearly civilized but missionaries could hardly penetrate Japanese society, and Korea was farther down the ladder but convertible. Strikingly, the conference spent a considerable amount of time worrying about "Mohammedism." Many missionaries reported considerable difficulty penetrating Islamic societies and that Christianity was losing ground to Islam for the souls of nonmonotheistic peoples in places like sub-Saharan Africa. Sounding alarmed and anxious, the conference highlighted the urgency of the task of confronting Islam, limiting its gains, and, if at all possible, sending it back to Arabia.

The WMC also dwelled on the complicated relationship between missionaries and political power. The heated consensus among the conference participants was that colonialism by the Christian powers provided an unprecedented opportunity for spreading the word, and they were brimming with the confidence of the period (little did they know, though, that this meeting was occurring at the twilight of the imperial era). National governments were not simply pursuing a secularized "national interest"; instead, they were helping to make possible a Christian world order. Consequently, while those in attendance may have been chauvinists and nationalists, they believed that the power of the state could and should be used to spread Christian civilization. The duty of governments, as they put it, is "to restrain evil and promote good," and "both missions and governments are interested in the welfare of nations."

However much affection the missionaries felt for the colonial powers, there were limits. Following the maxim, "Render unto Caesar the things that are Caesar's, and unto God the things that are God's," they attempted to maintain a line between themselves and politics. Matters of governance were the domain of the state and matters of religion were the domain of the church, and both the government and the church needed to recognize each other's sphere of authority. Critically, missionaries were not to engage in "political agitation" and instead had a duty to teach and practice obedience to "settled government." Reflecting their desire to respect a neutral zone, the participants identified a set of rules that resemble modern humanitarian principles. They expressed a principle of humanity, that all individuals had the right to hear the gospel and have the opportunity to convert, and they expressed a principle of neutrality, discouraging missionaries from confronting colonial governments, because doing so might jeopardize access to populations "in need."

Yet missionaries were not always pleased with the behavior of the colonialists and the capitalists and frequently intervened to stop the sinning in their midst. Specifically, they had a duty to "exercise their influence for the removal of gross oppression and injustice, particularly where the government is in the hands of men of their own race . . . provided that in so doing they keep clear of association with any political movement." Much like many relief organizations of today, missionaries were "rights-based" movements that wanted to protect certain fundamental rights of the population in ways that were *apolitical*, which they defined in ways that resemble our term *nonpartisan*. The conference singled out three activities for opprobrium: opium, liquor traffic, and enforced labor. Opiates and alcohol were particularly pernicious because they numbed the masses and were conduits of evil. Ever since the early nineteenth century and beginning with the abolitionist movement, missionaries had viewed slavery as a major evil. Importantly, colonial governments and foreign capitalists also had to be confronted because, in many cases, they had introduced and profited from these evils. A Christian, European international order, alongside its civilizing impulses, included principles of rights, justice, and compassion.

Although missionaries are perhaps the most vivid example of the relationship between the secular and the religious in the creation of the modern world order, religiously motivated action also was instrumental in creating the very international institutions, laws, and ethics that are frequently treated, at least today by those in the West, as quintessentially secular.[41] Consider the ICRC. The founders of the ICRC initially saw themselves as part of a civilizing mission—but one that worked within the existing boundaries of civilized society, that is, Christian Europe. Reflecting "the religious and moral assumptions of the nineteenth century European bourgeoisie . . . they had naturally assumed that mercy and compassion were uniquely Christian values. The first task for the Red Cross, they believed, was to propagate these virtues more widely within Christendom itself, especially among the common people whose weak moral sense seemed to them to need careful nurture."[42] The issue was not simply a matter of getting their priorities right—it also concerned whether and how these values might apply to those outside of Europe. Consistent with the notion, prevalent at that time, of a variegated humanity, the ICRC believed that while European Christians could comprehend and honor the Red Cross principles, those outside these boundaries probably could not. ICRC was surprised, therefore, when in 1865 the sultan of the Ottoman Empire communicated his willingness to accept the Geneva conventions; it could not believe that the Ottoman Empire, a Muslim state, understood or was prepared to honor these conventions. The controversy continued when the Ottoman Empire notified Geneva that it would not adopt the symbol of the cross. While the delegates to the Congress probably selected the cross because of its association with Christian charity and aspirations for a universal, enlightened humanitarianism (and not as a tribute to Switzerland), they nevertheless treated the symbol as nonsectarian and could not imagine how it gave offense.[43] After considerable discussion, though, ICRC authorized the Ottoman Empire to use the Islamic-based crescent.

This episode caused the ICRC to rethink its purpose and entertain the possibility of a civilizing mission beyond its borders. One founder stated in a newsletter in 1873 in the context of ICRC's discussions with Japan that, while it would be "puerile" to expect "the savages and barbarians, who are still singularly numerous on the face of the globe, to follow [Japan's] example, there is the possibility that there are races which possess a civilization, albeit one different from ours, that desire closer relations with Europe and might be brought into civilized society through the red cross societies."[44] Red Cross societies began to expand across the globe. For a dedicated colonialist like the ICRC's

Gustave Moynier, the ICRC could help perform a civilizing mission that would "humanize" the "savage peoples" by rescuing them from their "brute instincts." As the ICRC considered the speed with which it did so, it imagined not only the universalization of the laws of war but also the expansion of Christian notions of charity.

A similar story can be told regarding the creation and evolution of many of the original human rights documents. Missionaries, especially those who were outraged by slavery and the genocidal rule of King Leopold in the Congo, were at the forefront of defining and defending "native rights." At the turn of the century they were joined by activists motivated less by religion and more by a secularized humanity, and after World War I the latter became more prominent. Indicative is the story of Save the Children and the creation of the first convention on the rights of African children.[45] Although Save largely convened the preparatory meeting, around the table were missionaries from all over the continent, who could speak with considerable authority given their "field expertise." Although fully aware of Save's quasi-secular orientation, they nevertheless viewed the process as a vehicle for institutionalizing a set of rights that were founded on Christian principles but potentially had a greater chance of becoming institutionalized because they were now associated with a secular and universal agenda.

These sketches of the international humanitarian order suggest three ways of thinking about the changing relationship between religion, secularism, and world order. One, following the lead of sociologists of religion, is to consider the causes and consequences, and the varieties and vagaries, of the secularization of the world. However, if international relations theorists do this they will be adopting a position that was long ago found wanting by many of its founding advocates. Specifically, one of the important revisions of the secularization thesis is the assumption that the religious and the secular can be understood as binaries, and that the ascendance of one comes at the immediate expense of the other. Treating these spheres as distinct, indeed as rivals for supremacy, risks neglecting how the two can be co-constitutive and discursively related, how the secular might create the religious, and how the religious might underpin the secular.

A second way of thinking about this relationship might be to treat the secular as a "strategy" for managing the role of religion in world affairs. This possibility is offered by Elizabeth Shakman Hurd, who in this volume provocatively and persuasively argues that the modern secular order itself rests on a religious foundation. She argues that there are "two trajectories of secularism, or two strategies for managing the relationship between religion and politics." The first is laicism, "a separatist narrative in which religion is expelled from politics." The second is Judeo-Christian secularism, which is an accommodationist narrative to the extent that the Judeo-Christian tradition does not attempt to expel religion but rather sees it as very much a part of cultural life and, in fact, as helping to constitute modern secular life. Citing Samuel Huntington, Hurd argues that this narrative shows religion to be the common ground for Western democracy. Secularism, therefore, is a core value of a Judeo-Christian order, and basic liberal institutions are themselves shaped by, if not made possible by, Christian-Judeo values.[46] In this view, then, religion becomes either an element of Western secularism or makes Western secularism possible; in either case, the religious is part of the secular. As Hurd argues, such strategies for the domestic also appear in the international, in some ways consistent with the early findings of the English school regarding the importance of sovereignty and other international mechanisms that were designed to safeguard the state and codify a warmed-over realpolitik. But it would be critical to avoid seeing realpolitik as statecraft to the exclusion of "religiocraft."

A third possibility is that the religious helps to constitute the contemporary international order. For many scholars this requires upsetting some conventional wisdoms. International relations theorists are generally comfortable referring to a liberal world order, but because they generally equate liberal with secular, a liberal world order cannot also have a religious content. Does this mean that liberalism and other kinds of modernist projects might also have a religious dimension? Perhaps. This possibility is offered by many scholars of religion, including, most recently, Charles Taylor in his magisterial *A Secular Age*. Following on a centuries-long tradition, Taylor distinguishes between the immanent and the transcendental:

> The great invention of the West was that of an immanent order in Nature, whose working could be systematically understood and explained on its own terms, leaving open the question whether this whole order had a deeper significance, and whether, if it did, we should infer a transcendent Creator beyond it. This notion of the "immanent" involved denying—or at least isolating or perhaps problematizing—any form of interpenetration between the things of Nature, on the one hand, and the "supernatural" on the other, be this understood in terms of the one transcendent God or of Gods or spirits, or magic forces or whatever.[47]

But the immanent can never quite purge all vestiges of the transcendental, in large part because humans have a constant need to relate to something bigger than themselves. It is not simply the search for meaning, but rather a particular kind of meaning that allows them to imagine themselves as connected to a universe in existence and in emergence. Consequently, Taylor finds evidence of the transcendental in the immanent in various areas of life. For instance, British and American forms of patriotism have always projected a sense of the divine, or at least operated under the belief that each country was helping to further a civilizing process that was part of God's plan:

> The sense of superiority, originally religious in essence, can and does undergo a 'secularization', as the sense of civilizational superiority becomes detached from Providence, and attributed to race, or Enlightenment, or even some combination of the two. But the point of identifying here this sense of order is that it provides another niche, as it were, in which God can be present in our lives, or in our social imaginary; not just as the author of the Design which defines our political identity, but also of the Design which defines civilizational order.[48]

He similarly suggests that the the liberal order of equality, rights, and democracy might be sustained by more than a Rawlsian "overlapping consensus" based on Kantian utilitarian grounds and theological grounds. Secularization did not kill religion. Instead, projects that are viewed by many as quintessentially secular are sustained and given meaning by religious beliefs.

Although Taylor largely limits the transcendental to the religious, Craig Calhoun and others argue that the transcendental need not pivot on God, but can exist wherever there are collective beliefs that refer to the divine and that conceive of practical action as designed to transform oneself and the environment in order to bring about a greater good.[49] Consider human rights. Arguments about natural rights and human dignity are defended not only in terms of their instrumental value for other kinds of positive outcomes (including peace and prosperity) but also in terms of basic notions of justice and humanity that are part of the "divine." Humanitarian action is defended not only in terms of its contribution to international peace and security but also because it signifies the kind of world order that many would like to bring into existence. Many of the attributes of a liberal international order (and international ethics more broadly) are embedded in a cosmopolitanism and transcendentalism that is concerned not only with human flourishing but also the possibility of transforming oneself in relation to others and a broader moral universe. In short, modern day liberalism, this secularized liberalism, has a religious content because of its relationship to the transcendental.[50] If so, the modern liberal international order is not evidence of the triumph of secularism, as most international relations theorists assert, but rather the ascendance of a particular brand of secularism that itself has a strong religious content and is tied to the transcendental.

I must emphasize that the transcendental is not the universal — the transcendental is always historically and culturally situated. International ethics can have elements of the religious to the extent that those elements are constituted by the transcendental, but this is a transcendental born of a particular time and place, even if it is defined by its advocates as timeless. Consider, once again, humanitarianism. The idea of humanitarianism—the attempt to ameliorate the suffering of distant strangers—might appear to have an unambiguously universal character. Both Christian and Islamic aid agencies are inspired by religious commitments to help the poor and the suffering. Yet these different faith traditions also understand the purpose and principles of humanitarianism in fundamentally different ways, and tie them to very different understandings of a transcendental world order. For many Christian aid agencies it has been practically impossible to spread Christianity without also directly or indirectly transforming various aspects of social relationships and creating new kinds of transnational relations. The same is true for many Islamic aid agencies. In other words, the desire to relieve suffering, presumably a universal good and the purest expression of a transcendental ethic, is itself reflective of a particular understanding of order.

In sum, our contemporary world order might have a religious dimension in visible and veiled ways. International relations theorists have long been concerned with the production of order. A century ago that imagined order was assumed to have a Christian character, or at least most theorists believed that it should. The steady secularization of the world and the academic community that studies it has transformed the conceptualization of order as a result of rationality and the collective pursuit of interdependent interests. Indeed, not only did international order have little to do with religion, but increasingly religion was viewed as a destabilizing force. International relations theorists have become increasingly attentive to how order is accomplished not only by instrumental action but also by normative structures; as they have done so they have tacitly presumed that this order has a secular character. Yet the secular and religious elements of international order might not be as cleanly segregated as international relations theorists presume. Religious values might be part of our international ethics and international order, having become institutionalized in the world's governing institutions, and our liberal international order might itself have a religious dimension. If so, international relations theorists have much to learn about the world—and themselves.

DON'T LOOK TO "SCIENCE" TO FIND RELIGION

Recent scholarship on religion and international relations has been as methodologically and epistemologically diverse as the field of international relations. This secularist attitude toward the study of religion must continue. There is no single path to salvation and there is no single epistemological path to enlighten-ment. Yet the recent history of constructivism provides several cautionary les-sons about the dangers of attempting to study the social dimension of world affairs. Three stand out as particularly important.

DON'T ESSENTIALIZE

Social kinds do not have an essence. Instead they are social constructs whose meaning is historically and culturally situated in relationship to other discursive kinds. There is no essence to gender or religion. Critics might try and identify an essence, as will fundamentalists. But social scientists should know better. Islam does not have an essence and those that try to find it, whether they are critics wondering whether the world would be better without Islam or funda-mentalists who believe that Islam has an eternal meaning, are practicing their own forms of orientalism.[51] Religious discourse, like all cultures, is fractured; consequently, scholars need to trace these ever-shifting and never-stable cul-tural and religious fault lines. If a religious discourse appears to have an essence or fixed meaning, then this is a result of politics, and the job of the scholar is to understand how this appearance was achieved. For instance, Hurd expertly examines how social actors attempt to establish the meaning of the secular in relation to the religious, and do so for various politically motivated reasons.[52]

BEWARE OF BINARIES

In order for constructivists to make headway in the study of the social character of international politics, they had to overcome several hegemonic social theoret-ic binaries, including interests/norms, rationality/irrationality, and power/ethics. These binaries were an artifact of the dominant position of realism (or at least the Waltzian version) and individualism, and made it difficult for scholars to recognize that international relations, like all social relations, have a social char-acter. In response, constructivists argued that interests are socially constructed and are constituted by norms, that there is an important distinction between instrumental and subjective rationality, that too many scholars influenced by rational choice fail to recognize how rationality makes no claim regarding the preferences of actors, and that power is not limited to its material forms but instead some of the most enduring forms of power are found in discourse, ideas, and other ordering elements that direct action and shape self-understanding.[53]

International relations scholars should fight against binaries such as interests/religious values, rational/religious, and power/values because they undervalue the significance, both causal and phenomenological, of religion. Instead of asking how religion influences interests, we will assume that interests are material and that those who act in ways that seemingly go against their material interests will be viewed as irrational (or acting under forms of false consciousness). Fundamentalist Christians in Kansas and Wahabis in Saudi Arabia have much in common because they are willing to sacrifice their material interests for religion and fail to understand their true preferences.[54] The nation becomes part of the "national interest" that exiles the religious, while religious motivations become part of some ill-defined and amorphous community; patriots rationally sacrifice for the nation but suicide bombers are irrationally driven by visions of virgins. Such binaries can lead to ontological dead ends and alleviate analysts from the demand of having to understand actors in terms of their own interpretations of their actions and their constructed world.[55]

AVOID VARIABLE CENTRISM

The very desire to demonstrate that religion "matters" can encourage international relations scholars to transform religion into a variable. We cannot and should not avoid thinking in terms of variables. Yet a variable-centered world can omit four important features of many good explanations. First, it can lead scholars to fail to consider how actors make their actions and the world around them meaningful. Good explanations not only refer to interests but also to reasons, and the reasons that actors give for their actions provide important insights into how they make their world meaningful. Following Max Weber's insight that "we are cultural beings with the capacity and the will to take a deliberate attitude toward the world and to lend it significance," constructivists and others following an interpretive tradition attempt to recover the meanings that actors give to their practices and the objects that they construct. The meanings that actors lend to their activities derive not from private beliefs but rather from society or culture. In the United States a religious haze helped to define the meaning and significance of the terrorist attacks on September 11. Some religious figures posited that the attacks were divine retribution or a wake-up call to a dangerously irreligious country. The framing of the attacks and the post-September 11 climate as "good versus evil" drew from Christian discourse. Many other orienting concepts, which give meaning to events and inspire responses, also have religious foundations. Sin. Redemption. Sacrifice. Atonement. Forgiveness. These concepts are loaded with Christian meaning and can help legitimate foreign policy or even motivate it. In general, if international relations scholars look they are likely to find religion.

Second, a variable-centered approach to religion also neglects social constitution. Constitution is not mere description but is explanatory theory, of a particular sort. There are "why" and "how" questions.[56] Standard causal analysis asks "why" questions as it treats independent and dependent variables as unrelated entities. Constitutive theories instead ask "how" questions. They explore how structures constitute social kinds and make possible certain tendencies. Sovereignty does not cause states to act in certain ways; it helps to constitute them and endow them with certain capacities that make possible certain kinds of action. Being a sovereign state, after all, means having certain rights and privileges that other actors in world politics do not have. To what extent were/ are Western states Christian states and how does this identity make possible certain kinds of action? What does it mean to be an Islamic state? What kinds of historically situated social capacities does an Islamic state possess?

Third, variable-oriented analysis neglects discursive formations. We must be attentive to how historically and contingently produced discourses shape the subjectivity of actors, and how systems of knowledge and discourse shape categories of meaning and significance. Although some variable-oriented scholars turn gender into a variable that is reducible to biological categories—leading to questions like whether the world would be peaceful if women were in charge— scholars who understand that gender is socially constructed and a discourse are attentive to its historically situated meaning.[57] In a similar vein, a variable-centered scholar might be tempted to ask if the world would be more peaceful if Islam no longer existed, or more violent if Reverend Pat Robertson had his finger on the nuclear "button." The modern category of the religious is defined historically and in relation to the category of the secular; in some respects the secular is an invented term to help construct, codify, grasp, and experience a realm or reality differentiated from the religious. Consequently, we can speak not of secularism but rather of secularisms.[58]

Fourth, and following on the aforementioned points, the divisions between rationalism and constructivism are several and significant, but at times can be overhyped, to the detriment of creating sophisticated explanations of action and outcomes.[59] Constructivists made considerable headway in the discipline by demonstrating how thin understandings of action and stripped-down versions of methodological individualism omitted the various ways in which normative structures shape global life, including how actors make sense of the world and give it significance, the origins of beliefs, identities, and interests, and what counts as legitimate action. Yet as they have plowed ahead they have incorporated various enduring insights from rational choice, including that actors are goal oriented, self-reflective, strategic, and capable of using cultural resources for ulterior purposes. An approach that limits the place of the religious and the secular to discourse and normative structure leads to an impoverished account of human action, but an approach that fails to recognize how actors are able to instrumentalize religious beliefs and adopt interpretations of religious norms that are consistent with existing interests also yields an impoverished understanding of action.

It has been said often enough that scholars of international relations should be more attentive to the role of religion in world affairs, but it is not at all clear how we should do this. I am unconvinced that religion requires any special epistemology or ontology. Existing theoretical approaches provide a useful starting point. And while I suspect there will not be much enthusiasm for trying to develop a theistic theory of global affairs, there is considerable evidence that only by incorporating religion will we have a better understanding of how the world is constantly made and remade. As eloquently argued by Hurd in this volume and elsewhere, though, international relations theorists should not and cannot study the varieties of religion without also studying the varieties of secularism.

The religious and the secular have evolved in relation to one another and stand in a relationship of opposition and differentiation, as well as co-constitution. World leaders have used secularism as a strategy to try and define the political and the religious in ways that are hypothesized to be consistent with the requirements of international order. However, many "secular" global institutions have religious origins and continue to retain religious significance for many different groups. Many national and transnational projects have a high degree of support in part because of their relationship to religious discourses. And, lastly, there is the possibility that "we" will define order not only in terms of stability but also in terms of an ongoing search for enchantment, progress, and heaven on earth.

Yet as international relations scholars turn to the study of religion they also should bear in mind that religious faith is not the only kind of faith that exists in world affairs. The earlier discussion of the distinction between the transcendental and the immanent suggested that the transcendental can be either religious or nonreligious. There is of course no single, accepted definition of religion. Instead of trying to settle what will always be unsettled, scholars have favored formulations that identify "family resemblances," allowing them to identify a set of beliefs, commitments, and institutionalized practices that combine to produce an entity that can be defined as more or less religious.[60] So, for instance, religions have various characteristics—including an appeal to supernatural entities, conversion experiences, doctrines, rituals, understandings of the meaning of suffering, distinctions between the sacred and profane, and so on—but not all of these characteristics need be present in order to constitute a religion. Faith, on the other hand, can be generically understood as belief in the divine that does not depend on the existence of a God.[61] Liberal cosmopolitanism, particularly those versions that have shades of transcendentalism, can also be understood as part of a faith tradition. Nearly every aid worker I have ever met, from those who work for the evangelical World Vision International to the irreligious Doctors without Borders, expresses one kind of faith or another. While the humanitarian sector operates with a distinction between faith- and non-faith-based action, it is probably more accurate to acknowledge that its workers are inspired by different kinds of faith traditions. If so, then different kinds of faith—and not merely different religious denominations—exist in global politics.

NOTES

I would like to thank the many who indulged my attempt to work through a set of painfully unfamiliar ideas. In addition to those who contributed to this volume, I owe much to Al Stepan, José Casanova, Bud Duvall, Nicholas Guilhot, and those who attended my talks at Columbia University and Australian National University.

    1. There is a growing literature on religion and world affairs, but very little on religion and international relations theory. For important exceptions, see Fabio Petito and Pavlos Hatzopoulus, eds., *Religion in International Relations: The Return from Exile* (New York: Palgrave 2003); Scott Thomas, *The Global Resurgence of Religion and the Transformation of International Relations: The Struggle for the Soul of the Twenty-first Century* (New York: Palgrave, 2003); and Ron Hassner, *War on Sacred Grounds* (Ithaca: Cornell University Press, 2009), chapter 1. For a good overview of the challenge for theorists of IR and comparative politics, see Eva Bellin, "Faith in Politics: New Trends in the Study of Religion and Politics," *World Politics* 60, no. 2 (January, 2008): 315–347.
    2. Michael Barnett, *The International Humanitarian Order* (New York: Routledge, 2010), chapter 1.
    3. James Cockayne, "Islam and International Humanitarian Law: From a Clash to a Conversation Between Civilizations," *International Review of the Red Cross* 84, no. 847 (2002): 597–626.
    4. José Casanova, "Secularization Revisited: A Response to Talal Asad," in David Scott and Charles Hirshkind, eds., *Powers of the Secular Modern: Talal Asad and His Interlocuters* (Stanford: Stanford University Press, 2006), 24–28; Dominique Marshall, "Children's Rights in Imperial Political Cultures: Missionary and Humanitarian Con-

tributions to the Conference on the African Child of 1931," *International Journal of Children's Rights* 12, no. 3 (2004): 273–318.

5. Mark Lilla, *The Stillborn God: Religion, Politics, and the Modern West* (New York: Knopf, 2007).

6. John Mearsheimer and Stephen Walt, *The Israel Lobby* (New York: Farrar, Straus, and Giroux, 2007).

7. Ann Tickner, for instance, recently pleaded with international relations theorists to pay greater attention to religion by citing its importance for understanding violence. See Ann Tickner, "On Taking Religious Worldviews Seriously," in *Power, Interdependence, and Nonstate Actors in World Politics*, ed. Helen Milner and Andrew Moravcsik (Princeton: Princeton University Press, 2009), 223–42.

8. Thomas Haskell, "Capitalism and the Origins of the Humanitarian Sensibility, Part 1" *American Historical Review* 90, no. 2 (1985): 339–361.

9. Bernard Lewis, "Does Iran Have Something in Store?" *Wall Street Journal*, August 8, 2006; Daniel Pipes, "The Mystical Menace of Mahmoud Ahmadinejad," *New York Sun*, January 10, 2006.

10. Hedley Bull, *Anarchical Society: A Study of Order in World Politics* (New York: McMillan, 1977).

11. Hedley Bull and Adam Watson, *The Expansion of International Society* (New York: Oxford University Press, 1985); Gerrit Gong, *The Standard of "Civilization" in International Society* (New York: Oxford University Press, 1984).

12. I thank Paul Keal for bringing this possibility to my attention.

13. Hedley Bull and Martin Wight, *Diplomatic Investigations* (London: Allen and Unwin, 1966).

14. Although he might not care for being classified as a constructivist, Daniel Philpott's work is an important exception. See, for instance, "The Challenge of September 11th to Secularism in International Relations," *World Politics* 55, no. 1 (2002): 66–95; and "The Religious Roots of Modern International Relations," *World Politics* 52, no. 2 (January 2000): 206–45.

15. Joshua Mitchell, "Religion Is Not a Preference," *Journal of Politics* 69, no. 2 (May 2007): 351–62.

16. John Ruggie, "What Makes the World Hang Together? Neo-Utilitarianism and the Social Constructivist Challenge," *International Organization* 52, no. 4 (1998): 855–885.

17. Reinhold Niebuhr, *The Structure of Nations and Empires: A Study of Recurring Patterns and Problems of the Political Order in Relation to the Unique Problems of the Nuclear Age* (New York: Scribner's, 1959); *The Irony of American History* (New York: Scribner's, 1952); *Christianity and Power Politics* (New York: Scribner's, 1940); and, with Alan Heimert, *A Nation So Conceived: Reflections on the History of America from Its Early Visions to Its Present Power* (New York: Scribner's, 1963).

18. R. N. Leslie Jr., "Christianity and the Evangelist for Sea Power: The Religion of A. T. Mahan," in *Influence of History on Mahan: The Proceedings of a Conference Marking the Centenary of Alfred Thayer Mahan's "The Influence of Sea Power Upon History, 1660–1783,"* ed. J. B. Hattendorf (Newport, RI: Naval War College Press, 1991).

19. On the political economy, see Boyd Hilton, *The Age of Atonement: The Influence of Evangelicalism on Social and Economic Thought, 1795–1865* (Oxford: Clarendon Press, 1988).

20. C. Peter Williams, *The Ideal of the Self-Governing Church: A Study in Victorian Missionary Strategy* (Leiden: Brill, 1990). For general overviews of missionary movements, see Andrew Porter, *Religion Versus Empire? British Protestant Missionaries and Overseas Expansion, 1700–1914* (Leicester: Apollos Press, 1990); Brian Stanley, *The Bible and the Flag: Protestant Missions and British Imperialism in the Nineteenth and Twentieth Centuries* (Leicester: Apollos Press, 1990); and Sister Mary Casilda Renwald, *Humanitarianism and British Colonial Policy* (PhD dissertation, St. Louis University, 1934), especially chapters 2–4.

21. Porter, *Religion Versus Empire?* 32–38; Brian Stanley, *The Bible and the Flag*, 63, 161; Sister Mary, *Humanitarianism and British Colonial Policy*, 49.

22. Stanley, *The Bible and the Flag*, 63–64.

23. Porter, *Religion Versus Empire?* 32–38; Paul Varg, "Motives in Protestant Missions, 1890–1917," *Church History* 23, no. 1, (March 1954): 75–78.

24. Porter, *Religion Versus Empire?* 39–44.

25. Stanley, *The Bible and the Flag*, 68–69.

26. Ibid., 70–74.

27. Alison Bashford, *Imperial Hygiene: A Critical History of Colonialism, Nationalism, and Public Health* (New York: Palgrave, 2005); Douglas Haynes, *Imperial Medicine: Patrick Monson and the Conquest of Tropical Disease* (Philadelphia: University of Pennsylvania Press, 2001).

28. Porter, *Religion Versus Empire?* 92–115; Catherine Hall, *Civilizing Subjects: Metropole and Colony in the English Imagination, 1830–1867* (Chicago: University of Chicago Press, 2002).

29. Porter, *Religion Versus Empire?* 92.

30. P. M. Holt, *The Mahdist State in the Sudan* (Oxford: Clarendon Press, 1970), 32–44; Robin Neilands, *The Dervish Wars: Gordon and Kitchner in the Sudan* (London: John Murray, 1996), 23–34.

31. Varg, "Motives in Protestant Missions," 73; Stanley, *Bible and the Flag*, 73.

32. Stanley, *Bible and the Flag*, 78–83; Sister Mary, *Humanitarianism and British Colonial Policy*, chap. 6.

33. Sister Mary, *Humanitarianism and British Colonial Policy*, chapter 6; Stanley, *The Bible and the Flag*, 90; Hall, *Civilizing Subjects*; Claire McLisky "'Due Observance of Justice, and the Protection of Their Rights': Philanthropy, Humanitarianism, and Moral Purpose in the Aborigines Protection Society circa 1837 and Its Portrayal in Australian Historiography, 1883–2003," *Limina: A Journal of Historical and Cultural Studies* 11 (2005): 57–66.

34. Nancy Cassels, "Bentinck: Humanitarian and Imperialist—The Abolition of Suttee," *Journal of British Studies* 5, no. 1 (November 1965): 77–87; Peter van der Veer, *Imperial Encounters: Religion and Modernity in India and Britain* (Princeton: Princeton University Press, 2001), 41–43; Jennifer Pitts, *A Turn to Empire: The Rise of Imperial Liberalism in Britain and France* (Princeton: Princeton University Press, 2006), 13.

35. Frederik Cooper and Ann Stoler, *Tensions of Empire: Colonial Cultures in a Bourgeois World* (Berkeley: University of California Press, 1997); A. Lester, "Reformulating Identities: British Settlers in Early Nineteenth-Century South Africa," *Transactions of the Institute of British Geographers* 23 (1998): 515–531; A. Lester, "Settlers, the State and Colonial Power: The Colonization of Queen Adelaide Province, 1834–37, *Journal of African History* 39, (1998): 221–246, and *Imperial Networks: Creating Identities in Nineteenth Century South Africa and Britain* (London: Routledge, 1991); David Lambert, "Geographies of Colonial Philanthropy," *Progress in Human Geography* 28, no. 3 (2004): 320–341.

36. Stanley, *The Bible and the Flag*, 75; Varg, "Motives in the Protestant Missions," 75–78.

37. Amanda Porterfield, "Protestant Missionaries: Pioneers of American Philanthropy," in *Charity, Philanthropy, and Civility in American History*, ed. Lawrence Friedman and Mark McGarvie (New York: Cambridge University Press, 2003), 64–65. See also Emily Rosenberg, "Missions to the World," in Friedman and McGarvie, *Charity, Philanthropy, and Civility in American History*, 245; Porter, *Religion Versus Empire*, 328.

38. Brian Stanley, "Defining the Boundaries of Christendom: The Two Worlds of the World Missionary Conference, 1910," *International Bulletin of Missionary Research* 30, no. 4 (October 2006): 171–6, "Africa Through European Christian Eyes: The World Missionary Conference, Edinburgh 1910," in *African Identities and Global Christianity in the Twentieth Century*, ed. Klaus Herausgegeben von Koschorke (Wiesbaden: Harrassowitz Verlag, 2005), 165–80, "Twentieth-Century World Christianity: A Perspective from the History of Missions," in *Christianity Reborn: The Global Expansion of Evangelicalism in the Twentieth-Century*, ed. Donald M. Lewis, (Grand Rapids, MI: Eerdmans, 2004), 52–83, "Church, State, and the Hierarchy of 'Civilization': The Making of the Commission VII Report, 'Missions and Governments' Edinburgh, 1910," in *The Imperial Horizons of British Protestant Missions, 1840–1914: The Interplay of Representation and Experience*, ed. Andrew N. Porter (Grand Rapids, MI: Eerdmans, 2003), 58–84, and "Edinburgh 1910 and the Oikoumene," in *Ecumenism and History*, ed. Anthony Cross (Carlisle, UK: Paternoster Press, 2002), 89–105. See also W. H. T. Gairdner, *Echoes from Edinburgh 1910: An Account and Interpretation of the World Missionary Conference* (n.p.: Gairdner Press, 2008); Charles Clayton Morrison, "The World Missionary Conference," *Christian Century*, July 7, 1910.

39. Dana Robert, *Occupy Until I Come: A.T. Pierson and the Evangelization of the World* (Grand Rapids, MI: Eerdmans, 2002).

40. For constructivists interested in the life cycle of norms and normative diffusion, the conference in particular and missionary activity more broadly represents a fascinating and understudied topic, potentially illuminating various features of normative diffusion, including its altered meaning as it becomes localized and institutionalized in the context of existing cultural practices.

41. Jennifer Beard, *The Political Economy of Desire: International Law, Development, and the Nation State* (New York: Routledge-Cavendish, 2007).

42. John Hutchinson, *Champions of Charity* (Boulder, CO: Westview Press, 1997), 203.

43. Ibid., 143.

44. Ibid., 204. See also Caroline Moorehead, *Dunant's Dream: War, Switzerland and the History of the Red Cross* (London: Carroll and Graf, 1999), 122.

45. Marshall, "Children's Rights in Imperial Political Cultures."

46. Hurd, *The Politics of Secularism in International Relations* (Princeton: Princeton University Press, 2007), 5–6.

47. Charles Taylor, *A Secular Age* (Cambridge, MA: Harvard University Press, 2007), 15–16.

48. Ibid., 456.

49. See also Craig Calhoun, "A Secular Age: Going Beyond," *The Immanent Frame: Secularism, Religion, and the Public Sphere*, Social Science Research Council blog, http://blogs.ssrc.org/tif/2008/01/28/going-beyond/.

50. Nicholas Guilhot, "Secularism, Realism, and International Relations," *The Immanent Frame*, http://www.ssrc.org/blogs/immanent_frame/2007/10/31/secularism-realism-and-international-relations/; Elizabeth Shakman Hurd, "The Other Shore," *The Immanent Frame*, http://www.ssrc.org/blogs/immanent_frame/2007/12/18/the-other-shore/.

51. Graham Fuller, "A World Without Islam," *Foreign Policy*, January/February 2008, 46–53.

52. Hurd, *The Politics of Secularism in International Relations.*

53. One of the normatively desirable consequences of rationalist approaches is that they foreclose the possibility of the most pernicious forms of ethnocentrism.

54. Thomas Frank, *What's the Matter with Kansas?* (New York: Holt, 2005); Bernard Lewis, *What Went Wrong? The Clash Between Islam and Modernity in the Middle East* (Harper Perennial, 2003).

55. Talal Asad, *On Suicide Bombers* (New York: Columbia University Press, 2007).

56. Alexander Wendt, "On Constitution and Causation in International Relations," *Review of International Studies* 24, no. 5 (1998): 101–118.

57. The debate over gender raises the need to note that the study of religion does not need any special epistemology. However, see Mitchell, "Religion Is Not a Preference," for an argument regarding the near impossibility of contemporary models to capture the "religious experience."

58. José Casanova, "Secular, Secularizations, Secularism," *The Immanent Frame*, http://www.ssrc.org/blogs/immanent_frame/2007/10/25/secular-secularizations-secularisms/

59. James Fearon and Alexander Wendt, "Rationalism Versus Constructivism: A Skeptical View," in *Handbook of International Relations*, ed. Walter Carlsnaes, Thomas Risse, and Beth Simmons (Thousand Oaks, CA: Sage Publications, 2002), 52–72.

60. For a recent and good example of this exercise, see Jonathan Benthall, *Returning to Religion: Why a Secular Age Is Haunted by Faith* (London: Taurus, 2008).

61. There are a bevy of other concepts that are used to signify nonreligious faith, including *spirituality*.

5. RELIGION, RATIONALITY, AND VIOLENCE

MONICA DUFFY TOFT

Although there has been a great deal written on religion, there has been relatively little written on the relationship between organized religion and international politics.[1] Perhaps more glaringly, there have been only a few systematic analyses of the relationship between religion and war.[2] Most students of both international politics and war appear to take for granted the fact that when religion is involved in a conflict, it generally acts as a catalyst: religion makes deterrence more difficult, escalation to violence more likely, and wars more intense and more difficult to halt once under way.[3]

This chapter explores the connections between religion and war. As defined here, religion can be usefully seen as a system of practices and beliefs sharing most of the following elements: (1) a belief in a supernatural being or beings; (2) prayers or communication with those beings; (3) transcendent realities, including "heaven," "paradise," or "enlightenment"; (4) a distinction between the sacred and the profane and between ritual acts and sacred objects; (5) a view that explains both the world as a whole and humanity's proper relation to it; (6) a code of conduct in line with that worldview; and (7) a temporal community bound by its adherence to these elements.[4] Like nationalism, religion importantly shares the quality of imagined community and of a community that not only exists across space but also time.[5] As such, religion can aid in the rationalization of self-sacrifice in support of a larger community and its ends.

Unlike nationalism, in which self-sacrifice can be rationalized in terms of a community only, religious practice holds out the additional possibility of individual salvation; and also unlike nationalism, religion tends to be less attached to specific territory.[6] A final and crucial difference between nationalism and religion is that nationalists do not proselytize: one is unlikely to encounter a Serb, for example, trying to convince a Frenchman to become a Serb. One either is a member of a nation or one is not (and in some instances cannot become one). By contrast, most religions hold out the prospect of conversion to nonmembers, and some even demand that their members convert others as part of their conception of right practice in faith.

My focus is on the impact of religion on violence, and as such I restrict myself to two core questions. First, are religious adherents, or states whose governments identify closely with a religious tradition, rational actors? Although we can all recognize many differences between established religions, as social scientists we build *general* theories by abstracting from the details of our chosen unit of analysis. The process of abstraction invariably results in lost information, but if undertaken carefully, the rewards can be great, allowing us to see connections that cannot be appreciated without some distance from the particulars of each individual subject of analysis.

Second, assuming religious actors are rational, how might religion intersect with rationalist explanations for war such as issue indivisibility, commitment problems, private information, and asymmetric time horizons? If religious adherents are rational actors, why shouldn't war be as inefficient in affirming coveted values as it is for nonreligious actors? I argue that finding answers to both questions will go a long way toward allowing the useful incorporation of religious belief and practice into theories of political interaction, intelligent theory building, and, by extension, into policy making where religion is a central issue.

WHY RELIGION, WHY NOW?

The global resurgence of religious faith is an empirical trend with important political implications.[7] This resurgence can be seen in a number of ways. First, by nearly any measure, the distribution of people who identify as "more religious" or as "born again" into a new religion has risen steadily in the past three decades, and shows no sign of slackening.[8] Muslims and evangelical Christians appear to make up the lion's share of the phenomenon, with strains of Christianity making headway in formerly Catholic and mainline Protestant areas of the globe (e.g., Latin America and Africa) and Muslims attracting more followers to the faith and having more children on average than their non-Muslim counterparts. Given conversion and population trends, it is not surprising that some predict that the religious shall inherit the earth.

The increase in religious adherents has been accompanied by another trend: democratization. Throughout the globe the pressure for political systems to become more transparent and accountable to their populations has meant that different sectors of society have been able to advance their agendas in the political sphere. What this means in practice is that as religious populations have grown, so too have their influence in politics. A simple metric captures this opening up of politics globally. In just one decade, from 1990 to 2000, the average polity score of states jumped more than two points: whereas the average was .76 in 1990, by 2000 it was 2.83. Admittedly, most states remain on the autocratic side of the spectrum (a score of 6 is typically when scholars code countries as democratic). Nevertheless, increasing levels of democratization at the global level do seem to form a trend, and this trend has allowed for religious actors and issues to enter politics more readily.

A final trend is the decline in the legitimacy of secular ideologies. Although the collapse of colonialism in the late 1940s and 1950s ushered in the departure of the Western powers, the legacies of communism and socialism remained. These ideological systems promised much, but delivered little. By the late 1960s and early 1970s, alternatives to these secular ideologies were being sought. Religion had never disappeared, and thus those elites and organizations that survived were in a good position to deliver what these other systems failed to. In Iran, what started as a middle class struggle against a corrupt state resulted in the transformation of a state and society according to theological principles. Although Poland's overthrow of communism was not based in theology, the willingness of Pope John Paul II to condemn this political system provided needed legitimacy to challenge these systems and eventually led to their downfall.

What is important to note about each of these indicators of the religious resurgence is that they did not begin in the 1990s. Rather, the global resurgence can be traced back to the late 1960s and early 1970s. This is not a post–Cold War phenomenon. If you consider, for example, the proportion of civil wars with a religious dimension, an upsurge in relation to all types of civil wars began in the 1970s, when religious actors and institutions started to demand changes to their political systems.

RELIGION IN CIVIL WARS

Here I address a number of questions about the contemporary relationship between religion and war in the context of substate violence, which, as compared to interstate violence, has become much more common. Although my interest in this section is religion in civil wars, it hardly follows that its implications are limited to war within rather than between states.

For purposes of analysis, a civil war is large-scale violence in which two sets of organized combatants fight it out within the borders of the state, and each side suffers a significant number of casualties, with the war overall resulting in at least 1,000 deaths on average per year of combat. A civil war is a religious civil war if it is the case that (1) the combatants identify with a different faith tradition, as in Sri Lanka, with Buddhist Sinhalese fighting against Hindu Tamils, or (2) the combatants are of the same faith but contest the role of their religion vis-à-vis society and the state, as in the Tajik civil war, which pitted a formerly communist and secular group against a group wanting to impose an Islamic regime. In the first type religion features as a peripheral issue, while in the second, religion is central.

In relation to civil wars more broadly, the proportion of civil wars in which religion is a core issue of contention has risen. From the 1940s to the 1950s, the figure rose from 19 to 30 percent. The 1960s witnessed a modest decline to 22 percent, but in the 1970s this figure grew to 36 percent and continued to climb: in the 1980s to 41 percent, and in the 1990s to 45 percent. Religious civil wars made up a majority of the wars started after 2000.

WHERE RELIGIOUS CIVIL WARS HAPPEN

Most religious civil wars have occurred in four regions of the world: Asia and the Pacific, the Middle East, Europe, and Africa. From 1940 to 2008, Latin America and North America have experienced no religiously based civil wars. Asia and the Pacific experienced twenty religious civil wars, or 45 percent of all religiously based civil wars, the Middle East eight (18 percent), Europe eight (18 percent), and Africa eight (18 percent).

More than half of Europe's civil wars (eight of thirteen, or 62 percent) had a religious component. Asia and the Pacific hosted a somewhat smaller proportion: twenty of their forty-one civil wars (49 percent) were religious. The Middle East follows with eight of twenty-one (40 percent), and Africa with eight of forty-six (15 percent). These figures are presented in Table 5.1.

Table 5.1 shows that from 1940 to 2008, Asia and the Pacific experienced a disproportionate number of religious civil wars, and Europe experienced proportionately more religious civil wars than did other regions. These findings, however, do not reveal whether religion was a central or peripheral issue in these wars.

Table 5.2 provides data on the global distribution of wars with religion as a central or peripheral element. Recall that wars in which religion is central are

Table 5.1

Global distribution of religious civil wars, 1940–2008				
Region	Number of civil wars	Number of religious civil wars	Percentage of all religious wars	Percentage of wars in region with a religious component
Africa	46	8	18	17
Asia and the Pacific	41	20	45	49
Europe	13	8	18	62
Latin America / Caribbean	14	0	0	0
Middle East	21	8	18	38
Total	135	44	100	NA

Table 5.2

Global distribution of civil wars with religion as a central or peripheral factor, 1940–2008				
Region	Number of wars with religion central	Number of wars with religion peripheral	Percentage of all religious civil wars with religion central	Percentage of religious civil wars in region with religion central
Africa	5	3	19	63
Asia and the Pacific	15	5	56	75
Europe	1	7	4	13
Latin Ameica / Caribbean	0	0	0	0
Middle East	6	2	22	75
Total	27	17	100	NA

cases in which the parties in the war are fighting for the imposition of a given religious tradition throughout the state. So, for example, the wars in Afghanistan involved an insurgent group, the Taliban, fighting for the imposition of a legal code that strictly adhered to Islam. Wars in which religion is peripheral are those in which the parties follow different religious traditions in the broadest terms. So, for example, Muslims in Bosnia fought against Christian (Catholic) Croats and (Orthodox) Serbs during the Yugoslav wars in the 1990s. In this case religion was not central to the fight, but it was used by elites and masses to identify friend from foe. Most religious civil wars, two-thirds, involve religion as a central issue (n = 27). Only seventeen of forty-four had religion as peripheral.

The third column of Table 5.2 shows that the vast proportion of wars with religion as a central issue took place in Asia and the Pacific (56 percent), the Middle East (22 percent), and Africa (19 percent). Only one of Europe's religious wars featured religion in a central role. So, although most of Europe's wars involved religion, religion featured only peripherally. This is not the case for Africa, Asia and the Pacific, and Middle East: in these regions religion featured centrally.

Although there were a total of 44 religious civil wars from 1940–2008, only twenty-four states were responsible for them. Table 5.3 provides the distribution of wars across states. Three states experienced 3 or more wars. India experienced 6 wars, 5 of which involved religion as a central feature, followed by Indonesia and Yugoslavia with 3 each. An additional eleven states experienced 2 of the 44 religious civil wars, and the remaining 10 wars occurred within other states.

PARTICULAR RELIGIONS IN CIVIL WARS: A COMPARATIVE PERSPECTIVE

If we look at which of the many religions is most apt to be engaged in a religious civil war, a striking finding emerges: one or both parties adhered to Islam in 82 percent of all religious civil wars (thirty-six of forty-four cases);[9] Christianity was involved in twenty-three cases (52 percent); Hinduism was involved in six cases (14 percent); and other religions were involved in only a handful.

Another way to examine the connection between individual religions and civil war is to look at the religious makeup of the states involved. Table 5.4 shows that 58 percent of the states (14 of 24) that have experienced civil war have Islam as a dominant religion, where dominance is defined in terms of a majority of the population with a given religious identity. Christianity is a dominant religion in 21 percent of these states, while Buddhist, Hindu, Jewish, and Taoist states make up the remainder.

Table 5.3

State	Number of civil wars with religion as central	Number of civil wars with religion as peripheral
Distribution of religious civil wars across states, 1940–2008		
Afghanistan	2	0
Algeria	1	0
Azerbaijan	0	1
Bangladesh	0	1
Burma	2	0
Chad	0	1
China	2	0
Cyprus	0	2
Ethiopia	0	1
Georgia	0	1
India	5	1
Indonesia	1	2
Iran	2	0
Iraq	2	0
Israel	1	0
Lebanon	0	2
Nigeria	2	0
Philippines	2	0
Russia	1	1
Sri Lanka	0	1
Sudan	2	0
Syria	1	0
Tajikistan	1	0
Yugoslavia	0	3
Total	27	17

Table 5.4

Dominant religion of states experiencing civil war

State	Dominant religion	Percentage of population
Afghanistan	Islam / Sunni	84
Algeria	Islam / Sunni	99
Azerbaijan	Islam / Shia	>50
Bangladesh	Islam / Sunni	88
Burma	Buddhist	89
Chad	Islam / Sunni	50
China	Taoist	95
Cyprus	Christian / Greek Orthodox	78
Ethiopia	Islam / Sunni	50
Georgia	Christ / Georgian Orthodox	65
India	Hindu	80
Indonesia	Islam	88
Iran	Islam / Shii	89
Iraq	Islam / Shii	60
Israel proper	Judaism	80
Lebanon	Islam	70
Nigeria	Islam	50
Philippines	Christian / Catholic	83
Russia	Christian / Russian Orthodox	85
Sri Lanka	Buddhist	70
Sudan	Islam / Sunni	70
Syria	Islam / Sunni	74
Tajikistan	Islam / Sunni	80
Yugoslavia	Christian / Eastern Orthodox	49

So why is Islam so much more likely than other religions to be involved in religious civil war?[10] Consider religious influence among states and their populations. Of 192 states that are members of the United Nations, 27 (14 percent) have a clear orientation toward Islam,[11] while 25 (13 percent) have regimes in which Islam is defined as the state religion.[12] Population data reveal that in 48 countries (about 25 percent of all states), at least 50 percent of the population adheres to Islam, while globally the number of adherents to Islam in mid-2003 was approximately 20 percent of the worldwide population.

In contrast, 32 states (17 percent) have a clear Christian orientation, and 13 (7 percent) have declared Christianity as the official state religion. Population figures show that in 103 countries (54 percent of states worldwide), Christianity is a majority religion, and in mid-2003, Christians represented 33 percent of the worldwide population.[13]

Orientation of states, therefore, does not offer much help in explaining why Islam is disproportionately involved in religious civil wars, because a nearly equal proportion of states have an Islamic or Christian orientation (14 and 17 percent respectively). With regard to regimes that define themselves religiously, nearly twice as many are Islamic—13 percent, compared with 7 percent that are Christian. But this statistic does not offer much help either. Despite the differences, there remain relatively few Islamic- and Christian-oriented countries.

Yet, if the majority of the population of a state adheres to a particular religion, religious minorities are apt to be insecure. This likely explains why we find that as compared to civil wars more generally, religious civil wars were far more likely to involve groups seeking independence from the state. Whereas 66 percent of nonreligious civil wars (sixty of ninety-one cases) involved a centralist fight in the takeover of the government, 73 percent of religious civil wars (thirty-two of forty-four) involved fights over greater territorial autonomy or outright independence.[14] Of these, about half involved Muslim minority groups such as Palestinians, Chechens (twice), Somalis in Ogaden, Moros (twice), Kashmiris (twice), Bosnian Muslims, Abkhaz (the extent of their Muslim background is questionable), Kosovar Albanians, Turkish Cypriots, Achenese, and Hyderabadi Muslims. The remaining cases of self-determination involved a mix of Christians, Hindus, Buddhists, and Sikhs.

Finally, it might be worth considering whether it is "Arab" ethnicity that is driving the finding about Muslims in religious civil wars. For example, it turns out that, overall, twenty civil wars (15 percent) occurred in Arab states. Of the forty-four religious civil wars, only four (9 percent) took place in Arab states. The other sixteen cases involving Arab states did not have a religious dimension. Most religious civil wars involving Islam took place outside of the Arab world. Thus, Arab race/ethnicity is unlikely to be responsible for the finding, since most of these fights took place beyond the Arab world in such places as Bangladesh, Cyprus, Indonesia, and Tajikistan.

One of the common reasons given for the presumption that an "Arab" factor can explain the violence is the fact that there is much debate about whether there is actually an Arab-democracy deficit and not a Muslim one. Scholars such as Alfred Stepan point to Mali and Indonesia as prime examples of Islam and democracy coexisting quite well. This might be the case; indeed it might also explain why we see Islam disproportionately involved in civil wars. We know civil wars do not happen in highly autocratic states, and that states undergoing transitions are the most likely to suffer from violence. Most Arab states are autocratic; only a few are transitioning to greater openness and accountability (e.g., Algeria). Given this, Arab states should be underrepresented in terms of civil wars. Indeed, consider that there are 23 Arab states (22 in the Arab League plus Palestine), making up 12 percent of the total number of states (assuming 192 states with UN membership). There have been only 9 Arab states involved in the twenty Arab civil wars: Algeria, Egypt, Iraq, Morocco, North and South Yemen, Yemen, Syria, and Jordan. And of these states, three fought wars of independence (Algeria, Morocco, and Tunisia) during times of transition, when we expect violence to occur. Iraq is an anomaly, having suffered five different civil wars. However, an examination of these wars shows that they tended to occur when there was a breakdown in central authority, as in 1991 with the Shia revolt following the Persian Gulf War, and in 2004 with the American invasion.

Given this, there does not seem to be an Arab problem or an Islam problem per se. Rather, it appears to be the interaction of Islam with democracy, secular ideologies, and the right to self-determination, among other things, that implicates religion (or more accurately, allows adherents, elites, and masses to draw on it) in civil wars. In other words, it is not Islam, but Islam in relation to its current trends, trends that began in the 1970s.

THE DEADLINESS OF RELIGIOUS CIVIL WARS

One explanation for an increased interest in religious civil wars might be that they are more deadly than nonreligious civil wars. Are religious civil wars costlier than other kinds of civil war, and does it matter whether religion features centrally or peripherally? In terms of the intensity of religious civil wars, three aspects are worth reporting: (1) war duration, (2) whether the war recurred, and (3) noncombatant deaths. Religious civil wars tend to last longer than nonreligious civil wars. Whereas nonreligious civil wars last on average 81 months, religious civil wars last 105 months, or about two years longer.[15] The same holds true if one compares central religious civil wars with all other civil wars: central religious civil wars last on average 92 months; all others last about 87 months. Surprisingly, these data reveal that cases in which religion is peripheral are the longest, lasting on average 120 months (this is not statistically significant, however).

Furthermore, religious civil wars are about twice as likely as nonreligious civil wars to recur: nine of thirty-five (26 percent) recurred, compared with ten of eighty-two (12 percent) nonreligious wars.[16] Wars in which religion features centrally are a bit more likely to recur (six of nineteen, or 32 percent),[17] while religious civil wars in which religion plays only a peripheral role are no less likely to recur than nonreligious civil wars. Thus, when religion is central, we do find evidence for greater intractability, as the parties seem more willing to reengage in war after the first round of fighting is thought to have ended.

In addition, civil wars in which religion is central are two times deadlier to noncombatants than civil wars in which religion is peripheral (31,000 versus 14,000 average deaths per year for central and peripheral religious involvement respectively).[18] To the extent that we care about noncombatant mortality, this finding makes it clear that the movement of religion from a peripheral to a central issue in a civil war can be expected to have dire consequences.[19]

Since the Second World War, at least as many human beings have perished in civil wars as did during the six years of world war. Interstate wars—and in particular world wars—are never something to take lightly, but civil wars appear to be the most likely type of war we are apt to see. This, along with the fact that there are simply more cases of civil than interstate war available for comparison and analysis, justifies a close look at the links between religion and civil war.

Three important facts about religion and civil wars emerge from this analysis. First, religious civil wars made up one-third of all civil wars fought from 1940 to 2000, and there is little sign that this proportion will decline any time soon. Second, among the world's major religions, Islam was involved in just over 80 percent of these civil wars. Third, religious civil wars in some instances are more costly than nonreligious civil wars: they last longer, and when religion is central they are more intractable and deadlier to noncombatants than wars in which religion is peripheral.

FAITH, RATIONALITY, AND DETERRENCE

Clearly religious engagement in civil war is on the rise, and in many cases this increasing engagement is associated with longer wars, greater harm to noncombatants, and greater difficulties halting ongoing wars (or keeping those halted from reigniting). A key issue is whether these associations are due to an increase in the number of irrational actors in a system or whether something else is going on. From both a theoretical and a policy standpoint, the idea that religious actors are irrational is of little use. Although religious actors are different than secular actors in key ways, they remain rational actors, and this is good news for theorists and policymakers: religious actors' motivations can be understood, and their behavior manipulated. The bad news is that it will be more difficult to develop theories as broadly general as those based on a more restrictive understanding of rationality.

A key difference between religious actors and secular actors, however, is that the level of generalization and abstraction in anticipating action is not as broad in the case of religious actors. So, for example, in neorealist or neoliberal international relations (IR) theory, one may assume key features of a "state" in the abstract, and still generate stable predictions about how that abstract, idealized state might react to a given stimulus. With religious actors this will not be possible to the same degree: it matters whether the actor in question is a Christian, Hindu, or Jew in a way that has no analogue in secular international relations theory.

RATIONALITY AND DETERRENCE

A core concern of those dealing with religiously motivated actors is whether such people or groups can act rationally: can, in other words, their behavior be altered by inducements such as threats or bribes? Can religious actors be deterred? For example, after the ouster of the Shah of Iran in 1979, and the subsequent establishment in Tehran of an Islamic theocracy, could the Iranian government be engaged as any other government? Or did the fact that its leaders identified as Muslims leading an Islamic state mean that in terms of coercion and deterrence Iran was a radically different sort of state, with and against which the traditional tools of statecraft did not apply?

For many in the United States and Israel, both often the target of hostile and religiously charged rhetoric from Tehran, this is a crucial question, not least because Iran is on the threshold of developing a nuclear capability—perhaps even the capacity to build a nuclear weapon. If Iran were any other state, one might at least have the confidence that it could be dissuaded from weaponization or, failing that, incorporated into a preexisting structure of nuclear deterrence. In Washington and Tel Aviv, however, the feeling is that Iran may not be a rational state, and that therefore it cannot be allowed to develop a nuclear weapon, even if that means launching a preventive war to halt that development. The stakes in this question of rationality and deterrence are therefore extraordinarily high.

By definition, a rational person balances potential costs and benefits by attempting to arrive at outcomes that result in a net benefit. When religious faith is introduced into the calculation of net benefit, two subsidiary questions attach themselves. First, does the benefit affect primarily the individual or a group of some sort (family, clan, tribe, nation, and so forth)? Leaving aside for the moment the question of variation in how humans actually imagine themselves (we can assume that in some places and times there are no meaningful distinctions between "I" and "we"), this is an important dimension of calculation because, as observed earlier, actions that result in a net cost to individuals might nevertheless confer a net benefit on a family or larger group. Second, there remains the question of whether the benefits and costs taken into consideration have empirical or tangible artifacts. Problems arise when one set of actors imagines that certain types of cost and benefit are necessarily valid and universal. So for example, the idea that a given delimited territory, an amount of rare metal, access to scarce natural resources, or "life" narrowly restricted to a biological component are the only sorts of interests over which a rational person might struggle (and that this is universal or axiomatic) can limit our ability to understand the wide variety of interests and values that have no tangible or existential counterpart—no empirically verifiable referent.

I mention this because when thinking about deterrence as an enduring pillar of political action, the rise of religious faith, which while recognizing the importance of physical existence and values nevertheless systematically discounts these in favor of intangible costs and benefits, can complicate deterrence, especially when one actor—instead of inquiring—attempts to alter another's behavior by manipulating expected costs and benefits without first understanding how the target actor defines costs and benefits.

In attempting to understand and imagine rationality, however, we are not without a set of useful tools. In the late nineteenth century, the German sociologist Max Weber introduced four ideal-types of rational social action. Two of these are particularly relevant to the discussion here: what Weber called *Zweckrationalität* (instrumental rationality) and *Wertrationalität* (values rationality). The basic differences between these are that in instrumental rationality, there is no necessary link between the means a given actor chooses to employ and the ends sought. It is therefore possible to judge means separately from ends. In instrumental rationality, the core concern is not limited to a single goal, and is described most succinctly as practical or pragmatic: "maximizing results at a minimum cost." By contrast, values rationality is concerned with what we today would call identity. As such, means and ends are an irreducible set.[20]

The key feature then of values rationality, which clearly links it with religious belief and practice, is that the actions themselves constitute the value being sought. We can therefore think of both forms of social action as fundamentally rational. But the most important point is that today we are apt to have forgotten the existence of values rationality. It follows that our ability to understand, predict, and engage peoples for whom values rationality shares a stage with instrumental rationality is compromised.

A PUZZLE RESOLVED BY WEBER'S CONCEPTION OF RATIONALITY?

A chief reason the leaders and publics of advanced industrial states worry about a rise of religion may have to do with their inability to recognize values rationality as a form of rational social and political action. The withering away of *Wertrationalität* and its replacement by *Zweckrationalität* were not an accident. Wilfred Cantwell Smith, for example, goes to great lengths to explain that understandings of religion that emerged from the eighteenth century skeptical movement are responsible for current, narrow conceptions of religion, faith, and transcendence.

> We are now in a position to recognize that it was not fortuitous that the religion concepts, having arisen in Western Europe, are inherently depreciative. For the Christian tradition, particularly in its Protestant form, has historically been unusually disparaging of other religious traditions; and the rationalist academic tradition has been skeptical, if not disparaging, of all . . . This has to do with the fact that Christians have regularly failed or refused to recognize that the faith of non-Christians has that transcendence; that God does in fact encounter men in Buddhist, Muslim, and Hottentot forms, as he does in Christian. Secular academics have regularly failed or refused to recognize that there is a transcendent dimension to human life at all.[21]

Thus Smith not only holds Christian thinkers responsible for denying the faith and logic of other traditions, but he also holds academics with Western—or more accurately, post-Westphalian[22]—conceptions of the separation of church and state responsible for steadily eroding our understanding of how religion engages the public, political sphere.

All of this is important because the fading away of values rationality and its replacement by instrumental rationality as *the* sole conception of rationality led to the assumption that only instrumental rationality counts as true rationality, and all else falls into the error term (is irrational). This has created a blind spot. In other places, values rationality coexists with instrumental rationality (or even predominates). So a better way to reframe our analysis of the relationship between religion and war is to recognize that instrumental rationality is neither natural, inevitable, nor universal, but rather shares the stage with values rationality.

It is therefore unwise and in most cases counterproductive to argue that people of passionate religious faith act irrationally. Instead a more useful set of generalizations, those that are capable of generating effective policy recommendations, focuses on how values rationality works, and how the spread (or perhaps the resurgence) of values rationality in tandem with the spread of religious belief and practice is likely to affect conflict between and within states.

The key thing to remember is that, in terms of forming a stable, predictable *system* of states (which is what eventually emerged following the signing of the Treaties of Westphalia), the chief advantage of rationality conceived of as interests was that it provided a basis to *predict* what others would do given a certain stimulus.[23] One need not know the details or history of a given state to understand that all states maintained an interest in survival, for example.[24] That stable interest, it so happened, implied other interests. And again, if one accepted a set of simple initial assumptions, a stable set of predictions about how others might react to a given initiative, bribe, threat, attack, conciliation, and so on, could and did emerge.[25] One could make predications in the abstract, knowing few if any of the details of a target polity's culture, language, or history. But values rationality has a similar character: once one takes the trouble to ask and listen and learn, the actions of an ardent nationalist or evangelical Christian each become as predictable and stable as rational action via instrumental rationality. So, for example, learning about the role of Islam in policy making in Egypt will allow us to make stable predictions about Egypt's foreign and domestic policy. However, it will tell us much less about Syria's policy unless we ask and answer a similar set of questions. So the stability and predictability are there, but they are not as general as presupposed under instrumental rationality.

From this perspective it becomes more difficult to say whether the implications of resurgent religion are positive or negative vis-à-vis intrastate war. On the one hand, as we will see, religious rationality may act to undermine key pillars of deterrence and accommodation in the contemporary states system, so in that sense the global religious resurgence seems threatening. On the other hand, many religions place limits on what adherents may do, as well as what they may not do. We should therefore, a priori, expect to find cases in which war might have been an ideal response from an instrumental rationality point of view, but was ruled out due to a religious objection, i.e., a values rationality calculation.

RELIGION, BARGAINING, AND WAR:
FOUR OBSTACLES

Religion can make war more likely in a number of ways, but it may also prevent war when war seems imminent. As most students of conflict and conflict bargaining know, the costs of war generally exceed the benefits for all participants. Even winners often find that the benefits of victory could have been obtained more efficiently without war. This leaves the puzzle of explaining war when key decision makers on both or all sides are rational actors.[26] If war always results in a net loss for combatants as compared to other means, why ever resort to it? In 1992, James Fearon's review of the literature on barriers to conflict resolution short of war highlighted three key explanations, to which I have added a fourth.[27]

First, rational actors might go to war when they have misrepresented—either deliberately or inadvertently—their own interests in the outcome. For example, the United States did not appear to consider the fate of South Korea to be a vital security interest in 1950, and this made it easier for Kim Il Sung to convince Joseph Stalin to lend him the weapons and diplomatic support North Korea would need in order to forcibly unify the Korean Peninsula. Yet once the attack was under way, the United States revised its calculations and determined that "halting communist aggression in Asia," whether in South Korea or elsewhere, was in fact a vital U.S. security interest. Had both Stalin and Kim Il Sung understood this clearly, the attack might not have happened, or it might not have happened as or when it did. Fearon calls this a problem of private information.

Second, rational actors might go to war when one or both sides—typically the stronger side—cannot credibly commit to uphold an agreement in the future. The lack of a third party to guarantee compliance with a present agreement may make it rational for even a weaker actor to initiate or continue a war, for fear that it may be even more disadvantaged in a future engagement. Fearon calls this a commitment problem.

Third, rational actors might go to war when they cannot agree that an issue of contention is divisible. Some kinds of values have a continuous quality that allows for their division into subsets that retain their value to those seeking them—money is the classic example. Other kinds of values, however, have a lumpy quality: most can be literally divided, but those seeking such goods no longer consider the thing divided as retaining its value or identity. Children, divine-right titles, and national homeland territories all share this characteristic. Thus, two rational actors who might otherwise agree to share a sought-after value find it impossible to agree on an acceptable division, and choose war in order to gain unfettered control of the person, place, or thing in dispute. Fearon calls this a problem of issue indivisibility.

In addition to Fearon's summary of three rationalist explanations for war, contemporary work on conflict bargaining has posited a fourth: asymmetric time horizons.[28] Rational actors may share information about their true objectives, have the assistance of a third party in guaranteeing their contracts, and consider the issue of contention at least partly divisible; however, if each discounts the present at a different rate, war can appear to be a good gamble. In conflict bargaining, "the shadow of the future" argument posits a situation in which actors choose to forego the capture of short-term gains from defection (and sustain the perceived costs of not obtaining those gains) because in a relationship expected to endure over many exchanges, the benefits of cooperation are expected to far outweigh the short-term gains of defection.[29] For example, in the context of his fight with the secular and "corrupt" West, Osama bin Laden speaks of needing two hundred years to overthrow the West's influence in the Middle East. Given this, we are most likely to find asymmetric time horizons when religious adherents clash with nonreligious opponents.

Religion intersects each of the four obstacles to nonviolent conflict resolution in important ways.[30] First—and to take only the Abrahamic religions as an example—the quality of salvation tends to be indivisible. One cannot be partly sinful or partly holy in one's conduct, and the end state of one's existence is discrete rather than continuous: one's conduct is either sanctioned or censured; one goes to heaven or not. In addition to salvation being indivisible, physical locations have come to be seen as sharing this indivisible quality.[31] Examples include the Q'aba in Mecca; the Temple Mount, or Haram al-Sharif, in Jerusalem; and ancient American Indian sites that contain sacred clays used in religious rituals. Thus, issue indivisibility is closely associated with religion, and may account for the perception that religious belief or motivation makes escalation of a conflict to war more rather than less likely. Finally, interpretations of holy texts often share this indivisible quality. It matters, for example, whether a given Arabic passage of the Quran directs a husband to "beat" his wife or force her to "go away" when he calculates that she has not obeyed the commandments of God.[32] Scholars and practitioners who cleave to the former view will often not accept arguments to the effect that the original word in Arabic has another meaning or, more accurately, has another meaning in the specific context in which it was originally written.

Second, the start or resolution of a violent fight may not last when a dominant religion—dominant in terms of numbers of followers and control of government—cannot credibly promise not to renege on governmental agreements or a negotiated settlement with the followers of a minority religion in the same state. If it is the case that a regime has established itself on the basis of a particular faith, yet has a large portion of its population that is not of the same faith, then problems may arise if the state commits itself to upholding and defending only one tradition. This is what happened when the Sudanese government abrogated the Addis Ababa Agreement in 1983 as part of an Islamization campaign through all of Sudan, including the non-Muslim south. The situation does not look better with the recent 2005 Comprehensive Peace Agreement between the still-conservative Islamic government of Khartoum and the Southern resistance (SPLM/A) in Sudan, which continues to fear a Muslim-dominated North.

Third, people of faith often have private information about their true interests or capabilities in a conflict. This may be perhaps religion's oldest and most frequent association with conflict. Typically, a given correlation of forces makes attack or defense appear hopeless, but the belief that "god is on our side" (private information about a religious sanction) encourages conflict when it otherwise would have been avoided. In Islamic law, for instance, if the leadership is seen to be corrupt and not representing the true faith, the individual has a duty to overthrow the government. This is the rationale behind war in Algeria, Egypt, and Tajikistan. Perhaps the most striking example is the Iranian Revolution and its associated theology, which permitted the Shia to take a more aggressive political role; no longer were they to be victimized martyrs, but hero-martyrs.

Fourth, religious adherents often appear to discount the present in favor of the future. In other words, they may welcome tangible individual or group costs that are frightful in anticipation of future and intangible benefits. For example, a rational individual might seek his own death (a very high cost) under circumstances expected to result in long-term extra-temporal benefits, such as eternal paradise.[33] Note that in neither the "shadow of the future" nor the "martyr" case are the expected benefits guaranteed, yet we may still consider those who calculate in this fashion to be rational actors.

In addition to issue indivisibility, commitment problems, private information, and asymmetric time horizons, two related factors may also help explain the common association of religious zeal with increased frequency or intensity of war: dehumanization and compulsory proselytization. As a matter of record, most males—and males overwhelmingly make up the world's fighting forces[34]— have a difficult time killing other humans.[35] Historically, one important way to facilitate killing has been dehumanizing the adversary. The principle is simple and powerful: the more closely the target resembles "me," the more difficult it will be for me to muster the will to kill. Most people, for example, experience some discomfort killing animals for food, yet very few experience any discomfort killing plants for food. By imagining one's human adversary as less than human or nonhuman, the moral difficulty in killing is reduced, and as a result killing is facilitated (possibly even difficult to deter, depending on the nature of the characterization invoked by the dehumanizing effort).[36]

Religious belief has unfortunately facilitated this line of thinking in some cases.[37] Some of the earliest "human rights" debates were provoked by the "discovery" of natives by the Spanish Empire in the fifteenth century.[38] Spanish Catholic missionaries and soldiers had to wrestle with the status of natives, who were most often referred to as "savages." From a Christian point of view, each human possesses a soul that is God's business, not man's. But the rights that attach to the person as a result generally were held to depend upon acceptance of the Christian faith. Those who heard the word of God and *then* rejected Christian tenets, or the authority of the church more generally, were dispossessed of all rights and protections under the law. They could be killed without moral or legal consequence to the killer. Moreover, where "unbelievers" were held to be a systematic threat to believers, killing them was not only permissible, but might take on the character of a religious obligation. Such sentiments continued well into the twentieth century. American president William McKinley, for example, justified the conquest, occupation, and conversion of the Philippines as part of a divine plan: "There was nothing left for us to do but to take them all, and to educate the Filipinos, and uplift and civilize and Christianize them."[39] Christianity in its multiple forms is hardly unique in this, and the stripping away of moral consequence and protections from unbelievers and apostates is something many religious faiths share.

Second, and as observed above, in some religions whether one goes to paradise or heaven depends upon a relationship between the individual worshipper and his or her god(s). Sometimes that relationship is mediated by a priest or interpreter, and sometimes not. In other religions, however—in particular Evangelical religions—one's salvation depends not only on one's own conduct, but on the successful conversion of others to one's own faith. Functionally, these types of religion are more likely to be associated with violence, because some proportion of those sought as converts are apt to view the attempt at conversion as an act of coercion even when it has no physical component.[40]

In this chapter I have sketched a number of important ways international relations theorists and foreign policy students can understand the relationship between religion and war. Although, as with nationalism, there is a gap between the degree to which academic and policy audiences are likely to attach the assumption of rationality to actions (policy makers are apt to assume that religiously motivated actors are irrational, academics less so), I argue that religiously inspired actors are rational actors: firstly, they calculate; and secondly, they seek net gains from interactions. A key difference between secular and religious rational actors, however, is the degree to which the latter are apt to count the intangible, as well as the tangible, as significant.

Religiously inspired actors are apt, as individuals, to practice both of the types of rational action Weber introduces as instrumental rationality (*Zweckrational-ität*), and values rationality (*Wertrationalität*). My argument is that once understood (and generalization *across* religious faiths may or may not be productive in this sense), religiously inspired actors may be seen to act in accordance with a stable set of preferences, implying there will be ways to alter their behavior by manipulating a different set of costs and benefits.

That said, in other ways religious belief and practice as currently interpreted appear to make war more likely than nonreligious practices for two reasons. First, the leaders and states of the advanced industrial world (which I have called "the West" at times, but which includes Japan and South Korea, to name but two states that are industrialized but not Western) have lost their understanding of the systematic bases of religious belief and practice, and are therefore likely to rely on an inappropriate set of cost and benefit inducements in their efforts to secure themselves from perceived threats based in the developing world. By systematically ignoring this noninstrumental rationality, these actors are apt to rely on coercion by threat of physical destruction, which may ultimately make war between the advanced industrial states and their often non-state adversaries more, rather than less, likely.

The second pathway to a higher incidence of war is demographic. Like political affiliation, most young people adopt their parents' religious views (not unalloyed, but in the main). At the same time, many of the world's religions—and some of the largest denominations, such as Roman Catholicism—prohibit birth control. Where birth controls are lax, populations increase at a faster rate, and as a result the process of democratization worldwide promises to give members of fecund religious groups increasing political power.[41] Since members of rival religious groups are apt to gain increasing leverage over state foreign and domestic policies, it may be only a matter of time before the nation-state as a core actor in interstate politics is superseded by the "religious state." Given the similarities between nationalism and religion, and given the intensity of violence that characterized (and continues to characterize) nationalist conflicts, one can only expect the incidence of war—and perhaps its intensity—to rise over time as the world's religions continue to expand, first demographically and then geopolitically.

With the exception of (parts of) Europe and Japan, religious practice and identity are on the rise globally.[42] To the extent that intergroup and interstate conflict bargaining may be compromised in the future as a result of religious adherents gaining an increasing share of political power within states, the implications for peace between and within states may be negative, and the likelihood of war may rise.

Currently, the majority of religion's direct associations with war are represented at the substate level: first in civil wars, such as Sudan's, between the predominantly Muslim North and predominately Christian and animist South, and Iraq's, between Shiites and Sunnis; and second in religiously inspired terrorism, such as that directed by Al Qaeda and Islamic Jihad (to name but two groups). But religion affects interstate conflicts of interest as well: most famously, those between predominantly Hindu India and predominantly Muslim Pakistan. Additionally, the Russian Federation's increasing association with Orthodox Christianity has already complicated its relations with Europe and the United States over the fate of predominantly Muslim Kosovo's independence from Eastern Orthodox Christian Serbia. On the other hand, as highlighted by the long conflict between the Catholic Irish Republican Army and Protestant Ulster Unionists, and between Israeli Jews and Muslim and Christian Palestinian Arabs, it can often be difficult to disentangle nationalist and religious motives and effects, especially when religion becomes a part of national identity itself. But since nationalism and religion both share key functional aspects—demonization of the "other" and issue indivisibility, for example— once again, the prospects for keeping conflicts from escalating to violence and war may be diminishing.

My argument for why this may be happening is speculative at this point, but focuses on the hidden benefits of an expectation of interstate war. Since there are far more religions and nations than states, and since national self-determination has become an established norm of interstate politics, one puzzle is why there are not more states than there are.

My answer, in keeping with realist tradition, is that only a few homogeneous nation-states are viable in security terms (to say nothing of economies of scale). Thus, so long as invasion and conquest are a real fear, small nations and religious groups have a strong incentive to bury their differences and coexist productively within states. As noted above, however, different nationalities and religious groups have different capacities for coexistence.[43] More to the point, given that since the end of the Cold War the apparent threat of interstate war (invasion and conquest from another *state*) has diminished (or appeared to), it may be less surprising that in the absence of a common threat, groups within states—and here I focus on religious groups—may feel more confident in seeking a greater voice *as* groups. For the state's part, the persecution or restriction of religious group access to political power may be weakening as well, and for the same reasons.

Finally, and most broadly, the implications of the rise of religious identity and practice worldwide demand more focused scholarly attention—especially, I would argue, from students of conflict and violence. While religion has often been associated with war, there is an equally long association between religious practice and peace and nonviolence. A key issue will be whether religion hinders or catalyzes escalation of conflicts to violence. The answer is far from clear.

Consider that while many religions call for peace and condemn violence, these same religions are often involved in violence of the most extreme sort, including torture and mass murder. In terms of philosophy, religious prohibitions against violence (and war) count as tacit acknowledgment that "men" often seek violence and delight in conquering and subjugating other men. Thus, the rise in religious identity and its marriage to politics worldwide may be a measure of a rise in the number of persons with a desire to conquer others, who are at the same time seeking a way to govern or discipline that fundamental human desire. Moreover, when religion disciplines violence, its success depends on how closely the person so restricted may be identified with the faith in question. Unbelievers, in other words, do not benefit from prohibitions on violence to the same degree that co-religionists do.

All in all then, we may greet the rise of religion with regard to the likelihood of intergroup war with the same trepidation we would greet a similar rise in nationalism. While, like nationalism, religious faith per se is no indicator of an increased likelihood of a will to harm others, some percentage of religious adherents will cleave to a faith that functionally duplicates what we think of as hypernationalism, and with the same violent outcome: an increased likelihood of war. Understanding which religions are most likely to cultivate such adherents, and under what circumstances, should be a major preoccupation of students of interstate and intrastate violence.

NOTES

1. An exception is Scott M. Thomas, *The Global Resurgence of Religion and the Transformation of International Relations: The Struggle for the Soul of the Twenty-first Century* (New York: Palgrave MacMillan, 2005). See also Douglas Johnston, *Religion: The Missing Dimension of Statecraft* (Oxford: Oxford University Press, 1994); the special issue of *Millennium: Journal of International Studies* 29, no. 3 (December 2000); and Daniel Philpott, *Revolutions in Sovereignty: How Ideas Shaped Modern International Relations* (Princeton: Princeton University Press, 2001).

2. Exceptions include Kalevi J. Holsti, *Peace and War: Armed Conflicts and International Order, 1648–1989* (Cambridge: Cambridge University Press, 1991); and Samuel P. Huntington, *The Clash of Civilizations and the Remaking of World Order* (New York: Simon and Schuster, 1996). On civil war, see Jonathan Fox, *Religion, Civilization, and Civil War: 1945 Through the New Millennium* (Lanham, MD: Lexington, 2004); and Monica Duffy Toft, "Getting Religion? The Puzzling Case of Islam and Civil War," *International Security* 31, no. 4 (Spring 2007): 97–131.

3. One of the best treatments of the "ambivalence" of religion can be found in R. Scott Appleby, *The Ambivalence of the Sacred: Religion, Violence, and Reconciliation* (New York: Rowan and Littlefield, 2000).

4. William P. Alston, "Religion," *Encyclopedia of Philosophy*, vol. 7 (New York: Macmillan, 1972), 140–145.

5. Benedict Anderson, *Imagined Communities*, rev. ed. (New York: Verso, 1991).

6. Christianity and Hinduism, for example, each acknowledge holy places, yet the control or possession of a specific territory is not necessary to the practice of either faith. By contrast, many in Islam hold that territory does matter: control of the lands surrounding the Q'aba in Mecca and the Haram al-Sharif in Jerusalem, for example, are material to the practice of Islamic faith and often analogized to the body. This is why for many Muslims, even the nonviolent occupation of territories linked to the holy sites can be akin to an act of violence or sacrilege: a blind-spot for members of other religious communities who seek to control or share the same territories.

7. Timothy Samuel Shah and Monica Duffy Toft, "Why God is Winning," *Foreign Policy*, July/August 2006, 39–43.

8. The most comprehensive assessment of religious values can be found in Pippa Norris and Ronald Inglehart, *The Sacred and the Secular* (Cambridge: Cambridge University Press 2003). An exception to this rule is some of the Western European states; they are outliers relative to the rest of the world.

9. For a similar finding about ethnic conflicts in the early 1990s, see Huntington, *The Clash of Civilizations*, 269.

10. For a full explanation, see Monica Duffy Toft, "Getting Religion?"

11. Assaf Moghadam, "A Global Resurgence of Religion?" (Working Paper 03-03, Weatherhead Center for International Affairs, Harvard University, Cambridge, MA, August 2003), 46–54. Religious orientation refers to states in which a given religion is accorded preferential treatment in terms of a disproportionate allocation of state funds to religious institutions or groups when compared with state allocation to other religions and groups.

12. Ibid., 53.

13. Ibid., 46–53.

14. Pearson chi2(1) = 17.8118 Pr = 0.000.

15. The overall mean is 88 months.

16. Pearson chi2(1) = 3.2960 Pr = 0.069.

17. Pearson chi2(1) = 3.9241 Pr = 0.048.

18. To calculate whether religious civil wars are more brutal toward civilians, I subtracted the average number of battlefield deaths per year for each war from the total deaths per year, thereby obtaining an average nonbattlefield annual death count. Note that nonreligious civil wars seem to brutalize civilians even more than central religious wars, accounting for 51,000 nonbattle deaths per year on average.

19. I confirm this finding about the deadliness of religious civil wars in a paper in which I examine religiously based violence in the Caucasus region of Russia from 2000–2008: religiously based acts of violence produced far more deaths than those that did not have a religious basis. See Monica Duffy Toft and Yuri Zhukov, "Religious

Violence in the Caucasus: Global Jihad or Local Grievances?" (paper presented at the annual conference of the International Studies Association, New Orleans, February 17–20, 2010).

20. David Little, "Max Weber and the Comparative Study of Religious Ethics," *Journal of Religious Ethics* 2, no. 2 (Fall 1974): 5–40; Bradley Starr, "The Structure of Max Weber's Ethic of Responsibility," *Journal of Religious Ethics* 27, no. 3 (Fall 1999): 407–434.

21. Wilfred Cantwell Smith, *The Meaning and End of Religion* (1962; repr., Minneapolis, MN: Fortress Press, 1991).

22. The Romans, to cite but one important example, maintained neither a strict separation of church and state nor a bright line between mortality and divinity. See Christopher Kelly, *The Roman Empire: A Very Short Introduction* (New York: Oxford University Press, 2006).

23. Albert O. Hirschman, *The Passions and the Interests:Political Arguments for Capitalism Before Its Triumph* (Princeton: Princeton University Press, 1997).

24. Kenneth Waltz, *Theory of International Politics* (New York: McGraw Hill, 1979).

25. John Mearsheimer, *The Tragedy of Great Power Politics* (New York: Norton, 2001).

26. This is one of the main puzzles that motivates most international relations theorists. For a classic treatment, see Geoffrey Blainey, *Causes of War* (New York: Free Press, 1988)

27. James D. Fearon, "Rationalist Explanations for War," *International Organization* 49, no. 3 (Summer 1995): 379–414; Monica Duffy Toft, "Issue Indivisibility and Time Horizons as Rationalist Explanations for War," *Security Studies* 15, no. 1 (January–March 2006): 34–69.

28. Toft, "Issue Indivisibility and Time Horizons"; Jack S. Levy and Philip Streich, "Time Horizons, Discounting, and Intertemporal Choice," *Journal of Conflict Resolution* 51, no. 2 (April 2007): 199–226.

29. Robert Axelrod, *The Evolution of Cooperation* (New York: Basic Books, 1984).

30. I suspect that the range of circumstances under which commitment and private information obstacles apply to religious disputes is narrower than for secular disputes. Most religions, for example, hold that an all-knowing, all-powerful supreme being guarantees their agreements, so that a temporal third-party guarantee to enforce contracts would not be necessary. Private information, while clearly affecting some religious conflicts, is also less of a problem, since the stakes in a religious conflict are generally zero sum, such as salvation or paradise.

31. See, for example, Ron E. Hassner, "To Halve and to Hold: Conflicts Over Sacred Space and the Problem of Indivisibility," *Security Studies* 12, no. 4 (Summer 2003): 1–33; and Toft, "Issue Indivisibility and Time Horizon."

32. Lelah Bakhtiar, *The Sublime Quran* (New York: Kazi, 2007). Bakhtiar, an American woman who has translated the Quran into English, has stirred controversy over her arguments concerning the meaning of the Arabic word most often translated as "to beat," which she argues should be translated as "to go away."

33. See, for example, Monica Duffy Toft, "Getting Religion?" 100.

34. Joshua S. Goldstein, *War and Gender* (Cambridge: Cambridge University Press, 2001); Joanna Bourke, *An Intimate History of Killing: Face to Face Killing in 20th Century Warfare* (New York: Basic Books, 1999).

35. On this startling line of argument, see David Grossman, *On Killing* (New York: Little and Brown, 1996). Grossman shows that up until the Korean Conflict (1950–1953), only one in two U.S. infantry soldiers fired their weapons at the enemy while in combat. S. L. A. Marshall's research in World War II confirmed this finding, and the U.S. military subsequently overhauled its training program so that by the time of the Vietnam War (1965–1973), well over 98 percent of U.S. combat infantrymen were able to fire their weapons at the enemy. Grossman estimates that in the general population, only two percent suffer no psychological or emotional discomfort in killing other humans. The other 98 percent do suffer some degree of psychological or emotional injury as a result of killing.

36. The Nazis, for example, worked hard to indoctrinate average German citizens and convince them of the existential threat posed by Jews (among others). Even where such indoctrination was successful, however, the murder of defenseless human beings took a fearful psychological and emotional toll on most perpetrators. Two factors facilitated what we now think of as the Holocaust: (1) the organization in charge, the SS, worked tirelessly to identify and retain that tiny minority of Germans who were not traumatized by the act of killing; and (2) the industrialization of murder turned what began as a labor-intensive effort by Hitler's *Einsatzgruppen* into the capital-intensive effort (e.g., gas chambers) most people commonly associate with the Holocaust. See Richard Rhodes, *Masters of Death: The SS-Einsatzgruppen and the Invention of the Holocaust* (New York: Vintage, 2003).

37. Religion is hardly alone in this aspect. Nationalist and other secular training systems seek similar results, some more successfully than others. On the power of communist and leftist ideologies to dehumanize adversaries, see Elisabeth Jean Wood, *Insurgent Collective Action and Civil War in El Salvador* (Cambridge: Cambridge University Press, 2003). On the war-causing effects of hypernationalism, see John J. Mearsheimer, "Back to the Future: Instability in Europe After the Cold War," *International Security* 15, no. 1 (Summer 1990): 25, 35, 55–56; and Stephen van Evera, "Hypotheses on Nationalism and War," *International Security* 18, no. 4 (Spring 1994): 5–39.

38. Anthony Pagden, *The Fall of Natural Man* (Cambridge: Cambridge University Press, 1987).

39. As recounted and quoted in Madeleine Albright, *The Mighty and the Almighty: Reflections on America, God, and World Affairs* (New York: Harper Collins, 2006), 23.

40. See, for example, the most recent efforts of the Russian Orthodox Church and the Russian state in partnership to limit the activities of non-Russian Orthodox traditions in the country. Clifford J. Levy, "At Expense of All Others, Putin Picks a Church," *New York Times*, April 24, 2008, A1.

41. Monica Duffy Toft, "Differential Demographic Growth in Multinational States: The Case of Israel's Two-Front War," *Review of International Affairs* 56, no. 1 (Fall): 71–94, and "Population Shifts and War: A Test of Power Transition Theory,"

International Interactions 33 (2007): 243–269; Eric Kaufmann, "Breeding for God," *Prospect Magazine*, November 2006; Monica Duffy Toft, "Wombfare: The Politics of Fertility," in *Political Demography: Identity, Institutions, and Conflict*, ed. Jack Goldstone, Eric Kaufmann, and Monica Duffy Toft (Boulder, CO: Paradigm, 2011).

42. Pippa Norris and Ronald Inglehart, *The Sacred and the Secular: Religion and Politics Worldwide* (New York: Cambridge University Press, 2004); Shah and Toft, "Why God is Winning."

43. For a general theory of the conditions under which violence will emerge when identity groups challenge states, see Monica Duffy Toft, *The Geography of Ethnic Violence: Identity, Interests, and the Indivisibility of Territory* (Princeton: Princeton University Press, 2003).

6. RELIGION AND INTERNATIONAL RELATIONS

No Leap of Faith Required

DANIEL H. NEXON

After decades of discounting—if not simply ignoring—the significance of religion in world politics, many international relations scholars have now seen the light.[1] Indeed, most of those involved in the attempt to "bring religion into international relations theory" agree that intellectual and disciplinary blinders explain the field's decades-long failure to take matters of faith seriously. Some go further, however, and argue that "the global resurgence of religion confronts [international relations] theory with a theoretical challenge comparable to that raised by the end of the Cold War or the emergence of globalization" (Hatzopoulos and Petito 2003, 3). Others, shockingly enough, disagree. In a recent review article, for example, Eva Bellin evinces frustration with continued "exhortion[s] for a paradigm shift" in international relations theory and implores the field to "get on with the project of puzzle-driven research that might shed light (and middle-range theoretical insights) on questions of when and how religion matters in international affairs" (Bellin 2008, 316).

In this chapter I argue against the proposition that religion requires a "paradigm shift" in international relations theory.[2] Many scholars use religion as nothing more than a new vehicle for long-standing criticisms of the field, for example, that it pays inadequate attention to cultural forces, non-state actors, or even specific social-theoretic traditions. But I also dissent from Bellin's view that we should simply bracket epistemological questions and "get on with" constructing middle-range theories involving religion. Disputes over the importance of religion do highlight a number of ongoing problems with the way that the field handles not only religion but a host of cognate phenomena.

In particular, many substantive debates in the field pivot over the relative importance of "material" and "ideal" forces in international politics. For example, realists argue that the imperatives of relative military power matter more than ideological orientations in determining how states relate to one another. Thus, arguments for the importance of religion in international politics quickly become a specific instance of arguments for the importance of cultural forces vis-à-vis material ones.

This has two major consequences. First, it makes it difficult for us to assess the importance of complicated sociocultural forces, including religion. Religion shapes how humans behave via a wide variety of processes and mechanisms. It establishes basic conceptual categories and symbolic orders. It empowers some individuals to speak and act authoritatively in specific settings. It supplies justifications for social and political claims, such as calls for specific policies, acts of resistance, and demonstrations of obedience. It structures, and manifests in, a wide variety of social relations.

Even particular religions—ones recognized by adherents, for example, as forming a singular community of believers—are rife with ambivalent and ambiguous theological principles, practical instructions for daily conduct, and specified social roles. For all these reasons, we cannot resolve a debate over the relative importance of religious and material factors by looking to see if a particular international actors' behavior better correlates with some "religious norm" or "power-political interests."

Second, framing this debate in terms of material versus cultural distracts us from a more interesting set of questions involving the relative importance of social forms and cultural content. Indeed, most of the factors that international relations theorists define as "material," such as economic interests and relative material power, are really manifestations of social position and relation. Although international relations scholars have paid inadequate attention to religion itself, religious forces manifest in a variety of social forms that are both familiar to international relations scholars and generate comparable dynamics to their secular cousins.

In the pages that follow, I review the putative challenges posed by religion to international relations theory. I then use evidence from the Reformations era to illustrate what these challenges get right, and what they get wrong. I next discuss the aforementioned problems with material/ideal framings of the significance of religion in international relations. Here I highlight an implicit theme of this chapter—that we face greater danger of treating religion as sui generis than not taking it seriously enough. I end with some concluding words concerning the "old wine in new bottles" character of much of the paradigm-change literature on religion and international relations theory.

THE CHALLENGES POSED BY RELIGION

The last decade has seen a growing body of scholarship that accuses international relations theory, whether directly or indirectly, of suffering from a "secularist bias." My reading of relevant literature suggests that we can distinguish four distinct, if sometimes overlapping, lines of criticism. In order to adequately grapple with the place of religion in international relations, scholars argue, we must:

- Avoid treating material forces as more important than meanings, ideas, and beliefs;
- Abandon state-centric accounts of world politics that ignore the importance of non-state religious actors;
- Eschew secularist understandings of "religion" and "politics" as distinctive zones of activity; and
- Rethink our tendency to analyze religion primarily in terms of categories such as preferences, norms, and identities.[3]

MATERIALISM

Not a few scholars charge that the materialist bias of many international relations theoretical traditions renders them unsuited to understanding religious phenomena. If we accord causal priority to material factors — such as the military capabilities of states, economic interests, and so forth — then we immediately downplay the importance of symbols, meanings, and, for believers, matters of the spirit that comprise religious worldviews and motivations. Realists, for example, tend to argue that religious factors only matter at the margins; that leaders of states — and other political elites — deploy religious claims to mask or forward their self-interested pursuit of wealth, power, and status; and that religion is, in fact, epiphenomenal to the real drivers of international political processes.[4]

To the extent that liberals privilege economic interests and adopt a narrow understanding of social action as the product of rational, self-interested utility maximization, they similarly cannot adequately theorize religious phenomena. And Marxist accounts, critics contend, also raise problems in that they treat religion as a form of false consciousness epiphenomenal to class politics and the workings of modes of production.[5] As Hurd argues, "Conventional understandings of international relations, focused on material capabilities and strategic interaction, exclude from the start the possibility that religion could be a fundamental organizing force in the international system" (Hurd, 2008, 1).

STATE-CENTRISM

Many of the most important religious actors in world politics are non-state in character. Al-Qaeda and nonviolent Islamic revivalist movements, Falun Gong, the Church of Jesus Christ of Latter-day Saints, Evangelical churches, the Church of Scientology, and a host of Christian missionary movements all operate within and across state boundaries. The Catholic Church has its own state, controls a transnational organization, and acts as an interest group in many political communities. Religious organizations and movements participate in the formulation of state policies through various routine and contentious activities, including lobbying officials, electing representatives, sitting on administrative bodies, mobilizing for protest, and even wielding violence.[6]

It follows that international relations theories that focus on states as the only, or at least primary, actors of significance in world politics erase religious forces from the map. Adopting a weaker form of state-centrism—one that rejects that treatment of states as unitary actors and considers how their domestic politics profoundly shapes their behavior—fails to solve this problem, insofar as religious norms, identities, values, interest groups, and societal actors merely become influences on state foreign policy. Such a blinkered framework, the argument goes, precludes us from locating religious forces, actors, and movements as part of the texture of international politics itself. Thus, international relations scholars downplay the influence of religious forces at the international and transnational level.[7]

SECULARISM AND THE DISTINCTION BETWEEN "RELIGION" AND "POLITICS"

State-centrism and materialism comprise, arguably, symptoms of a broader secularist bias in international relations theory. International relations scholars, according to this line of criticism, build a distinction between religion and politics into their theories, insofar as they treat the two as discrete phenomena that, under normal circumstances, designate separate zones of activity. But this line of thought stems from Enlightenment ideology, particularly in its secularist offshoots; it reflects a concerted effort to take religion out of the "public" sphere and relegate it to the "private" realm of personal convictions and practices.

This line of argument implies that, for example, the very act of defining some variables as "religious" and others as "political" may lead us to underestimate the significance of religious forces in international politics. We must also be careful about the way these categories lead us to describe religion as acting upon politics, as if the "natural" condition of politics is to be free from religious influence. Instead of allowing this distinction to inflect our analysis of religious phenomena, critics contend, we must treat the boundary between religion and politics as variable, contested, and contingent: in other words, as socially constructed.

The boundary itself, it follows, often comprises the relevant focus of scholarship on religion and international relations. Scholars should study the processes that sustain, transform, or reconfigure the relationship between religion and politics across time and space (Hallward 2008, 2, 4–6). In this light, the so-called resurgence of religion reveals itself not as an eruption of religiosity, but as "a series of challenges to the fundamental assumptions that sustain particular authoritative secularist settlements" (Hurd 2008, 143).[8]

SECULARISM AND THE ANALYTICAL REDUCTION OF RELIGION

Many of the scholars who best articulate the aforementioned secularist bias in international relations theory find fault with attempts to view religion primarily as a source of individual preferences and input into strategic choices. Kubálková, for example, criticizes "mainstream or soft constructivist" scholars for being "prepared to consider ideas, including religious ideas, and changing identities and state interests," but subordinating them to "the rational choice theory" (Kubálková 2000, 677). Contemporary rational choice methodologies, critics note, are rooted in Renaissance, liberal, and Enlightenment arguments concerning the necessity of taming passions—notably, religious passions— through interests. The rational, self-interested pursuit of worldly ends therefore entails a normatively laden set of claims about what politics *should* and *should not* entail.

Many of the international relations scholars who advance these claims rely, therefore, on analyzing religion as a set of norms, a discourse, or a basis of individual and group identity. But some argue against applying those categories to religious phenomena. One line of argument holds that religious orientations—unlike, for example, political ideologies—suffuse their adherents' entire lifeworlds. As Thomas argues, "What is distinctive about [religious non-state actors] . . . stems from the way religion is rooted in and constitutive of particular kinds of faith communities" (Thomas 2005, 98). Religion cannot be reduced to an idea, or even a social identity, that individuals adopt or discard with relative ease. Religious orientations produce fundamental categories of knowledge and practice that operate at a much "deeper" or "thicker" level than, for example, identification with a particular political party or ethnic group.

Mitchell, in contrast, agrees that many of these terms are themselves deeply inflected by secularist bias, but offers a different kind of objection. Writing in the idiom of Western Christianity, he argues that "to speak of 'religious values' [and here we might substitute 'norms' as used in international relations theory] is to speak incoherently, since a 'value' is something that a man has as his own." Religious experience, however, looks towards the transcendent, and "God is the Author of all things. . . . 'Value' is affirmative with respect to man; religious experience is deferential with respect to God" (2007, 356). The category "identity," moreover, implies an understanding of politics in which religion is merely a marker of a role in the world, a characteristic of individuals in their relation to one another. The terms "preference," "choice," "value," and "identity," argues Mitchell, "were generated to understand specific problems. As new problems arise, they must be seen as the historically contingent terms that they are, so that more adequate terms can be developed" (359).

Indeed, we might argue that most of the language used by international relations scholars who accuse the field of a secular bias—concerning ideas, identities, norms, and discourses—shapes our attempts to theorize religion with assumptions born from heuristics incompatible with important religious challenges to contemporary secularisms. It is not immediately clear why, if we accept other charges of secularist bias, we should be comfortable treating religion as another manifestation of identity politics, of the struggle over values and norms, or understanding it through post-structuralist categories such as "discursive configurations" that deny the stable relationship of signs and signifieds. As Gregory argues:

> [I]f the entire premise of a study on the Eucharist in the late Middle Ages is that it was "constructed as a symbol," and that religion is reducible to culture and "all culture, all meaning can usefully be studied as a language through its salient symbols," then one will necessarily miss the meaning of transubstantiated host for late-medieval people high and low, clergy and laity, according to whom the Eucharist was not merely symbolic. (Gregory 2006, 143)

TESTING THESE CRITICISMS: CAN MAINSTREAM INTERNATIONAL RELATIONS THEORY SURVIVE THE PROTESTANT REFORMATIONS?

If mainstream international relations theories falter in the face of contemporary religious forces, then we should have particular difficulty using their tool kits to make sense of the impact of the Protestant Reformations on early modern Europe. Not only did the international relations of the period take place in a pre-secular environment, but the Reformations gave rise to a number of non-state religious movements whose activities shifted the European balance of power.

The Reformations led, for example, to a series of military conflicts in the German Empire that, by the middle of the sixteenth century, forced Charles of Habsburg—ruler not only of the empire but also of a hodgepodge of dynastic holdings including Castile, Aragon-Catalonia, the Netherlands, and parts of Italy—to abdicate and divide his holdings between his son, Philip II of Spain, and his brother, Ferdinand, founder of the "Austrian" branch of the Habsburg dynasty. Not long afterwards, the spread of Calvinism plunged France into the decades-long Wars of Religion and sparked the Dutch Revolt, an uprising in the Netherlands that eventually mutated into an interstate war between the Dutch Republic and its erstwhile Spanish Habsburg rulers. Another series of religious conflicts in the Empire culminated in the 1618–1648 Thirty Years' War, which marked the end of Spanish Habsburg hegemony in Europe.

A variety of other reasons suggest that the Reformations era should be a particularly "easy" case for validating the challenges associated with religion and international relations theory. Religious claims and narratives played a major role in the legitimation of early modern authority, whether in the Holy Roman Empire, the French monarchy, or elsewhere. The papacy, for example, had the power to place monarchs under interdict—an act that, when exercised, created significant political difficulties for its targets. Individuals took oaths extremely seriously, as violating them without appropriate dispensation threatened the immortality of their souls. Obedience to temporal authorities was justified in profoundly religious terms. And so on and so forth.[9] Indeed, many who accuse modern international relations theory of having secularist bias invoke early modern Europe as an example of a pre-secular political order.[10]

MATERIALISM

Can we provide adequate explanations for the international politics of the early modern era that focus on the distribution of military capabilities or other putatively "material" factors? In some respects, such explanatory frameworks fare better than we might expect. Consider realist interpretations of the Reformations period, which focus on dynamics associated with balance-of-power politics and the rise and decline of hegemonic orders. Realists point to two processes in particular: First, increasing Habsburg power threatened other actors in Europe, such as the rulers of France and those German princes seeking to consolidate and expand their political autonomy. Second, Charles V and his Spanish Habsburg successors suffered from conventional problems of hegemonic overextension and decline in the face of strategic commitments that exceeded their underlying resources (Gilpin 1981, 120–121). Religion, in this interpretation, played at best a secondary role in the decline of Habsburg hegemony and the power-political struggles of the period.

We can, in fact, find a great deal of evidence that supports downplaying religious forces. Protestant German princes balanced with Catholic French kings against the Habsburgs. Philip II intervened in the French Wars of Religion to keep his primary rival politically fragmented, but failed to provide sufficient support to French Catholic parties to resolve the conflicts in their favor. Elizabeth Tudor initially resisted appeals from Protestants to support co-confessionals in the Netherlands against their Spanish overlords. She only swung decisively against Spain when power-political and economic considerations recommended English intervention in the conflict. The Thirty Years' War saw Protestants and Catholics fighting alongside one another in the various armies that clashed across Germany. And so on.[11]

In this reading, Europe during the sixteenth and seventeenth centuries thus demonstrates how, as Waltz puts it, through "all of the changes in boundaries, of social, economic, and political form, of military and economic activity[,] the substance and style of international politics remains strikingly constant" (Waltz 1986, 329).[12] Realism, properly understood, does not exclude the role of nonmaterial factors in shaping alliances, decisions to support opposition movements in other polities, or leading actors to adopt policies inconsistent with a "pure" form of realpolitik. One could also argue, quite plausibly, that the Habsburg experience reflects, in Gilpin's terms, how the "fundamental problem of international relations in the contemporary world is the problem of peaceful adjustment to the consequences of uneven growth or power among states, just as it was in the past" (Gilpin 1981, 230).

Realism, of course, comprises only one variation on the materialist theme. A broader materialist bias might lead us to conclude that if we scratch the surface of apparently religious motivations and forces, we find economic and other materialist interests. Religion is, in this way, epiphenomenal to political outcomes. Such claims are not at all uncommon in analysis of the Reformations era. Over the last two decades, however, a number of historians have placed great emphasis on the religious character of rule, conflict, and resistance in the period. In doing so, they have actively contested what was the dominant trend in historical interpretations of the period: to treat political, economic, and class interests as much more important than autonomous religious forces. Unsurprisingly, many of those international relations theorists who consider religion a significant force in the period draw on such recent scholarship.[13]

It isn't difficult to understand why many historians downplayed, and continue to deemphasize, the significance of nonreligious forces. Most rebellions in early modern Europe were, at their heart, disputes over taxes, disagreements about rights and privileges, conflicts over the balance between central authority and local autonomy, rivalries between court factions, struggles over succession, or some combination of all five. Tabulating the number of these issues at stake, in fact, provides a decent indicator of the likely severity of any given conflict. The more of them in play, the more destructive and prolonged the struggle.

Some combination of these disputes were almost invariably present in the "religious" civil wars of the period, whether in Germany, Britain, France, the Netherlands, or elsewhere. The French Wars of Religion, for example, overlaid a confessional dispute on a struggle for influence among court factions; the untimely death of Henry II and his rapid succession by two young and inexperienced sons led to high-stakes conflict between rival noble families, most notably the Guise and the Bourbons. Factional struggles for influence in the government of the Netherlands, disputes over taxation, and fears of Spanish encroachment on local privileges played major roles in the Dutch Revolt. Hence, we do not need to stretch matters much to characterize most of the "religious" conflicts within early modern polities as tax revolts or struggles for the control of government. Most of the interstate wars involving confessional differences involved, for their part, preexisting dynastic rivalries and dynastic claims.

But we also confront strong evidence against those who would accord overwhelming weight to power-political and material forces. The French Wars of Religion owed much of their intensity and intractability to the presence of religious disputes. Foreign princes and religious authorities intervened, either directly or indirectly, to support their co-confessionals. Religious affiliations motivated burghers and other ordinary people to commit their money and their lives to the cause of noble factions whose rivalries they usually greeted with indifference (Kingdon 1967; Parrow 1993, 9; Wood 1996, 5; Elliott 2000, 74–75).

Arguments over the status of the Eucharist between Heinrich Zwingli and Martin Luther nearly doomed the emergence of a German Protestant alliance; only Zwingli's death and a significant growth in the threat posed by Habsburg power to the survival of Protestantism broke the deadlock (Dueck 1982; Christensen 1984). German Protestant princes, of course, allied with Catholic France against Charles. Yet their concerns about French persecution of Protestants often shaped their relations with France, even precluding an alliance at inopportune times. Confessional concerns led the Spanish, for their part, to delay critical support for French Huguenot rebels during the Thirty Years' War. The major political pressure on Elizabeth Tudor to support the Dutch emanated from hard-line supporters of the Reformation; without such pressure, support for the Dutch might have been a nonissue (Parker 1977). In fact, the earlier alliance between Madrid and London might have still been in force.

Although Catholics fought on both sides of the Dutch Revolt, religion drove many of the dynamics of the conflict. Persecution of Reformation movements inevitably reduced local autonomy in the Low Countries. It not only went against the grain of local norms, but also required reorganizing the existing Ecclesiastical system in ways that cut out local interests (Nierop 2001). Indeed, as Antonio Ortíz argues, "but for the indignation of Philip II at the excesses of the Calvinists the established order might have been maintained indefinitely in the Netherlands; it was the Calvinists, albeit a minority, who succeeded in giving coherence to the resistance of those who were initially lukewarm." The conflicts in the Netherlands "were not exclusively religious, but it is unlikely they would have broken out if there had not been religious disaffection. Catholics and Protestants were at one in their indignation at the new taxes and the presence of foreign troops, but it was the Protestants who first resorted to arms" (Ortíz 1971, 73–74).

Indeed, religious disputes ultimately destroyed the unity of the revolt. Many moderate Catholics defected to the Habsburgs in reaction to acts of iconoclasm, religious persecution, and a number of urban coups carried out by Calvinist rebels. Calvinism provided the backbone of the organization and resources for revolt; it also made surrender a difficult proposition for those towns where Calvinists had put down significant institutional roots. In the end, the question of toleration—on both Catholic and Calvinist sides—prevented the kind of negotiated settlement to the revolt that might have left Habsburg sovereignty intact (Rowen 1972, 42; Parker 1977, 195; Israel 1995, 183–184).

What should we do in the face of such discrepant evidence? We might argue that religious forces mattered enough that a focus on material interests and capabilities still leads us to unacceptably downplay the role of religion. We might, alternatively, conclude that the existence of a great deal of realist-style power politics in the period provides some support for realism's claims about fundamental continuities in the texture of international politics. In fact, the importance of power-political calculations *despite* the pre-secular and religious-ly inflamed character of the Reformations era arguably provides rather strong evidence against the need for a religion-inspired paradigm shift in international relations theory.

However, as I will argue later on, we should avoid this particular debate alto-gether. It reflects a basic misconception: that the significance of religion should be evaluated by comparing the relative importance of material and ideational factors in any particular outcome. It also tests the relative importance of these factors by means of questionable assumptions about the relationship between ideas and human behavior.

STATE-CENTRISM

Early modern Europe provides, at first glance, convincing evidence for the limitations of state-centric international relations theory in the face of religious forces. The period witnessed a spread of non-state religious movements—which modern scholars would describe as "subnational" and "transnational"—that brought about shifts in the European balance of power.

Consider the Netherlands during the sixteenth century. There, Dutch Cal-vinists operated as part of a network of transregional and trans-state members of the Reformed Church and other Protestant groups. The network included not only Geneva, the base of the Reformed Church, but also French Huguenots, English sympathizers, and German princes. Geneva provided financial and military aid to co-confessionals in the Netherlands and France, and it negoti-ated loans and agitated for external intervention on their behalf. These linkages proved key to the success of the revolt, allowing it to escape defeat at critical moments and generally to maintain sufficient revenue and manpower to com-bat the superior resources of the Spanish monarchy. Furthermore, many of the conflicts engendered by the Reformations involved not simply non-state actors, but individuals and factions embedded within the organs of early modern Euro-pean states. In other words, state actors and different levels of governance fought against one another.[14]

A great deal hinges, however, on what we actually mean by *state-centrism*. It should be pretty obvious that claims along the lines of "only states matter" or "states should be treated as unitary actors" falter when dealing with the Ref-ormations—and, arguably, with the contemporary period as well. But weaker forms of state-centrism hold up a good deal better, such as the notion that states represent the most significant repositories of power. In the Reformations era, many major religious conflicts involved a mixture of interstate conflict and struggles within composite states for control over governance—whether over the whole polity or a segment thereof (Zagorin 1982). Indeed, one of the most successful rebellions, that of the Dutch, led to the creation of a new state. Even before the widespread recognition of the Dutch Republic by dynastic rulers, Holland and Zeeland—among others—managed to hold off the Spanish Habsburgs because they functioned as states in the sense usually understood by international relations theorists: they raised armies, floated debt, and regulated internal violence.[15]

In fact, one could make a strong case for applying Mearsheimer's comments about contemporary violent religious transnational movements to the early modern period: "My theory and realist theories don't have much to say about transnational actors," but their activities "will be played out in the state arena and, therefore, all of the Realist [sic] logic about state behavior will have a significant effect on," for example, "how the war on terrorism is fought" (Mearsheimer 2002). The decisions of rulers about which confession to adopt, which movements to support, and how far to crack down on the spread of heterodox beliefs arguably determined the fate of the Reformations. How important were these decisions? In the absence of external or state support, *not a single conflict* centering around a Protestant-Catholic struggle resulted in a Protestant victory. Territories with a significant Protestant population that remained under the control of Catholic rulers—such as Bohemia, Hungary, and parts of France—ultimately succumbed to counter-reformation (te Brake 1998).

But there's a more profound way in which I find myself troubled by criticisms of state-centric frameworks. I find it difficult to make sense of the impact of non-state actors during the Reformations *without* placing the structure of early modern states at the center of analysis. Some reflections on the conflicts that led to Charles of Habsburg's defeat in Germany illustrate this point.

The German Empire comprised an extremely decentralized composite political community, one involving important organs of federative governance, such as that of the emperor and the Imperial Diet, with some degree of rule-making and enforcement capability. Relatively uniform shared rights and privileges among members of the same orders—electors, princes, imperial cities, and the like—coexisted with heterogeneous contracts between them and the empire. Various leagues and other "self-help" arrangements within Germany, such as the Swabian League (which collapsed under the strain of religious conflict), created additional variations in formal and informal relations. Corporate and individual actors such as princes, magistrates, and the regional leagues occupied various intermediary positions between the emperor and his subjects (Wilson 1999).

In some respects, the general parameters of German religious politics in the first half of the sixteenth century shared important features with later politics in the Netherlands. In both cases, religious movements and orientations created networks that often crossed key divisions within composite polities—those of class and region, as well as those within distinctive regions. Rulers of early modern European states normally contained and suppressed resistance by exploiting these divisions.

As te Brake argues, "The fact is that the political bargains by which dynastic princes typically constructed their composite states created local privileges that distinguished one piece of the composite from another" (te Brake 1998, 28). The chances of serious resistance increased when rulers faced cross-class and cross-regional mobilization, and when movements received indirect or direct support from external actors (Elliott 1970, 112; Zagorin 1982; Koenigsberger 1986, 164). The spread of Reformation religious movements produced these conditions in both the German Empire and the Netherlands. In the German Empire, for example, Charles met defeat at the hands of an alliance of Protestant towns and princes; this coalition brought together individuals and political communities that generally disagreed with one another more than with their emperor (Nexon 2009, chap. 5).

Some might argue that this kind of argument—which focuses on the way that state institutions structure political relations—resembles the ones associated with state-centric theories. I agree. It has more in common with historical institutionalist accounts than with standard variants of state-centrism in international relations theory (Katznelson 1997; Thielen 1999). But the fact remains that the structure and organization of early modern European states explains a great deal about why the spread of transnational religious movements led to conflict, territorial adjustments, and changes in the European distribution of power.[16] Indeed, much of the structure of the early modern "international system" can be understood as emerging from the organization of the states that resided within it (Nexon 2009, chaps. 2–4).

Where does this leave us? We have confronted evidence for and against state-centrism. Attention to religious forces certainly rules out the most blunt forms of state-centrism. Yet these forms of state-centrism enjoy virtually no support in contemporary international relations theory, let alone among those who consider themselves realists.[17] Once again, I submit, the argument that state-centric approaches cannot be effectively applied to religion hints at underlying problems with the common ways of framing such debates.

THE RELIGION-POLITICS DISTINCTION

Does drawing a distinction between religion and politics necessarily marginal-ize religion by rendering it external to our disciplinary object of analysis, i.e., politics? In some respects it does. We frame arguments in terms that replicate secularist assumptions about religion: religion "impinges upon," "shapes," or "intersects" with political phenomena. Even some proponents of "bringing re-ligion into international relations" adopt this framework, arguing that "the key is to focus . . . on what religion . . . does," and that we should "stress what role religion plays in society." But even such scholars admit that it can be difficult to draw the line between religion and politics (as well as culture and society): "the fact that [religion] is sometimes a tool and sometimes an autonomous force blurs the line between religion and other social and political forces" (Fox and Sandler 2006, 176, 177).

Evidence from the Reformations era reinforces the socially and historically contingent nature of the distinction between religion and politics. Most actors in the period did not differentiate between the two spheres of action, as should be clear from Protestant debates over the formation of a defensive alliance in Germany (discussed earlier), as well as the myriad ways in which questions of taxation, central authority, and other supposedly "political" matters were caught up in religious claims and counterclaims. Indeed, even the so-called *politique* position during the French Wars of Religion did not amount to a kind of proto-secularism (Holt 1995, 109).[18] As Roelker notes, the politiques believed that "in the circumstances of civil war, it was preferable to make *temporary* concessions on confessional uniformity rather than to suffer the destruction of the national com-munity" (Roelker 1996, 238). The key debate centered upon whether *some* tolera-tion of religious dissent best served the objective of building a just, peaceful, and unified Christian social order, rather than a reliance on violence and coercion.[19]

The frequent misinterpretation of the politique position demonstrates the dangers of a secular bias concerning the distinction between religion and poli-tics. Hall, for example, seeks to explain how France could violate its Catholic "corporate identity" by supporting Protestant powers against the Habsburgs. His answer is that the victory of religious pragmatists, combined with the severity of religious violence in France, meant that France "excised religious identity," at least in a comparative sense, "from its collective identity," and thus "emerged into the thoroughly modern era a bit earlier than the rest of Europe, as indi-cated by the earlier decoupling of religious identity from French foreign policy" (Hall 1999, 57–58).

French Catholic *devouts*, in fact, voiced opposition to Richelieu's anti-Habsburg policies on the grounds that they undermined the Catholic cause.

They accused him of adopting politique and Machiavellian principles of state-craft. But Richelieu, in turn, justified his policies on the grounds that they would best serve the long-term interests of the Catholic cause. Richelieu's Castilian counterpart, the Count-Duke Olivares, himself authorized support for French Protestant rebels in order to weaken the Bourbon cause. True, he convened a junta of theologians to justify his actions, but the rationales they provided were strikingly similar to those embraced by Richelieu (Elliott 1984, 125–127).[20] As Elliott remarks, "It seems necessary . . . to discard any straightforward picture of a Spanish foreign policy dictated by purely confessional considerations and a French foreign policy operating in conformity with the unvarnished require-ments of *raison d'état.*" The fact that France crossed confessional lines far more systematically than the Spanish, he concludes, was because they had more opportunities to do so in support of their strategic goals (Elliott 1984, 127).

But why isn't this evidence in favor of a trans-historical distinction between religion and politics? One might argue, with some justification, that French and Spanish authorities provided rationales for supporting actors from opposing confessions that were religious-political in character; since defense of dynas-tic interests also amounted to a religious imperative, theological considerations recommended, under certain circumstances, in favor of assistance to heretics and infidels. In other words, they approached the decision whether to support heretics not just in terms of expediency, but whether doing so was "acceptable to God." And that question, rather than a "modern" appeal to the interests of the state qua state, framed subsequent debate.

However, I do see problems with this line of argument. If we want to ask specific questions about contestation over the boundary between religion and politics, then we obviously cannot assume a fixed relationship between the two (Hallward 2008). But if we don't assume such a fixed relationship, than what exactly do we need to change about contemporary international relations the-ory? I suppose, as I noted with respect to French and Spanish policy during the Reformations, that realists (or anyone else) should be wary of arguing that evidence of power-political behavior cuts against the significance of religious forces. But here we are back to the same concern raised by the materialist bias claim: that we too readily downplay the importance of religion. The obvious solution, then, is for us to be on our guard against doing so.

To put it another way, an analyst suffering from a strong secularist bias on these issues might wrongly conclude that conflicts over taxation in early mod-ern Europe were political rather than religious. But a scholar overly concerned about displaying symptoms of secularist bias might have difficulty recognizing that the Reformations often injected high-stakes religious disputes into conflicts over taxation—and therefore produced an extremely combustible admixture of the sacred and the profane.

THE ANALYTIC REDUCTION OF RELIGION

The fourth set of criticisms are much more serious than the ones we have looked at so far.[21] As I noted when I introduced them, they apply even to the work of some of the most prominent critics of the field's supposed secular bias. Insofar as such critics embrace, for example, linguistic-turn and identity-centric frameworks for making sense of religion, they arguably provide alternatives no more or less tainted by secularist ideologies than strategic-choice approaches. All of these forms of analysis fail, as Mitchell argues, to take religious experience seriously.[22]

Many of the contexts in which we study religion, however, do not require us to understand the nature of religious experience. They involve the *translation* of religious experience into the kinds of activities we associate (rightly or wrongly) with politics. I would never claim to understand, for example, how Francis I experienced religion. But I feel confident that I can make sense of the elaborate steps he took to negate his oath in support of a punitive treaty dictated by Charles V after the 1525 French defeat in Italy. Francis feared that failing to do so would condemn his soul to hell. Moreover, the political (or, if you prefer, "religious-political") significance of his actions depended not one whit on Francis's experience of religion: given that he intended to nullify the treaty the moment he returned to France, it was rather prudent of him to find a way to justify his future actions to his subjects and to the church (Knecht 1996, 35–38).

As Wilcox and colleagues argue, "Religion is not simply a set of preferences, choices, values, or identities," but religion does shape, inform, produce, and otherwise translate into preferences, choices, values, and identities (2008, 878). The problem rests less on applying particular (possibly anachronistic) frameworks to understanding religion than it does on reducing the causal and constitutive role of religious forces to a particular social-scientific heuristic.

WHAT'S REALLY AT STAKE?

A critical evaluation of the secular bias literature leads, I believe, to a number of conclusions about the status of religion in international relations theory. Most important, I think, is the notion that religion cannot be reduced to preferences, choices, values, and identities. Religion not only inflects preferences, choices, values, and identities, but also manifests itself in habits, material practices, and styles of argument. Thus, we need to be careful about what frameworks we use to assess the influence of religion on global politics.

RELIGION AS CONTEXT

We should often approach religion as something akin to a discursive context.[23] Rather than supply efficient causes of behavior, religion creates conditions of possibility for action. This means that we are unlikely to make much progress if we attempt to "test" whether, for example, material interests or religious ideas explain particular outcomes.

This point deserves some elaboration. I have already noted how the Reformations era witnessed a wide range of behaviors with respect to religious, economic, and power-political aims. Even individual rulers, officials, nobles, theologians, and ordinary people might privilege one set of interests at a particular moment, then another at the next. Such variation complicates attempts to use the standard logic of appropriateness–logic of consequences framework that many international relations theorists use to evaluate claims made by constructivists, realists, rationalists, and proponents of other broad approaches. This framework holds that norms and identities matter to the extent that actors are willing to pursue them even in the face of deleterious consequences (Elster 1989; March and Olsen 1998). Thus, we might see the refusal of German princes to form a defensive alliance due to theological disputes as evidence of the importance of religious norms; after all, it left them vulnerable to pro-Catholic forces.[24] But periods of French support for German Protestants, which involved sacrificing confessional concerns in order to weaken Habsburg power, would provide evidence that "necessity and reason of state trump morality and ethics when those values conflict" (Schweller and Wohlforth 2000, 69). Similarly, situations in which actors placed economic considerations— overtaxation, trade, and so forth—over confessional ones would also constitute evidence against the constructivist position and, more broadly, the significance of religious forces.[25]

At one level, this kind of reasoning makes perfect sense: the presence of conflicting behavior simply represents variation in individual preferences and level of commitment to religious concerns. Some individuals are just more "religious" than others, and even those individuals face disparate constraints and opportunities for realizing their aims and values at any given moment. At another level, though, it creates real difficulties. It may lead us to underplay the importance of religious forces, or to treat religion as an overly deterministic source of human behavior.

Recall Francis I's repudiation of his treaty with Charles V, Richelieu's justifications for supporting Protestants, and Olivares's decision to convene a council to rule on the appropriateness of supporting Huguenot rebels against France. It isn't so much that necessity and reason of state trumped ethics in such cases, but that religious beliefs proved flexible enough to accommodate a range of actions—most of which were also seen as religious imperatives. But more striking, I think, are the ways in which theologians adjusted their views on the right to resist duly constituted authority. Lutherans and Calvinists, in particular, shifted their positions in light of changing circumstances. But they *always* felt compelled to couch their positions, at least in part, in terms of religious principles. Religious beliefs also never provided unlimited flexibility for participants in these debates; they did not allow, for instance, for resistance to a rightful prince on just any grounds.[26] And they also proved quite sticky, such that the lag between religious sanction for resistance and the onset of civil conflict might reduce the scope and chances of successful mobilization against rulers.

But this is exactly what we should expect. Religious orientations supply ways of apprehending the world, which, in turn, constitute conditions of possibility for social action. Actors operating within a particular set of religious frameworks have a limited number of scripts, rhetorical commonplaces, and styles of reasoning available to them. Religious beliefs, experiences, and frameworks draw boundaries, however blurred, around what constitutes acceptable arguments and warrants.[27]

Thus, in early modern Europe, the same basic religious experiences suggested, at one time, obedience to temporal authority and, at other times, resistance to rulers unwilling to accommodate confessional concerns. It isn't so much that actors deployed these resources in purely instrumental terms—although sometimes they did—but that they combined and recombined them in the face of shifting circumstances. In many respects, John Shotter's understanding of nationalism applies well to religion: as a "way for people to argue about who and what they are, or might be. And the very fact of their arguing about it sustains their form of [religion] in existence" (Shotter 1993, 201). As such, although it is far more than a source of identity, preferences, and norms, religion also manifests itself in a variety of different sources of behavior.

AVOIDING CULTURAL REDUCTIONISM

Unfortunately, the way of thinking about religion that I just outlined remains overly limited in at least one crucial respect: it emphasizes the cultural content of religion. We often conceptualize religion as something solely in the realm of ideas—or of the spirit, if you will—and that's one reason we test its significance against that of material forces.[28] But religion often manifests itself in terms of how it patterns social relations. In that sense, religious phenomena have a dimension of "form" as well as "content," and religion implicates social relations that take forms quite familiar to international relations theorists.

We often identify Georg Simmel with one of the stronger versions of this kind of claim. As he argues, "In any given social phenomenon, content and societal form constitute one reality" (Simmel 1971, 25). But our ability to extrude, at least analytically, content from form allows us to abstract general patterns that obtain despite variations in constitutive ideas and beliefs. "Superiority, subordination, competition, division of labor, formation of parties . . . and innumerable similar features are found in the state as well as in a religious community, in a band of conspirators as in an economic association, in an art school as in a family. However diverse the interests that give rise to these sociations, the forms in which the interests are realized are identical (Simmel 1971, 26).

Although the example is a bit simplistic, recall one of the reasons the Reformations led to such significant political upheaval in early modern Europe: some of the movements it generated crossed the boundaries of composite polities and their constitutive segments, while linking together otherwise adversarial class and status groups. In other words, it produced broad-based transnational movements. These movement are comparable to both secular and religious ones found in other times and places; some even had underground cells, propagandists, and other features of what Koeningsberger calls "revolutionary parties" (Koenigsberger 1955; Nexon 2006). Others displayed patterns consistent with other well-rehearsed forms of collective mobilization (te Brake 1998). We can make sense of much of their impact on patterns of resistance and rule in early modern Europe by analyzing only their formal properties, rather than focusing on the specific content of their ideas.[29]

Indeed, while international relations scholars need to take religion seriously, they should also be careful about treating religious phenomena as sui generis. We most often study religion in settings where it supplies part of the cultural content of movements, political parties, insurgencies, states, and other phenomena well known, if not always well theorized, by scholars of international relations. There's no reason to suppose the politics and dynamics of those phenomena will be so profoundly different from their secular cousins as to render the two noncomparable. At least, that is my reading of how best to understand the impact of the Protestant Reformations on early modern European political relations.

I do not mean to suggest that religious content makes no difference whatsoever; indeed, my sense is that much of what interests us concerns whether (and how) religious claims and contexts intersect with more general dynamics to trigger differing processes or produce different outcomes. It would also be a mistake to view religion as a purely "cultural" phenomenon. Religious practices, institutions, and activities have material properties; they involve exchange, social performances, and so on. In consequence, shoehorning religion into the "ideas" side of the material/ideal debate unacceptably restricts our ability to analyze the impact of religious forces on world politics.

But, yet again, we are ultimately talking about a broader set of problems with contemporary international relations theory. On the one hand, we tend to conflate social processes with cultural ones. Much of the research that goes on under the name of constructivism, for example, drops the "social" from "social construction" in favor of studying the impact of symbols and meanings on world politics, i.e., the causal and constitutive role of culture. On the other hand, we tend to describe social phenomena as material. For example, economic exchange and extraction is not a material process, but a social one. Most of the objective and material economic interests studied in contemporary political economy, for example, stem from where actors are situated in trade and production networks, that is, their social location.

The net effect is that we focus our energies on a putative material/ideal dichotomy and mostly ignore the relationship between the social and the cultural. As a consequence, we risk rendering religion overly mysterious, when much of what we study under the rubric of "the impact of religion on world politics" involves rather familiar forms of social organization.

NO LEAP OF FAITH REQUIRED

The field has long-standing traditions of complaining about state-centrism and about the field's preference for material explanations over ideational ones.[30] Even criticisms of the religion-politics distinction—let alone the use of specific modes of analysis for assessing the impact of religion on world politics—echo larger debates between, for instance, so-called rationalists and constructivists. Claims concerning the historical specificity of the religion/politics distinction, for example, bear more than a passing resemblance to well-worn criticisms of international relations scholars for smuggling historically specific conceptions of state sovereignty into their theoretical frameworks.[31]

Thus, the challenge posed by religion to the study of international relations turns out to be, more or less, *exactly comparable* to that supposedly produced by the end of the Cold War and processes of globalization, insofar as the resurgence of religion (or, at least, the field's renewed attention to religion) provides another opportunity to score the same basic points in ongoing disciplinary debates. None of this suggests that we should reject secular bias arguments out of hand. Rather, we need to be sensitive to the very real risk that religion becomes yet another vehicle for advancing the agenda of, variously, constructivists, post-structuralists, interpretivists, and adherents to other "dissident" positions in the field.[32]

There is, of course, nothing wrong with arguing that developments in the field or in world politics provide warrants for one's preferred analytic framework. That is, in essence, what I did in the preceding section. But, at the end of the day, none of these putative challenges suggest much that is special about religion, and we should not, based upon them, elevate religion to the next great challenge facing some aggregated body of approaches called "international relations theory." Indeed, if our brief forays into the Reformations era elucidate anything, it is that fetishizing religion is as much a danger as not taking it seriously enough.

NOTES

1. The growing availability of funding for grants and institutes related to religion and politics likely played some role in their conversions.

2. I should note that such uses of the term *paradigm shift* usually obscure more than they reveal. The issues at stake here are less tendentious than those associated with paradigm shifts of the sort analyzed by philosophers of science (see Jackson and Nexon, 2009).

3. See, for example, Kubálková 2000; Lautsen and Wæver 2000; Thomas 2000; Hatzopoulos and Petito 2003; Byrnes and Katzenstein 2006; Mitchell 2007; Hallward 2008; Hurd 2008.

4. For further discussion, see Hasenclever and Rittberger 2000.

5. These approaches, Hurd argues, reach this conclusion because they start from secularist premises. See Hurd 2008, 31–32, and my discussion in this chapter.

6. See, for example, Wilcox 2000; Fox and Sandler 2006.

7. See, for example, Kubálková 2000, 694–695.

8. See also Philpott 2002.

9. See, in general, Elton 1964; Grimm 1965; Lambert 1977; Tracy 1999; Kamen 2000; Gregory 2006, 143–145.

10. See, for example, Thomas 2005; Hurd 2008.

11. See, for example, Parker 1977; Elliott 1984; Knecht 1989; Elliott 2000; Bonney 2002.

12. See also Mearsheimer 2001, 365. Although Mearsheimer believes that anarchy inclines states to maximize power, and thus sees regional hegemony rather than balances of power as the norm in world politics, his theoretical architecture tracks closely to that found in conventional structural-realist approaches.

13. See, for example, Holt 1993.

14. See, for example, Parker 1977; Israel 1995.

15. Indeed, their experience in these activities while under Habsburg rule contributed greatly to the viability of the revolt. See Tracy 1985; Tracy 1990.

16. It also helps explain their spread in the first place, but that's another matter entirely.

17. As William Brenner notes, even "within the realist research program there is a grudging acknowledgement of the increasing importance of nonstate actors," (Brenner 2006, 504). And the dominant forms of realism — neoclassical and defensive — place a great deal of emphasis on domestic politics and domestic structures. See, for example, Snyder 1991; Rose 1998; Snyder 2000; Schweller 2006.

18. Cf. Hall 1999: 57–58; Philpott 2001, 116–117.

19. For discussions, see Holt 1986: 76–85; Bettinson 1989; Beame 1993; Holt 1995, 108–109, 168–169; Roelker 1996, 326–328. For the standard view of the politiques, see Philpott 2000; Philpott 2001.

20. See also Le Roy Ladurie 1996, 37, 42–47.

21. The forms of secularist bias we have explored cut much less deeply than some of their advocates imply. The first two comprise sins of omission rather than of commission: many international relations theorists habitually focus on variables and actors that lead them to neglect the significance of religious phenomena. Criticisms of the religion-politics distinction, in contrast, tackle an apparent sin of commission. But, as we have seen, the main implication of this assumption is the same as for other forms of secularist bias: it facilitates relegating religious phenomena to second-class status in international relations theory. The ultimate correctives, as best I can tell, are to take religion more seriously, recognize that politics and religion need not be distinctive arenas of practice, and so forth.

22. Mitchell admits that his arguments work best in the context of specific Protestant understandings of religious experience. See Mitchell 2008, 883.

23. On this point, I echo Lautsen and Wæver 2000; Hurd 2004.

24. As is usually the case, this example is complicated by the existence of a variety of factors, some of them decidedly profane, that also worked against the alliance.

25. One contemporary variant of this kind of argument dismisses the importance of ethnic identity in civil conflicts and argues, based on large-n studies, that economic factors provide one of the best predictors of intrastate conflict. See Fearon and Laitin 2003.

26. For discussions, see Sutherland 1967; Shoenberger 1977; Shoenberger 1979; Knecht 1989; Parrow 1993.

27. For discussions of this theoretical point, see Jackson and Nexon 2001; Jackson 2006; Krebs and Jackson 2007.

28. I find it odd that so much of the work on identity in the field seeks to determine whether "identity mattered" by posing rival hypotheses focused on material interests,

but so little tries to ascertain *which* identities mattered most for explaining a particular phenomenon. Much of the politics of identity, after all, concerns conflict between rival claims concerning the (1) relevance of particular identities and/or (2) what those identities imply for political action. When, for example, early modern rulers were forced to choose between (at least in the short-term) advancing their confessional interests or their dynastic ones, they were, in a sense, trying to reconcile conflicting social roles.

29. For an elaboration of this argument, see Nexon 2009.

30. For example, Keohane and Nye 1971; Ruggie 1982; Kratochwil and Ruggie 1986; Onuf 1989; Koslowski and Kratochwil 1994.

31. For example, Biersteker and Weber 1996.

32. Thus, for example, Kubálková's call for an "International Political Theology" turns out, rather unsurprisingly, to also be an argument in favor of Onuf-style "rule-oriented constructivism" against its realist and "soft" constructivist interlocutors. See Kubálková 2000, 677ff.

REFERENCES

Beame, E. M. 1993. "The Politiques and the Historians." *Journal of the History of Ideas* 54 (3): 355–379.

Bellin, E. 2008. "Faith in Politics: New Trends in the Study of Religion and Politics." *World Politics* 60 (2): 315–347.

Bettinson, C. 1989. "The Politiques and the Politique Part: A Reappraisal." In *From Valois to Bourbon: Dynasty, State and Society in Early Modern France*, ed. K. Cameron. Exeter: University of Exeter Press, 35–50.

Biersteker, T., and C. Weber, eds. 1996. *State Sovereignty as Social Construct*. Cambridge: Cambridge University Press.

Bonney, R. 2002. *The Thirty Years' War, 1618–1648*. Oxford: Osprey.

Brenner, W. J. 2006. "In Search of Monsters: Realism and Progress in International Relations Theory After September 11." *Security Studies* 153 (3): 496–528.

Byrnes, T. A., and P. J. Katzenstein, eds. 2006. *Religion in an Expanding Europe*. Cambridge: Cambridge University Press.

Christensen, C. C. 1984. "John of Saxony's Diplomacy, 1529–1530: Reformation or Realpolitik." *Sixteenth Century Journal* 15 (4): 419–430.

Dueck, A. J. 1982. "Religion and Temporal Authority in the Reformation: The Controversy Among the Protestants Prior to the Peace of Nuremberg, 1532." *Sixteenth Century Journal* 12 (2): 55–74.

Elliott, J. H. 1970. "Revolts in the Spanish Monarchy." In *Preconditions of Revolution in Early Modern Europe*, ed. R. Forster and J. P. Greene. Baltimore: Johns Hopkins University Press, 109–130.

——. 1984. *Richelieu and Olivares*. Cambridge: Cambridge University Press.

——. 2000. *Europe Divided, 1559–1598*. Oxford: Blackwell.

Elster, J. 1989. *Nuts and Bolts for the Social Sciences*. Cambridge: Cambridge University Press.

Elton, G. R. 1964. *Reformation Europe: 1517–1559*. Cleveland: World Publishing Company.

Fearon, J. D., and D. D. Laitin. 2003. "Ethnicity, Insurgency, and Civil War." *American Political Science Review* 97 (1): 75–90.

Fox, J., and S. Sandler. 2006. *Bringing Religion into International Relations*. New York: Palgrave.

Gilpin, R. 1981. *War and Change in World Politics*. New York: Cambridge University Press.

Gregory, B. S. 2006. "The Other Confessional History: On Secular Bias in the Study of Religion." *History and Theory* 45 (4): 132–149.

Grimm, H. J. 1965. *The Reformation Era, 1500–1658*. New York: Macmillan.

Hall, R. B. 1999. *National Collective Identity: Social Constructs and International Systems*. New York: Columbia University Press.

Hallward, M. C. 2008. "Situating the 'Secular': Negotiating the Boundary Between Religion and Politics." *International Political Sociology* 2 (1): 1–16.

Hasenclever, A., and V. Rittberger. 2000. "Does Religion Make a Difference? Theoretical Approaches to the Impact of Faith on Political Conflict." *Milennium: Journal of International Studies* 29 (3): 641–674.

Hatzopoulos, P., and F. Petito. 2003. "The Return from Exile: An Introduction." In *Religion in International Relations: The Return from Exile*, ed. P. Hatzopoulos and F. Petito. New York: Palgrave Macmillan, 1–20.

Holt, M. P. 1986. *The Duke of Anjou and the Politique Struggle During the Wars of Religion*. Cambridge: Cambridge University Press.

Holt, M. P. 1993. "Review Article: Putting Religion Back in the Wars of Religion." *French Historical Studies* 18 (2): 524–551.

Holt, M. P. 1995. *The French Wars of Religion, 1562–1629*. Cambridge: Cambridge University Press.

Hurd, E. S. 2004. "The Political Authority of Secularism in International Relations." *European Journal of International Relations* 10 (2): 235–262.

Hurd, E. S. 2008. *The Politics of Secularism in International Relations*. Princeton: Princeton University Press.

Israel, J. 1995. *The Dutch Republic: Its Rise, Greatness, and Fall 1477–1806*. Oxford, Oxford University Press.

Jackson, P. T. 2006. *Civilizing the Enemy: German Reconstruction and the Invention of the West*. Ann Arbor, MI, University of Michigan Press.

Jackson, P. T., and D. H. Nexon. 2001. "Whence Causal Mechanisms? A Comment on Legro." *Dialogue IO* 1 (1): 1–21.

——. 2009. "Paradigmatic Faults in International-Relations Theory." *International Studies Quarterly* 53 (4): 907–930.

Kamen, H. 2000. *Early Modern European Society*. New York, Routledge.

Katznelson, I. 1997. Structure and Configuration in Comparative Politics. In *Comparative Politics: Rationality, Culture, and Structure*, ed. M. I. Lichbach and A. S. Zuckerman. Cambridge, Cambridge University Press: 81–112.

Keohane, R. O., and J. S. Nye. 1971. Introduction to *Transnational Relations and World Politics*. Cambridge, MA, Harvard University Press: xii-xvi.

Kingdon, R. M. 1967. Calvinist Religious Aggression. In *The French Wars of Religion: How Important Were Religious Factors?* ed. J. H. M. Salmon. Boston, Heath: 6–10.

Knecht, R. J. 1989. *The French Wars of Religion, 1559–1598*. New York, Longman.

——. 1996. *The Rise and Fall of Renaissance France*. London, Fontana Press.

Koenigsberger, H. G. 1955. "The Organization of Revolutionary Parties in France and the Netherlands During the Sixteenth Century." *Journal of Modern History* 27 (4): 333–351.

——. 1986. *Politicians and Virtuosi: Essays in Early Modern History*. London, Hambledon Press.

Koslowski, R., and F. V. Kratochwil. 1994. "Understanding Change in International Politics: the Soviet Empire's Demise and the International System." *International Organization* 48 (2): 215–247.

Kratochwil, F., and J. G. Ruggie. 1986. "International Organization: A State of the Art on an Art of the State." *International Organization* 40 (4): 753–775.

Krebs, R. R., and P. T. Jackson. 2007. "Twisting Tongues and Twisting Arms: The Power of Political Rhetoric." *European Journal of International Relations* 13 (1): 35–66.

Kubálková, V. 2000. "Towards an International Political Theology " *Milennium: Journal of International Studies* 29 (3): 675–704.

Lambert, M. 1977. *Medieval Heresy: Popular Movements from the Gregorian Reform to the Reformation*. London, Blackwell.

Lautsen, C. B., and O. Wæver. 2000. "In Defence of Religion: Sacred Referent Objects of Securitization." *Milennium: Journal of International Studies* 29 (3): 705–739.

Le Roy Ladurie, E. 1996. *The Ancien Régime: A History of France, 1610–1774*. Oxford, Blackwell.

March, J. G., and J. P. Olsen. 1998. "The Institutional Dynamics of International Political Orders." *International Organization* 52 (4): 943–969.

Mearsheimer, J. 2001. *The Tragedy of Great Power Politics*. New York, Norton.

——. 2002. "Through the Realist Lens: Conversation with John Mearsheimer." *Conversations with History*, http://globetrotter.berkeley.edu/people2/Mearsheimer/mearsheimer-cono.html (retrieved December 14, 2006).

Mitchell, J. 2007. "Religion is Not a Preference." *Journal of Politics* 69 (2): 349–360.

——. 2008. "A Reply to My Critics." *Journal of Politics* 70 (3): 880–883.

Nexon, D. 2006. Religion, European Identity, and Political Contention in Historical Perspective. In *Religion in an Expanding Europe*, ed. T. A. Byrnes and P. J. Katzenstein. Cambridge, Cambridge University Press: 256–282.

——. 2009. *The Struggle for Power in Early Modern Europe: Religious Conflict, Dynastic Empires, and International Change*. Princeton, Princeton University Press.

Nierop, H. v. 2001. Alva's Throne—Making Sense of the Revolt of the Netherlands. In *The Origins and Development of the Dutch Revolt*, ed. G. Darby. New York, Routledge: 29–47.

Onuf, N. 1989. *World of Our Making: Rules and Rule in Social Theory and International Relations*. Columbia, University of South Carolina Press.

Ortíz, A.D. 1971. *The Golden Age of Spain, 1516–1659*. New York, Basic Books.

Parker, G. 1977. *The Dutch Revolt*. Ithaca, NY, Cornell University Press.

Parrow, K. A. 1993. "From Defense to Resistance: Justification for Violence During the French Wars of Religion." *Transactions of the American Philosophical Society* 83 (6): i-v, 1–79.

Philpott, D. 2000. "The Religious Roots of Modern International Relations." *World Politics* 52 (1): 206–45.

——. 2001. *Revolutions in Sovereignty: How Ideas Shaped Modern International Relations*. Princeton, Princeton University Press.

——. 2002. "The Challenges of September 11 to Secularism in International Relations." *World Politics* 55:66–95.

Roelker, N. L. 1996. *One King, One Faith: The Parlement of Paris and the Religious Reformations of the Sixteenth Century*. Berkeley, University of California Press.

Rose, G. 1998. "Neoclassical Realism and Theories of Foreign Policy." *World Politics* 51 (1): 144–172.

Rowen, H. H., ed. 1972. *The Low Countries in Early Modern Times*. New York, Harper & Row.

Ruggie, J. G. 1982. "International Regimes, Transactions, and Change: Embedded Liberalism in the Postwar Economic Order." *International Organization* 36 (2): 379–415.

Schweller, R. L. 2006. *Unanswered Threats: Political Constraints on the Balance of Power*. Princeton, Princeton University Press.

Schweller, R. L., and W. C. Wohlforth 2000. "Power Test: Evaluating Realism in Response to the End of the Cold War." *Security Studies* 9 (3): 60–107.

Shoenberger, C. G. 1977. "The Development of the Lutheran Theory of Resistance: 1523–1530." *Sixteenth Century Journal* 8 (1): 61–76.

——. 1979. "Luther and the Justifiability of Resistance to Legitimate Authority." *Journal of the History of Ideas* 40 (1): 3–20.

Shotter, J. 1993. *Cultural Politics of Everyday Life*. Toronto, University of Toronto Press.

Simmel, G. 1971. *On Individuality and Social Forms*. Chicago, Chicago University Press.

Snyder, J. 1991. *Myths of Empire: Domestic Politics and International Ambition*. Ithaca, NY, Cornell University Press.

——. 2000. *From Voting to Violence: Democratization and Nationalist Conflict*. New York, Norton.

Sutherland, N. M. 1967. Calvin's Idealism and Indecision. In *The French Wars of Religion: How Important Were Religious Factors?* ed. J. H. M. Salmon. Boston, Heath: 14–23.

te Brake, W. 1998. *Shaping History: Ordinary People in European Politics, 1500–1700*. Berkeley, University of California Press.

Thielen, K. 1999. "Historical Institutionalism in Comparative Politics." *Annual Review of Political Science* 2 (1): 369–404.

Thomas, S. 2000. "Taking Religious and Cultural Pluralism Seriously: The Global Resurgence of Religion and the Transformation of International Society." *Milennium: Journal of International Studies* 29 (3): 815–841.

——. 2005. *The Global Resurgence of Religion and the Transformation of International Relations*. New York, Palgrave Macmillan.

Tracy, J. D. 1985. *A Financial Revolution in the Habsburg Netherlands: Renten and Renteniers in the County of Holland, 1515–1565*. Berkeley, University of California Press.

——. 1990. *Holland under Habsburg Rule, 1506–1566: The Formation of a Body Politic*. Berkeley, University of California Press.

——. 1999. *Europe's Reformations, 1450–1650*. Lanham, MD, Rowman & Littlefield.

Waltz, K. 1986. Reflections on Theory of International Politics: A Response to My Critics. In *Neorealism and Its Critics*, ed. R. O. Keohane. New York, Columbia University Press: 322–346.

Wilcox, C. 2000. *Onward Christian Soldiers? The Religious Right in American Politics*. Boulder, CO, Westview.

Wilcox, C., K. D. Wald, and T. G. Jelen. 2008. "Religious Preferences and Social Science: A Second Look." *Journal of Politics* 70 (3): 874–879.

Wilson, P. H. 1999. *The Holy Roman Empire, 1495–1806*. London, Macmillan.

Wood, J. B. 1996. *The King's Army: Warfare, Soldiers, and Society During the Wars of Religion in France, 1562–1576*. Cambridge, Cambridge University Press.

Zagorin, P. 1982. *Rulers and Rebels, 1500–1600*. 2 vols. Cambridge, Cambridge University Press.

7. IN THE SERVICE OF STATE AND NATION

Religion in East Asia

IL HYUN CHO AND PETER J. KATZENSTEIN

Theories of international relations share a unifying assumption that is rarely, if ever, questioned in their frequently recurring paradigmatic debates—the irrelevance of religion in international affairs.[1] The master narrative of international relations theory holds that the Peace of Westphalia privatized religion and left international relations to secular rulers and rules. The process of modernization thus did to believers what the Industrial Revolution did to peasants—it made them politically irrelevant. The effect of September 11, 2001, furthermore, has been to direct international relations scholars to a narrow slice of empirical reality, specifically the spectacularly violent acts of tiny jihadist sects. The flood of contemporary writings on terrorism and counterterrorism makes it easy to lose sight of the fact that only 15 percent of the world's Muslim population actually live in the Middle East, that Indonesia is the largest Muslim state in the world, and that only a miniscule proportion of Muslims are engaged in violence. This chapter inquires into this shaky foundation of international relations theory by seeking to broaden its substantive focus to take account of the role of religion in East Asia.

Religion is like the weather—a fact of life. If this causes discomfort to theories of international relations, as many of the contributions in this volume illustrate, then we should seize the opportunity to adjust our theories. That process of adjustment, we argue, might well start with three steps: scrapping reified distinctions between international relations and comparative politics; avoiding excessive abstractions by focusing on the regional context of international and global systems and processes; and sidestepping overly sharp distinctions between secular and religious orders.[2] These three adjustments clear the ground for an inquiry into the politics of religious syncretism in East Asia, a topic sidelined by the implicit Eurocentrism of American international relations theory and the centrality of Islam and the Middle East in contemporary foreign policy analysis.

The first adjustment is to take full account of the interpenetration of domestic and international affairs as a defining characteristic of contemporary world politics. As numerous realist, liberal, and constructivist critics of structural realism have pointed out, international anarchy no longer exerts a primary causal influence over world politics. And as many scholars of comparative politics now recognize, many important aspects of domestic politics can no longer be analyzed without taking into account transnational structures and processes. International relations theorists, who argue that in the academic division of labor their special contribution is to focus exclusively on international factors, remind us of those planners in the early 1950s who developed sophisticated models of the Dutch economy. In those models international trade was a residual variable not amenable to domestic planning. Within a few years, as that one residual variable accounted for more of the observed variation in Dutch economic life than the rest of the model, this exercise in planning was scrapped. Grand theories of international relations are less susceptible to empirical disconfirmation. Thinking about religion in world politics, however, offers us the opportunity to shift our attention. Religious politics is best analyzed in such integrated rather than neatly compartmentalized international and domestic domains. In the case of East Asian religion, this means not losing sight of the regional meeting place of domestic and international influences.

A second adjustment is to sidestep the excessive abstractions of international and global styles of analysis.[3] Even though they refer to very different phenomena, because they are highly abstract these terms are often used interchangeably. Globalization refers to processes that transcend space and compress time. It has novel and potentially transformative effects on world politics. Internationalization refers to territorially based exchanges across national borders that increase the dynamic density of a system that is not being transformed. The politics of East Asian religion shows much more readily processes of internationalization and the power of the state than processes of globalization and the power of transnational religious movements. Yet it also illustrates that, under the label of "Asian values," Confucian variants of religious politics have profound implications for regional identity that encompass both global and international processes and structures.

A third conceptual adjustment is to recognize that East Asian states have always been deeply involved in religious politics and thus to avoid drawing overly sharp distinctions between secular and religious orders in world politics. From the ancient era of imperial dynasties to modern times, both foreign and indigenous religions have been part and parcel of East Asian politics. In contrast to Islam and Christianity, the central actors behind the politics of religion in East Asia have rarely been conventionally understood religious entities such as priests or sects. Instead it was the state that typically shaped the contours of religious politics in East Asia. Fluid and syncretic East Asian religions have put a strong emphasis on public rituals and never-ending political contestations and manipulations.

Religions in general have a transcendental dimension that East Asian civil religions with their focus on the here and now lack. Both, however, inform the moral and ethical precepts and sensibilities that shape the range of options available to political decision makers at any given time.[4] We thus include in our analysis not only conventionally understood religions but also Confucian thought and practice as East Asia's most important civil religion. Confucianism differs from conventional American understandings of religion. It does not make metaphysical claims that appeal to transcendental life, as do Christianity, Judaism, Islam, and Buddhism. But it does embody moral debates, a moral code of conduct, and core ethical beliefs about the most basic aspects of society. And, as is true of East Asian religions such as Buddhism, it puts the state center stage. In short, we should think of Confucianism as a civil religion that embodies a history of intellectual and philosophical debate and social practice that can be compared meaningfully to conventionally understood religious faiths. In brief, these three conceptual adjustments help us to accommodate East Asia's historical and contemporary experiences with religious politics within American international relations theory.

As is true of other world regions, religion is resurfacing in East Asia today. Throughout the region various local sects of Buddhist and Confucian origins are flourishing. In contemporary China the government is elevating Confucianism once again to a central place. In Japan traditional religions such as Shintoism and Buddhism are now vying for public attention with thousands of small religious sects, known as "the new religions" (shinkoshukyo). And in South Korea Christianity is flourishing as the nation's most popular religion, while at the same time Buddhism and Confucianism are also gaining increasing prominence. And a region-wide terminology of Asian values has helped create an identity that enjoys public resonance.

This chapter uses East Asia as a template for the argument that, European exceptionalism aside, there was never any good reason for grounding international relations theory on the dubious assumptions of the secularization thesis that provides the foundation for all major theories of international relations. As we argue here, East Asia's historical experience suggests that religion was typically not confined to the private domain but always a matter central to the state. Modernization never led to secularization. We argue later on that religion in contemporary East Asia is a central tool for bolstering state legitimacy and national unity and that it has important domestic and region-wide political consequences.

RELIGION IN THE EAST ASIAN PAST: NO PRIVATIZATION OF RELIGION, NO SECULARIZATION OF POLITICS

Based on European experience, the secularization thesis that continues to inform the main branches of American international relations theory conceives of secular modernity as ridding world politics of religion, since religion "belongs to the childhood of the human race, and is destined to fade away with the rise of science."[5] Many scholars expected the path to modernity to be secular everywhere, marked by the "disenchantment of the world in the Weberian sense."[6] Pippa Norris and Ronald Inglehart, for example, contend that modernization in advanced countries such as Japan weakens religious influence, accelerating the trend toward secularization.[7] Sociologists of religion now doubt what theories of international relations still firmly believe—that secularization is the basis of modernity.[8]

NO PRIVATIZATION OF RELIGION

In East Asia state and religion have been indelibly fused. Rather than following the pattern of "prophetic religious politics" that separates religion and state, East Asia is an exemplar of "priestly religious politics," where state and religious faith have "a mutually supportive relationship."[9] But that relationship has been distinctively lopsided. Typically, the state has dictated the rules of the game. In each country political authorities were largely shielded from the influence of powerful external religious forces that posed threats to the political order and had to be destroyed, marginalized, or co-opted. With guile and luck, time and again, Chinese, Japanese, and Korean leaders maneuvered successfully to hijack religious principles and movements.

Stressing the importance of social order and stability, political elites in pre-modern China used Confucius's teachings of filial piety and loyalty to authority as the political foundation for imperial China.[10] In premodern Japan the ruling shogunate built Buddhist temples in Shinto shrines and thus promoted syncretism between indigenous religions and imported Buddhism. In the attempt to increase national unity, political leaders looked to universal Buddhist principles as a useful antidote to a combination of family-focused, traditional Shintoism and fervent localisms. Initially welcomed by Japanese officials as a source of advanced knowledge and techniques, Christianity met a different fate. It was banned in 1613 when Japanese court officials suspected foreign missionaries of lending support to feudal lords living in outlying areas.[11] In premodern Korea's changing political landscape, Buddhism also received varying treatments. After a successful coup against the Koryo dynasty (918–1392), which had made Buddhism the state's religion, the founder of the Chosun dynasty (1392–1910), Yi Taejo, intent on enhancing his legitimacy, persecuted Buddhism and promoted Confucianism instead. The Yi dynasty, however, maintained a cozy relationship with Korean shamanism by hiring several famous shamans within the royal court "to ensure the well-being of the royal family," and to get advice from them in times of national crisis.[12] In all of these episodes the state was the driving force behind the ebb and flow of religious politics in East Asia. It was not religious believers but political leaders who defined the parameters of religious life.

Indeed, often the very meanings of religion were subject to the interpretations and needs of political leaders. Political elites contested and defined the meanings of religious orthodoxy. The entire history of Confucianism, Chaibong Hahm writes, can be summed up as "a tale of powerful central states repeatedly appropriating key Confucian tenets for state ends."[13] When Buddhism made its first appearance in China during the Han dynasty, anti-Buddhists spread the notion that this Indian religion offered heterodox teachings and practices that could create social unrest and undermine the imperial state.[14] Similarly, the Confucian state relegated Buddhism and other teachings to the status of heterodoxy (yiduan, meaning heresy or strange principles) and various millenarian religious movements to the category of cults (xiejiao).[15]

Such categorizations always served political needs. For instance, in the mid-nineteenth century when a millenarian religious sect called Heavenly Kingdom of Peace (taiping tianguo) initiated the Taiping Rebellion, it was suppressed by the imperial state. A few decades later, in 1900, when another millenarian movement, Righteous and Harmonious Fist (yiho quan), launched the Boxer Uprising against foreign missionaries and imperialists, it enjoyed the support of the Qing dynasty, which found itself in complete disarray amid foreign intervention.[16] What mattered was not whether a religious movement was millenarian and thus deemed "a cult" (*xiejiao*), but whether such a movement was conducive to achieving the political ends of the state.

In East Asia no clear distinction separated the public from the private realms on matters of religion. Religion served as a medium of public rituals, rather than a source of private, spiritual salvation. Instead of Western notions of "the exclusivity of religious belief,"[17] the populace in East Asian polities were expected to embrace "the de facto control of the sovereign in the public realm," thus leaving little room for the private realm of spiritual yearning and salvation.[18] The state worked very hard to bring religious beliefs and rituals out of the private and into the public domain. Nationally sanctioned Confucian rituals in the Chinese and Korean dynasties—such as national civil service exams based on Confucian texts and various rituals linking filial piety (*xiao* in Chinese, *hyo* in Korean) and loyalty to political authority (*zhong* in Chinese, *chung* in Korean)—and Shinto rituals in Meiji Japan exemplified state-led campaigns for keeping religion in the public realm. Norihisa Suzuki thus concludes that as a consequence, "a group-oriented ethic aiming at social integration" prevailed over individually focused faith in East Asia.[19]

Furthermore, syncretism rather than fundamentalism was the East Asian norm. As long as other local and foreign religions did not challenge the imperial Chinese state, they were allowed to coexist with Confucianism.[20] In Japan, the phrase "Born Shinto, die Buddhist" captures an unproblematic "multiplicity of belongings."[21] In a 1965 study, for instance, Joseph Spae reported that about two-thirds of the Japanese public believed that all religions, including Shintoism, Buddhism, and Christianity, are the same.[22] Similarly, Christianity in Korea was infused with Confucian principles of hierarchy, authority, and orthodoxy. In general, "the fluid nature of religious theology," has enabled East Asian political elites to appropriate religious principles and traditions as part of the solutions to their political problems.[23]

NO SECULARIZATION OF POLITICS

In a standard narrative of modernity, religion is a "negative social force" that is opposed to "science, rationality, secularism."[24] In this view secularization is a necessary first step toward modernity. Such characterization, as Peter van der Veer observes, collapses multiple paths to modernity into "one narrative of secularization."[25] In East Asia, however, modernization did not move in lockstep with secularization. As was true of premodern politics, religion has played instead a vital role in East Asia's modernization process. No sharp break separates the state from the sacred.

In Japan modernization coincides with a rebirth of Shintoism as a state religion. In times of dramatic change Shintoism became the backbone of Japan's evolving national consciousness.[26] The phrase "Western techniques, Eastern spirit" (*wakon yosai*) pointed to the widely perceived need to adopt many Western practices, but with "an ideology that serves to unify the nation and enrich its sense of common purpose."[27] In this process, Buddhism, formerly a state religion, was forcefully separated from Shintoism. Infused with Confucian ethics, State Shinto became the basis for the national polity (*kokutai*) as an ideology that put the emperor at the political center.[28] Although Western knowledge and technologies were important, the Meiji reformers believed that one "national consciousness was a prerequisite to building a modern nation." Through public rituals of emperor worship and the Imperial Rescript on Education in 1890, nationalism and religion fused into State Shintoism.[29]

Particularly interesting in Japan's modernization was the creative use of past religious traditions. The Meiji reform was officially called a "restoration—incorporating traditional elements and a return to the ancient emperor system (*tenno*)."[30] Grounding rapid change in past tradition helped ameliorate the shock of transformation.[31] And it helped maintain unity among different political factions. Faced with the influx of Western knowledge and institutions in the late nineteenth century, some members of Japan's political elite were deeply troubled. A frequent lecturer on the West for the emperor, Nishimura Shegeki, for example, called for a return to the morality of Confucianism, angering reformist elites such as Ito Hirobumi.[32] State Shintoism and emperor worship were deemed crucial in maintaining national and elite unity.[33]

In contrast to Japan, Chinese and Korean elites were divided over the proper path to modernity; hence religion was politically more contested. The impetus "to smash temples and build schools" was strong and so was the lead of political over social secularization.[34] Instead of reincarnating religious traditions, political elites began to view Confucianism as a source of national weakness. In a battle for religious influence, the ruling elites in China vigorously defended Confucianism, while reformists turned to Western notions of secular modernity, calling for Confucianism and the feudal past to be "extirpated, annihilated, and replaced with science."[35] In nineteenth-century Korea a similar battle emerged between the conservative establishment, which defended Confucian orthodoxy (*choksa wijongpa*), and a reformist group calling for "enlightenment" (*kaehwapa*).[36] The reformists in the latter group, particularly members of the Independence Club (1896–98), depicted Confucianism "as an alien—hence bad—tradition."[37]

The commonality between Chinese and Korean modernization ends, however, with the rejection of Confucianism as a source of national weakness and social chaos. China and Korea took very different approaches toward Christianity. In Korea Christianity helped in building a modern nation. Chinese elites viewed Christianity instead with deep suspicion, calling it "irrational and super-stitious—unworthy of the attention of serious-minded people."[38] Furthermore, Christian missionaries were regarded as foreign agents working subversively for other states.[39] In the twilight of imperial China, anti-Christian sentiments served as a common ground for the local gentry and the general public. With help from millenarian religious movements, such sentiments erupted into the Boxer Uprising and subsequently infused the Kuomintang and the Communist Party in the post-Qing era.[40]

In contrast, despite earlier persecution of Catholics by the state, Korean reformists expressed great interest in Western science and technology and called Christianity "Western learning" (*seohak*).[41] The first Protestant missionaries in Korea were a main provider of much-needed medical and educational services, which reinforced the image of Christianity as a source of "enlightenment and national salvation."[42] And in the face of foreign encroachment, Christianity played a crucial role in fostering national consciousness.[43] For example, the use of the native *Hangul* alphabet by the church bolstered national unity under Japanese rule.[44] In the face of an imperial power which was neither Western nor Christian, Christianity served as "a rallying point for fervent nationalists striving for indepen-dence."[45] Their efforts culminated in the 1919 Independence Movement, through which nationalism began to take shape.[46] Sixteen of the thirty-three national rep-resentatives of the movement were Christians. In brief, Donald Clark writes that Christianity made Korean followers "feel both patriotic and modern at the same time."[47] In stark contrast, the pervasive antiforeign, anti-imperial sentiments in China put Christianity in direct opposition to patriotism and modernity. With the predominance of State Shinto, Christianity found only a small audience in Japan, where indigenous religious tradition accompanied modernization and the growth of a modern nation. On the path to modernity religion was a central marker in all three states, and secularization conspicuous only by its absence.

RELIGION IN EAST ASIA TODAY:
THE PRIMACY OF POLITICS

East Asia's syncretist religious politics fits into a world-wide ecumene of knowl-edge and practices that offers ample political space for both secular and reli-gious politics and the porous and shifting borders separating them. Distinctive of East Asia is the primacy of politics reflected in governmental concern over the twin issues of political legitimacy and national unity. Although transnational and region-wide religious politics exist, they have less far-reaching consequences than the infusion of religions and religious elements into issues of government legitimacy and national unity.

LEGITIMACY

From the vantage point of East Asia, the rise of religious extremism in recent years is not, as Scott Thomas writes, "an aberration in an otherwise 'modern' world."[48] Religious revival in East Asia is a story of continuity and gradual adaptation. As was true of prior decades and centuries, religious revival is to a large extent a politically engineered process. Political leaders in East Asia use religion as a tool for cementing their political authority and a means to enhance effective policy making. This is not to deny the fact that East Asian politics and religion are changing. Gone is the latitude during the Cold War enjoyed by China's communist regime, Korean military dictators, and a Japanese Liberal Democratic Party that maintained near-monopoly control. The state in East Asia is adapting to changing political contexts. But the script for and logic of power remains state-centric.

Considerations of regime legitimacy help explain a notable shift in China's position toward religion. President Hu Jintao and other Chinese leaders have reevaluated the Confucian tradition. They now concede that harmony as the central value of Confucian teachings is "something to be cherished."[49] Sensing wide-spread public concern about growing economic disparities amid rapid economic growth, the Chinese Communist Party focuses on Confucian harmony as "the ideological umbrella under which China has taken the first steps toward developing a redistributive welfare program."[50] Behind the familiar political rhetoric of achieving a well-rounded socialist country lies a broader ideational shift in thinking. The Chinese leadership appears to be ready to embrace Confucianism as a new conceptual foundation for reclaiming the political legitimacy of the Communist Party and the entire regime.[51] In a 2006 statement, for instance, President Hu Jintao urges Chinese to "love their motherland, serve the people and work hard—all typical Confucian notions."[52]

This Confucian revival is more pronounced in the public than in the private realm. For the first time in sixty-six years, for example, the party organized a lavish worship ceremony at Tianjin's Confucius Temple in November 2004. In the town of Qufu, the birthplace of Confucius, the official ceremony commemorating his birthday has, since 2004, become an important public ritual, broadcast live on state television. The Ministry of Education is encouraging numerous courses in Confucian culture.[53] Long cherished by China's past regimes, the state-led public ritualization of religious traditions is promoted precisely because it helps strengthen government legitimacy.

In Japan the end of the Cold War coincided with a decline in the postwar dominance of the Liberal Democratic Party (LDP). Conservatives have thus looked to a revival of Shintoism as a way to reassert their political authority. Along with the passage of legislation requiring "patriotic expression" such as the national anthem (*kimigayo*) and the raising of the sun flag (*hinomaru*) at school ceremonies,[54] conservatives have devoted their energy to the resurrection of the Yasukuni Shrine as a new nationalist symbol. Established in 1869 as a site to honor those who died in the service of the Meiji emperor, the shrine became the spiritual center of Meiji Japan.[55] In the early postwar years leftist opposition parties were able to block conservative efforts to pass a bill to "renationalize the shrine." But in 1985 conservatives finally succeeded in having Prime Minister Nakasone visit the shrine, and the issue has remained a highly visible point of contestation ever since.[56]

The Yasukuni issue has established a symbiotic relationship between the LDP and various conservative groups seeking to "nationalize the management of the Yasukuni Shrine,"[57] such as the Japan Association of Bereaved Families (*Nihon izoku kai*), with one million members, and the Association of Shinto Shrines (*Jinjia honcho*).[58] Former prime minister Junichiro Koizumi played the Yasukuni card during his early bid for the LDP chairmanship in 2001. As a lesser-known politician within the LDP, especially compared to former prime minister and longtime LDP kingmaker Ryutaro Hashimoto, Koizumi relied strongly on the support of the Japan Association of Bereaved Families (JABF). Indeed, the JABF was the only powerful pressure group he really could count on. Koizumi let it be known that, if elected prime minister, he would visit the Yasukuni Shrine on August 15, the anniversary of Japan's surrender at the end of World War II.[59] He kept his promise throughout his five-year term as prime minister, endangering Japan's relationships with China and South Korea.

But Japan's multiple religious traditions also resulted in a very different, internationalist kind of religious politics. With its legislative majorities in the upper and lower houses declining after 1993, the LDP in 1999 formed a coalition government with the New Komeito Party, which is intimately linked to the internationally oriented religious group Soka Gakkai. Founded in 1930 as a small Buddhist-influenced sect, Soka Gakkai has blossomed into one of the major new religions in the postwar period, with members in eight million Japanese households.[60] Along with thousands of other new religions, Soka Gakkai has been successful in "filling gaps left by the discrediting of the traditional religions" in the wake of Meiji Japan's downfall.[61]

The Komeito's significance in Japanese postwar politics was illustrated dramatically during the 1993 parliamentary elections. The party won 52 seats in the Japanese Diet and thus helped end the LDP's four-decade run as Japan's ruling party. As the political wing of Soka Gakkai, the Komeito's platform is not well aligned with that of the LDP. Moreover, still fresh from the memories of the 1995 sarin gas attack in the Tokyo subway by the religious sect Aum Shinrikyo, the Japanese public was hostile to the New Komeito joining the LDP in 2000 as a coalition partner. Given wide-spread public suspicion of religious sects, the formation of a coalition with the Komeito was a risky political gamble for the LDP.[62] But the allure was too strong for the LDP to resist, since the Komeito had developed into "one of the largest vote-gathering machines in Japan."[63] In entering a coalition government, the Komeito helped bolster the LDP majority in the Diet. And the Komeito's endorsement has also helped immensely in getting LDP candidates elected in recent elections.[64] In contemporary Japan religious issues and parties thus proved to be central to LDP rule until the watershed electoral victory of the Democratic Party of Japan (DJP) in the fall of 2009.

In South Korea Christian churches have generally been considered active supporters for democracy. The Catholic Church's role in democratic progress is a case in point. Ever since the promulgation in 1972 of the draconian Yushin Constitution by the Park Chung Hee administration, the Myongdong Cathedral in Seoul has served as the main site and a national symbol of democratic protests.[65] Among Protestant organizations, however, there existed a split between politically active, radical Christian groups and conservative Christians who had cooperated for decades with the military dictatorship.[66] Under the ruthless crackdown by the Japanese occupation on all religions other than Shintoism, South Korean church leaders lost their political influence in the later years of Japanese colonial rule. They tried to "justify their apolitical stance by emphasizing the so-called pure faith (*sunsu sinang*)."[67] Political acquiescence during this period laid the foundation for close ties between mainstream Christian organizations and South Korea's authoritarian regimes in the postwar years.[68] The Christian leaders who were accused of collaborating with the Japanese were "groping for survival in the new era," and thus came to support Rhee "in the name of Christian unity and early independence."[69] After the end of the Korean War, the links between the Rhee government and the Protestant church grew even stronger, based on Rhee's Christian background and his strong anti-Communist stance. In return for their support, Rhee extended many favors to mainstream Christian organizations. This pattern also persisted through the later years of the military regimes of Park Chung Hee and Chun Doo Hwan.[70] As was true of China and Japan, in South Korea, especially under authoritarian regimes, legitimacy and religion have been closely intertwined.

NATIONAL UNITY

Along with the need for securing political legitimacy, the use of religion in promoting national unity is a second salient fact about religious politics in East Asia. As was true of State Shinto in Meiji Japan and Christianity in colonized Korea, religion in contemporary East Asia has been an important means to rejuvenate national consciousness in changing regional and global contexts.[71]

In China the Communist Party's drive for a "harmonious society" seeks to promote national unity on the basis of Confucian values that are enjoying growing popular appeal. As François Bougon, author of a recent bestseller on Confucius in China points out, the Chinese are increasingly turning to Confucian teachings in thinking about the quality of life and "what being Chinese really is."[72] But Confucianism is not the only religious tradition encouraged by the Chinese state for the purpose of improving national unity. Recently, the Chinese government has also promoted other religions, particularly Buddhism and Taoism. For example, in April 2006 China hosted an international meeting of Buddhist leaders brought together under the theme, "A harmonious world begins in the mind," echoing the party-driven campaign for a "harmonious society."[73] Similarly, party officials have promoted the wisdom of ancient Taoism. At an international forum held in April 2007, Jia Qinglin, member of the powerful Politburo Standing Committee of the Communist Party and chairman of the National Committee of the Chinese People's Political Consultative Conference (CPPCC), stressed Taoist principles of modesty and peacefulness as "an inspiring reference to China's ongoing construction of a harmonious society." The forum itself was significant since, with three hundred invited delegates from seventeen countries, it had become "the first international forum of its kind that China has organized for the last 50 years."[74] Citing the need to "meet the demands posed by the new situation and new tasks," at the 17th National Congress convened in October 2007, for the first time in its history, the Communist Party inserted the word *religion* in an amendment to its Constitution.[75] Drawing support from various religions, the Chinese government is eager to enhance national unity under the banner of a "harmonious society."

When Shintoism as the state religion and symbol of national unity was banned by the U.S. occupation authorities, Japan's postwar governments, Harry Harootunian writes, "sought first to recapture the lost unity by rehabilitating the economy under a 'dedivinized emperor.'"[76] Facing economic difficulties in the wake of the 1973 oil shock, the Japanese government found an increasing need for an adequate manner of self-representation. This prompted conservatives to launch a campaign "to restore the symbolic unity of prewar Japan represented by the Yasukuni Shrine."[77] This move was rooted in the belief that "some kind of sacred revitalization is necessary to fill the void at the nation's cultural core where a devotion to industrial capitalism and a 'yen for the yen' does not suffice."[78]

Nakasone's 1985 shrine visit stirred up a broad national debate over Yasukuni. In a symbolic move to reconnect state and shrine, Nakasone not only signed the guest register with his title as prime minister but also offered flowers using government funds. With this public ritual deliberately timed for August 15, he became the first Japanese postwar prime minister to pay tribute, in his official capacity, at the Yasukuni Shrine.[79] His visit aimed to reestablish Japan's national identity "by diluting the postwar Japanese separation of state and religion imposed by the occupation forces and upheld by Japanese centrists and leftists."[80] This bold political move backfired as China and South Korea harshly condemned the visit, effectively forestalling further visits by Nakasone. However, the political effort to galvanize national consciousness by politicizing the Yasukuni Shrine and emperor worship did not subside. In May 2000, for instance, then prime minister Yoshiro Mori, in his speech before a gathering of the Shinto Political Federation of Diet Members, declared that "Japan is a divine nation centered around the Emperor."[81] Coming only a year after Mori's "divine nation" speech, Prime Minister Koizumi's annual pilgrimage to the Yasukuni Shrine was a further example of political efforts to appeal to national solidarity in times of change. While Koizumi's successor, Shinzo Abe, did not make a visit to the Yasukuni Shrine while in office, he reportedly did visit secretly before he assumed his premiership. More recently, in April 2009, then prime minister Taro Aso caused a stir in the region by sending an offering to the shrine.[82]

In South Korea Christianity has been at the center of the search for national cohesion. The current popularity of Christianity stems in part from its role in promoting national consciousness during the colonial period. Although vying for followers and influence within South Korean society, Christian organizations continue to express "a patriotic fervor and an emphasis on Korea as Asia's first Christian nation."[83] With the ever-present nationalist focus, the mainstream Christian organizations, during the Cold War period, prayed for "security from a North Korean attack and for preservation of the South Korean state."[84] Such nationalist tendencies of Christian organizations persist in the age of globalization, symbolized in the growing number of South Korean missionaries abroad. Their numbers skyrocketed from 93 in 1979, to 3,272 in 1994, and about 16,000 in 2006, serving in more than one hundred and fifty countries.[85]

With its sunshine policy of engagement toward North Korea, the South Korean government has also become involved with religious politics in the issue of inter-Korean relations. For instance, during the Roh Moo Hyun government, the Ministry of Culture and Tourism supported various religious exchanges between the two Koreas.[86] The two inter-Korean summits included South Korean religious representatives as part of the official delegation. A panreligious consultative body, the Korean Conference on Religion and Peace (KCRP), convened its tenth anniversary of religious exchange between the two Koreas in Pyongyang in 2007.[87] Sensing a change in government policy and the public's perception toward North Korea, and also driven in part by organizational competition over resources, media attention, and followers, major religious organizations in South Korea have begun joining the new crusade. South Korea's largest Christian congregation, Yoido Full Gospel Church, with more than 800,000 followers, has recently started construction on a cardiology hospital in Pyongyang. Well known for his anti-Communist views, the church's pastor, Yongki Cho, explained his change of heart by emphasizing the goal of "enhancing national prestige, along with the need to win people's trust for Christianity in North Korea."[88] Similarly, in the name of contributing to "national unification and promoting Buddhist exchange between the two Koreas," the largest Buddhist organization in South Korea, Jogyejong, helped restore an old Buddhist temple in North Korea.[89]

DOMESTIC AND REGIONAL CONSEQUENCES

How does the religious revival in East Asia affect domestic and regional politics? At the domestic level governments have subjected revived religious movements to a mixture of lingering suspicion, intense scrutiny, and political persecution. While people across the region are increasingly free to follow their faiths to the extent that "they remained loyal to the state," some religious sects are not immune from intermittent persecution, especially when they appear "to threaten the state by denying its legitimacy or to threaten society by encouraging its members to act in ways contrary to accepted moral norms."[90] Broad labels, such as Christianity or Buddhism, are rarely helpful in identifying the targets of government concern. For instance, some Christian groups, especially mainstream Protestant organizations, have helped the government in South Korea; yet the government at times has viewed other Christian groups as problematic. In Japan Soka Gakkai is also often regarded with suspicion, while other groups have been ignored. And while Buddhist organizations play an increasing role in China's campaign for a "harmonious society," Tibetan Buddhism remains a major source of political concern for Chinese leaders.

The Chinese state retains substantial power to define the boundaries of organized religion and is quite selective in adopting different religious traditions. Daniel Bell, a philosophy professor at Tsinghua University, reminds us of a deliberate tendency to depoliticize Confucius in popular books and to downplay "Confucian values of social or political criticism."[91] Religious freedom is permitted only for groups that conform to government policy. The appointment of religious leaders and the sites of worship typically also remain in government hands.[92] Groups refusing to accept government guidance, such as Tibetan Buddhists under the Dalai Lama, are subject to suppression. In contrast, the Hui, China's largest Muslim minority, with an estimated 20 million followers, enjoy substantial religious freedom as long as they respect the rule of the party. Once they are deemed a threat to the political leadership, religious groups become the subject of persecution. The rise and fall of Falun Gong illustrates this point.

Founded by Li Hongzhi in 1992, Falun Gong is based on Qigong, a system of traditional breathing practices, and became widely popular in China in the 1990s. Li combined the Qigong practice with elements from Buddhism and Taoism to create his syncretic sect.[93] Initially, the Chinese government viewed the movement positively. In 1993 Li received praise from security organizations, while government officials even mentioned the contribution of Falun Gong's breathing practice to Chinese health care.[94] In the late 1990s conditions changed almost overnight. In April 1999 a physicist at the Chinese Academy of Sciences published an article criticizing Qigong practice as "a health hazard because adherents might forgo conventional treatment for serious illnesses."[95] The criticism prompted protests by Falun Gong members, resulting in arrests of several protestors. What followed was a massive silent sit-in in front of the Chinese leadership compound in Beijing on April 25, 1999, involving more than 10,000 Falun Gong practitioners who sought official recognition and the release of those arrested earlier. What alarmed the Chinese leadership was not the specific content of the appeal but the size and nature of the demonstration, through which a religious sect had suddenly become an overt political force. The sit-in was the largest demonstration in China since the 1989 pro-democracy movement.[96] At a special meeting with two thousand CCP officials, President Jiang Zemin reportedly "required each of the members of the Politburo Standing Committee to stand up and testify that they endorsed the necessity of the campaign to eradicate the Falun Gong . . . as well as the military crackdown on the Tiananmen demonstrators ten years earlier."[97]

Falun Gong was thus declared to be a dangerous cult threatening to disrupt social stability and challenge political authority. The government-affiliated Xinhua press referred to the protest as "the April 25 siege of the central leadership compound . . . [which] seriously disrupted the work of government departments and the daily routine of the general public, threatened social stability, and had negative political consequences."[98] The government's arrest warrant of Li Hongzhi was issued on the basis of his "disturbing public order."[99] Ye Xiaowen, director of the State Administration of Religious Affairs, summed up the government's case by saying, "Like every other cult in the world, the cult of Falun

Gong poses a great danger to society."[100] *People's Daily* also reported that China banned Falun Gong because it "[advocates] superstition and spreading fallacies, hoodwinking people, inciting and creating disturbances, and jeopardizing social stability."[101]

Nothing in Japan's recent history is readily comparable to the suppression of Falun Gong. In fact, Shintoism has in the last two decades received political support from the conservative wing of the LDP. In contrast, the government has approached thousands of new religious groups with evident suspicion. The spread of new religions began in the 1950s as rapid industrialization and urbanization severed many Japanese from their ties to traditional religions such as Buddhism and Shintoism. Living in a growing spiritual vacuum, the Japanese turned to these new religions, which have since sprouted with missionary zeal.[102] With their religious focus on worldly benefits (*genze rikyaku*) such as family and health, new religions are "continuations rather than aberrations of the Japanese religious tradition."[103] However, one commonality among the new religions sets them apart from Japan's more traditional religions: "A spirit of protest against the establishment." Representing those who suffer from unfair government treatment and fighting against government pressures became "a fundamental tradition of the new religions."[104]

Understandably, the government's skeptical view of new religious movements intensified in the wake of the Aum sarin gas attack of 1995. Founded in 1984 by Shoko Asahara as a yoga and meditation group, the Aum Shinrikyo became a highly organized religious sect with about 10,000 followers in Japan.[105] Prior to the 1995 gas attack the sect was linked to various crimes, including murder and kidnapping. But it had escaped careful scrutiny by the Japanese police, which since 1945 have been very reluctant to interfere in religious affairs.[106] Memories of the political manipulation of religion during the Meiji era supported the generally shared view in the postwar period that "in a modern, secular and liberal society, religious movements needed to be protected from state interference." But after the 1995 gas attack, the debate shifted to "whether the state and its citizens required greater protection from religious groups."[107]

Under the provisions of the Anti-Subversive Activities Law, the government initially tried to ban Aum altogether, only to forestall the ban once Asahara had stepped down as the leader of the sect, "a move designed to show that Aum no longer posed a danger to Japanese society."[108] Along with the dismantling of Aum Shinrikyo, the Japanese government also tried to change the hands-off "relationship between the state and religious organizations that has held in Japan since the end of World War II."[109] Government efforts to control religious affairs and to put them under the general supervision of the state took the form of requiring religious organizations to "annually submit a list to government authorities of all of their senior officials and of their assets." Since then, the government has had the right "to investigate religious organizations if there is some suspicion that they are abusing their status as officially recognized religious organizations."[110]

Under South Korea's authoritarian governments radical Christian groups developed a distinctive Korean theology, called *Minjung* (or masses) theology, with strong ties to the working class. Conservative Christian groups have remained largely apolitical.[111] In a striking similarity to the role played by Christianity during the early colonial period, various Christian activists have used a liberal church as the organizational base for protests against government.[112] Conservative Christian groups, especially those that are well established in society, have viewed the liberal church and Minjung theology as "having the potential to destroy social and political stability."[113] With close ties to mainstream Christian organizations, South Korean military regimes saw "a clear connection among Minjung theology, student activism, labor unrest and overseas criticism of the Seoul regime."[114] As a result, Christians following Minjung theology were the main target of government persecution. The suppression of religious groups was not limited to the case of Christianity. For instance, the Chun Doo Hwan government in the 1980s was particularly aggressive toward Buddhist organizations, which were viewed as uncooperative with the military regime. The Chun government eventually sent military and police forces to various Buddhist temples, including the headquarters of South Korea's largest Buddhist organization, and arrested hundreds of monks.[115]

What are the regional ramifications of religion in East Asia? No particular religion enjoys a region-wide resonance. China's religious revival is focused primarily on Confucianism, with some elements of Buddhism and Taoism added. Japan's religious revival centers on the resurgence of Shintoism and the appearance of various new religions. In South Korea Christianity is the most popular religion, but Buddhism and Confucianism are also enjoying a revival. In contrast to Islam in the Middle East, there is no single overarching religion in East Asia. However, states feel compelled to address regional and global audiences in the effort to create a favorable international image; this creates a regional dimension for East Asia's religious politics. Furthermore, transnational linkages connect some of these religious groups and movements on a regional and even broader scale.

East Asian states now more than ever must balance "the need to unify their nation[s] with the need to maintain friendly ties with the international community."[116] Governments thus cannot simply disregard the regional dimension of their quest for creating a favorable image through public diplomacy initiatives. For example, since 2004 the Chinese government has begun to establish Confucius Institutes around the world. Under the guidance of the Confucius Institute headquarters in Beijing, the spread of the institutes is "aimed at promoting friendly relationship with other countries and enhancing the understanding of the Chinese language and culture among world Chinese learners as well as providing good learning conditions for them."[117] While the main focus of the institutes is "to teach Chinese, train teachers, certify instructors, [and] conduct examinations," they also plan to "provide consultancy services on Chinese culture, the economy and society."[118] There exists a striking similarity between the Chinese government's use of Confucianism for fostering regime legitimacy and national unity under the banner of a "harmonious society," and its promotion of Confucian Institutes as a foreign policy tool to achieve what the Chinese call a "harmonious world." China's establishment of Confucius Institutes is a clear attempt to "reassure people that its drive to gain major-power status is based not simply on military and economic might but also on sound foundations of tradition and culture."[119] Thus far, for example, China's Confucian revival seems to have resonated well with South Koreans. Formally established in November 2004, the Confucius Institute in Seoul was the first of its kind in the world. By the end of 2007 eleven Confucian Institutes had been established in South Korea.[120]

The South Korean government also sponsors various religious events as a means to foster Korean culture and traditions in a globalizing world. During earlier years, as in China, the South Korean government deemed Confucianism to be nothing but "an obstacle to economic development."[121] For instance, in his 1962 speech entitled "Reflections on Our Nation's Past," then president Park Chung Hee echoed the logic of early reformers in the modernization period, criticizing "the corruption, irrationality, venality, and waste of the Confucian tradition."[122] Now the South Korean government supports various elements of traditional religions, especially Confucianism and Buddhism. A Web site for the South Korean Ministry of Culture and Tourism for instance claims, "Korea, even more than China or Japan, has been able to preserve Confucianism and Buddhism in their classical forms."[123] In 2001 the government sponsored an international Confucian cultural festival to commemorate the five hundredth anniversary of the birth of Toegye, one of the most renowned Korean Confucian intellectuals. The festival proclaimed that the Confucian tradition is not only "an alternative to the spiritual and moral deterioration of the present day" but also "at the center of [Korean] national culture."[124] With these government-sponsored events, the Korean state strives to "defend [Korean] identities and cultures from the encroaching forces of globalization."[125] Only Japan does not fit this pattern of relying on religious revival for public diplomacy. Although repeated invocations of Japan's respect for nature by many of its soft power advocates may recall the legacy of Shintoism, appealing to that tradition explicitly would be politically too charged. Rather than referring to old or new religions, Japan's government prefers to rely instead on popular culture as it seeks to improve Japan's international image.

Transnationalism is a second distinctive feature of East Asia's religious revival. In the past, despite the important role played by foreign missionaries, East Asian countries tended to undercut the transnational ties of foreign religions by "bring[ing] them within state corporatist regimes" and "allow[ing] them to operate on the condition that they sever foreign connections and communicate abroad only through state channels."[126] As people expand their contacts across borders, this transnational dimension offers East Asian states both opportunities and challenges. One such challenge is the growing presence of foreign workers/ residents in East Asia. In 2009, for instance, foreigners residing in South Korea for the first time exceeded one million.[127] The increasing number of foreign workers with various religious beliefs, including Catholicism (the Philippines), Buddhism (Bangladesh), and Islam (Pakistan), is slowly altering the South Korean religious landscape. This new reality may present new challenges to the South Korean government, a possibility also applicable to China and Japan.[128]

Generally speaking, the Chinese state has been successful in neutralizing foreign influences on religion in China while increasing its own "visibility in international religious circles."[129] Tensions between the Vatican and the Chinese government over the appointment of Catholic bishops illustrate this point.[130] Since the 1950s the Catholic Church in Rome and the Chinese government have had no diplomatic relations. As a result, eight million Chinese Catholics worship with the underground church, while another five million belong to the government-sanctioned Chinese Patriotic Catholic Association. The rift between the Catholic Church in Rome and the Chinese government became particularly acute in June 2004, when the Chinese authorities arrested three Roman Catholic bishops. The Vatican called the arrest "inconceivable in a country based on laws."[131] In May 2006 the Vatican threatened to excommunicate the two bishops ordained by the Chinese Catholic Church.[132] While defending its right to ordain Catholic bishops, the Chinese Catholic Church also called for "improvement of the relationship between China and the Vatican."[133] This was a far cry from its previous position that the appointment of bishops by the Holy See constituted "meddling in China's internal affairs."[134] In fact, over the past several years the Chinese government and the Vatican have reached "a tacit understanding," based on which "candidates for bishop have been vetted by each side." Since 2004 this practice has led to the approval of at least five bishops by the Holy See.[135] In June 2007 Pope Benedict XVI even sent a fifty-five-page letter to Chinese Catholics, acknowledging that there has been some improvement in religious freedom in China and expressing his hope to normalize diplomatic ties with Beijing.[136] In September 2007 the Chinese Catholic Church ordained the head of the Beijing diocese of the state-sanctioned church, reportedly with the Vatican's approval, while a vice chairman of the government-backed Chinese Patriotic Catholic Association spoke highly of the

Pope's letter.[137] The positive momentum continued in 2008. In May 2008, in a rare symbolic move, the China Philharmonic Orchestra performed for Pope Benedict XVI in Vatican City.[138] Three months later a Chinese bishop in Beijing, initially ordained without papal approval but later legitimized by the Vatican, was selected as a torchbearer for the Beijing Olympics, thanks in part to what the government called "the Church's contribution" to society.[139]

In the case of South Korea, its overseas Christian missions, especially those active in China, have become a main conduit for helping North Korean refugees defect to South Korea. In their relations with North Korea, this is creating political challenges for both the South Korean and Chinese governments. In the words of a Korean-American mission leader, "Christians have become the alpha and omega of the North Korean issue" by launching campaigns to "liberate" North Koreans from the totalitarian regime. Christian groups such as the Commission to Help North Korean Refugees view North Korea as "the biggest target" of Korean missionaries.[140] By 2005 Chinese authorities had arrested dozens of South Korean and American missionaries because they were helping North Koreans. Some of the North Korean defectors have also played a role in the United States, where they worked with American evangelical organizations in their efforts to facilitate the passage of the 2004 North Korean Human Rights Act by the U.S. Congress.[141] These efforts also have the potential to "complicate the talks to stop Pyongyang's nuclear weapons program or irk China or American allies like South Korea that favor a less confrontational approach."[142]

Another transnational implication of religion concerns the regional reverberations of Japan's Yasukuni Shrine controversy. Prime ministerial visits to the shrine have become a major source of regional tension. Part of the problem is that Japanese conservatives who seek to reconnect the state and the shrine are also the loudest critics of Japan's apology for its wartime aggressions.[143] China and South Korea vehemently protested Prime Minister Koizumi's visit to the Shinto shrine and, for several years running, canceled their bilateral summits with Japan.[144] Furthermore, there are 27,863 Taiwanese and 21,181 Koreans enshrined at Yasukuni.[145] In June 2001 relatives of these South Korean war dead filed a lawsuit requesting removal of their names from the shrine. In June 2005 a group of Taiwanese also attempted to protest at the shrine. Fearing a violent clash between them and Japanese right-wing groups who had placed several vehicles at the main gate of the shrine blocking the Taiwanese from entering, the Japanese police stopped the Taiwanese protesters.[146] In October 2005 the Committee of Anti-Yasukuni Joint Counteraction, a transnational movement involving groups from South Korea, Taiwan, Japan, and Okinawa, launched a joint campaign against the shrine. In 2006 the committee began an investigation of the enshrining of non-Japanese, and it started writing petitions addressed to the UN Secretary General and the UN Human Rights Commission.[147]

The immediate aftermath of World War II suggested that religion in East Asia had lost most of its ground in a dramatically altered political landscape. In China religion was all but banished by the Communist Party. The party viewed religion as a leftover from a feudal past, the proverbial "opium of the people."[148] Christianity in particular was problematic because it was viewed as an agent of Western imperialism.[149] During the upheavals of the Cultural Revolution, the party sought to exterminate religion altogether as the Red Guards smashed churches, temples, and other religious sites.[150] In Japan the U.S. occupation authorities banned State Shinto and put into the new constitution an article ensuring the separation between Shintoism and the state, leaving the war-torn nation in a spiritual vacuum.[151] In return for the prohibition of State Shintoism and emperor worship, the occupation authorities helped establish the principle of religious freedom, which eventually opened the way for "the emergence of a large number of competing new sects and movements and the secession of thousands of temples," collectively called the "new religions."[152] Finally, in South Korea, Christianity and other prominent religions did not recover fully from the long suppression during Japan's colonial rule. Although Christianity was a key source of national aspiration for independence in the early colonial period, Christian missionaries in Korea and most Korean Christian groups eventually acquiesced to Japanese rule.

These exceptional circumstances have now passed, and it is a mistake to read into them a larger secularization thesis. While the timing of religious revival differs in each country, permissive political conditions exist in each, including domestic political upheavals requiring close attention to the legitimacy of the state (China), a growing spiritual vacuum in an age of rapid economic growth and material prosperity that threatens national cohesion in the eyes of a conservative coalition (Japan), and state legitimacy and national cohesion in a period of democratic transformation (South Korea). "The secular form of Asian political institutions often masks a religious spirit," writes Richard Madsen, a leading scholar in the field of Chinese religion; "often, the secular political form is what outsiders see, while the spirit is what insiders apprehend."[153] To make his point, Madsen refers to the controversies over the Yasukuni Shrine. The pressure to visit the shrine is not merely to memorialize the names of those who died in the war, but to worship at a site that contains the actual spirits of the war dead.

The contemporary regional relevance of religion in East Asia is reflected nowhere more clearly than in the debates about Asian values. That concept and the values it refers to resonate deeply with Confucian traditions. An innovation by Singaporean intellectuals in search of a state identity in the 1970s, the concept of Asian values is readily understood and appreciated by many people in East Asia. The notion of a paternalistic leader, the rewards of wise and just leadership, and the merits of respect and loyalty are of course not unique to East Asia. But what is distinctive of East Asia is the attraction these ideas have had for many leaders and intellectuals, in particular as they have sought to engage the West on their own terms and with values and traditions that are distinctly "Eastern."[154] In this vein, some scholars suggest that Asian values represent a distinctive path to modernity. For instance, Tu Wei-Ming, a leading scholar on this subject, considers the grasping of Asian values to be a key to "an understanding of the political economy and the moral fabric of industrial East Asia."[155]

Such views are not confined to scholarly analysis. Former Singaporean prime minister Lee Kuan Yew attributes the region's rapid growth to Asian values. Even in the face of Western criticism leveled against Asian values and calls for political and economic changes during the Asian financial crisis, Lee refused to accept the Western impulse to lay blame on Asian values: "If it is Asian values that brought about this disaster, how come Hong Kong and Singapore have not been affected?"[156]

The political will to resist Western demands for social and political change has made Asian values language attractive. The availability of a shared religious vocabulary has thus provided ammunition for dispersed efforts to forge a common regional identity. Like all identity politics and projects, this one is marked by vigorous debate and acrimonious contestation, for example, between liberals and conservatives, and Japanese and Chinese. But the ubiquity and durability of the Asian values discourse is inseparable from the regional legacy of Confucian traditions. And that legacy now injects new vitality into efforts to build a regional community. Indonesian Vice President Jusuf Kalia, for example, directly links Asian values to the idea of an East Asian Free Trade Area, suggesting that they would help the region overcome various gaps in per capita income, development, and resource endowment. Highlighting Asian values as "a system of ethics that prioritize[s] cooperation over competition," he insists that Asian countries should turn to Asian values "rather than copying other systems and values."[157] To affirm an Asian values discourse against Western criticism thus points to the power of religion in East Asia, just as Western claims regarding, for example, human rights point to the power of a "secular religious discourse" that is trying to change the East.

Theories of international relations take for granted the secularity of international politics rather than tracking the ebb and flow of religious politics as do sociologists of religion. This is an intellectual shortcut grounded in a partial reading of European history, which has become enshrined in Eurocentric disciplinary assumptions that typically remain exempted from scrutiny. Yet contemporary Europe is not as secular as most scholars of Europe and international relations assume.[158] And neither is Asia, as we have argued here, concurring with Richard Madsen's assessment that "the secularity of modern Asian states has by no means led to widespread social secularity."[159] In looking for religion in Asia we should not search, as we are accustomed to in Europe and America, for private faith. Asian religion is neither private nor faith-based, argues Madsen. Instead of faith, Asian religion is fueled by the creation of collective rituals and the yearning for social myths that give some sense of order and meaning to individuals' lives. And that sense of order and meaning, Asian states realize, is of strategic importance and needs to be provided not by individuals or social movements but by governments dedicated to their specifically state-centric conceptions of the public good.

East Asia's religious politics suggests the promise of integrating international and comparative perspectives more fully and systematically into a disciplined analysis of world politics, of avoiding excessive abstractions of international and global theories by grounding them in regional structures and processes, and of avoiding hard and fast distinctions between secular and religious politics. If it made these three adjustments, international relations theory would no longer have its head stuck quite so high in the clouds. And that slight change in theory altitude might help us gain a better understanding of fair and foul religious weather in world politics.

NOTES

For their critical comments and helpful suggestions we would like to thank Michael Barnett, Richard Madsen, Katharine Moon, Seo-Hyun Park, Jack Snyder, and especially David Leheny. All the usual disclaimers obtain. Katzenstein would like to thank Louise and John Steffens, members of the Founders' Circle, who assisted his stay at the Princeton Institute of Advanced Studies during the 2009–10 academic year.

1. Peter J. Katzenstein, "Multiple Modernities as Limits to Secular Europeanization?" in Religion in an Expanding Europe, ed. Timothy A. Byrnes and Peter J. Katzenstein (London: Cambridge University Press, 2006), 1–33.

2. José Casanova, Public Religion in the Modern World (Chicago: University of Chicago Press, 1994); David Smilde and Matthew May, "The Emerging Strong Program in the Sociology of Religion" (SSRC Working Paper, New York, February 2010).

3. Peter J. Katzenstein, A World of Regions: Asia and Europe in the American Imperium (Ithaca: Cornell University Press, 2005), 13–19.

4. We are indebted to David Leheny for sharpening our thinking on this point.

5. Philip J. Costopoulos, introduction to *World Religions and Democracy*, ed. Larry Diamond, Marc F. Plattner, and Philip J. Costopoulos (Baltimore: Johns Hopkins University Press, 2005), ix.

6. Mark R. Mullins and Richard Fox Young, eds., *Perspectives on Christianity in Korea and Japan: The Gospel and Culture in East Asia* (Lewiston, NY: Edwin Mellen Press, 1995), xiv.

7. Pippa Norris and Ronald Inglehart, *Secular and Sacred: Religion and Politics Worldwide* (Cambridge: Cambridge University Press, 2004), 24–25.

8. Peter van der Veer, *Imperial Encounters: Religion and Modernity in India and Britain* (Princeton: Princeton University Press, 2001); Peter van der Veer and Hartmut Lehmann, eds. *Nation and Religion: Perspectives on Europe and Asia* (Princeton: Princeton University Press, 1999). See also Katzenstein, "Multiple Modernities."

9. Ted Gerald Jelen and Clyde Wilcox, eds., *Religion and Politics in Comparative Perspective: The One, the Few, and the Many* (Cambridge: Cambridge University Press, 2002), 7.

10. Maria Hsia Chang, *Falun Gong: The End of Days* (New Haven, CT: Yale University Press, 2004), 37–38.

11. Maria A. Toyota and Aiji Tanaka, "Religion and Politics in Japan," in Jelen and Wilcox, *Religion and Politics in Comparative Perspective*, 272–274; Norihisa Suzuki, "Christianity," in *Religion in Japanese Culture: Where Living Traditions Meet a Changing World*, ed. Noriyoshi Tamaru and David Reid (Tokyo: Kodansha International, 1996), 68; Chushichi Tsuzuki, *The Pursuit of Power in Modern Japan, 1825–1995* (Oxford: Oxford University Press, 2000), 19–20.

12. Yung-Chung Kim, *Women of Korea: A History from Ancient Times to 1945* (Seoul: Ewha Womans University Press, 1976), 21. On Korean shamanism, see also Dong-sik Yu, *Hankuk Mukyo ui Yoksawa Kujo* [The History and Structure of Korean Shamanism] (Seoul: Yonsei University Press, 1975). We thank Katharine Moon for pointing out the importance of Korean shamanism both in the daily lives of people and in the royal court during the Yi Dynasty.

13. Chaibong Hahm, "The Ironies of Confucianism," *Journal of Democracy* 15, no. 3 (July 2004): 105.

14. Paul A. Cohen, *China and Christianity: The Missionary Movement and the Growth of Chinese Antiforeignism, 1860–1870* (Cambridge, MA: Harvard University Press, 1963), 6, 16–17.

15. Chang, *Falun Gong*, 42, 44. The Chinese state was of course not always Confucian. The Tang dynasty was Buddhist. And when it was Confucian or neo-Confucian (amalgamating Confucian and Buddhist teachings), the Chinese state was at heart Legalist. The Confucian Ming and Qing dynasties regarded Buddhism as orthodox teaching as long as it was practiced in monestaries loyal to the state. Heterodox teachings were practiced by lay Buddhist sects that sometimes offered a political basis for rebellion. We are grateful to Richard Madsen for adding nuance to our analysis.

16. Ibid., 56–58.

17. Merle Goldman, "Religion in Post-Mao China," *Annals of the American Academy of Political and Social Science* 483, no. 1 (January 1986): 147.

18. Anthony C. Yu, *State and Religion in China: Historical and Textual Perspectives* (Chicago: Open Court, 2005), 43.

19. Suzuki, "Christianity," 65.

20. Goldman, "Religion in Post-Mao China," 147.

21. Ian Reader, *Religion in Contemporary Japan* (Honolulu: University of Hawaii Press, 1991), 7–8.

22. Joseph J. Spae, *Christian Corridors to Japan* (Tokyo: Oriens Institute for Religious Research, 1965), 168.

23. Donald N. Clark, *Christianity in Modern Korea* (Lanham, MD: University Press of America, 1986), 22; Toyota and Tanaka, "Religion and Politics in Japan," 269.

24. Van der Veer and Lehmann, *Nation and Religion*, 3.

25. Van der Veer, *Imperial Encounters*, 14–15.

26. Harry Harootunian, "Memory, Mourning, and National Morality: Yasukuni Shrine and the Reunion of State and Religion in Postwar Japan," in van der Veer and Lehmann, *Nation and Religion*, 153.

27. Stuart D. B. Picken, *The A to Z of Shinto* (Lanham, MD: The Scarecrow Press, 2006), 12.

28. Ian Reader, Esben Andreasen, and Finn Stefansson, *Japanese Religions: Past and Present* (Hawaii: University of Hawaii Press, 1993), 39.

29. Toyota and Tanaka, "Religion and Politics in Japan," 275–77.

30. Paul Kevonhorster, "Civil Society, Religion, and the Nation: The Case of Japan," in *Civil Society, Religion, and the Nation: Modernization in the Intercultural Context: Russia, Japan, Turkey*, ed. Gerrit Steunebrink and Evert van der Zweerde (Amsterdam: Rodopi, 2004), 91–92.

31. Parker Jay Palmer, *Religion, Political Modernization and Secularization: Case Studies in America, Turkey and Japan* (PhD dissertation, Department of Sociology, University of California, Berkeley, 1970), 166.

32. Donald Keene, *Emperor of Japan: Meiji and His World, 1852–1912* (New York: Columbia University Press, 2002), 408–410.

33. Christianity was one of many new religions officially permitted by the Meiji government. Entering the crowded field of religion, where Japanese had already been "embedded in familial (Buddhist), communal (Shinto), and eventually civil (State Shinto) religious obligations," Christian missionaries found it exceedingly difficult to overcome the public perception of Christianity as "a deviant religion." Mullins and Young, *Perspectives on Christianity in Korea and Japan*, xviii.

34. Peter van der Veer, "'Smash Temples, Build Schools': Comparing Secularism in India and China," in *Rethinking Secularism*, ed. Craig Calhoun, Mark Juergensmeyer, and Jonathan VanAntwerpen (Oxford: Oxford University Press, 2011); Richard Madsen, "Secularism, Religious Change, and Social Conflict in Asia," in Calhoun, Juergensmeyer, and VanAntwerpen, *Rethinking Secularism*. In an interesting twist on this state-driven secularization, in China today there has been a rebranding of "superstition" as "cultural heritage" that serves various political, economic, and social interests. Richard Madsen, "Back to the Future: Pre-Modern Religious Policy in Post-

Secular China" (unpublished manuscript, University of California, San Diego, August 2009), 7.

35. James Miller, "The Historical Legacy of China's Religious Traditions," in *Chinese Religions in Contemporary Societies* (Santa Barbara, CA: ABC-CLIO, 2006), 15.

36. Chung-Shin Park, *Protestantism and Politics in Korea* (Seattle: University of Washington Press, 2003), 119.

37. Vipan Chandra, *Imperialism, Resistance, and Reform in Late Nineteenth-Century Korea* (Berkeley: Institute of East Asian Studies, 1988), 126–148.

38. Cohen, *China and Christianity*, 268.

39. Kuang-sheng Liao, *Antiforeignism and Modernization in China, 1860–1980: Linkage between Domestic Politics and Foreign Policy* (Hong Kong: Chinese University Press, 1984); Cohen, *China and Christianity*, 267–68.

40. Liao, *Antiforeignism and Modernization in China*, 46–47. Not all Chinese leaders were anti-Christian, however. The founder of the Kuomintang, Chiang Kai-shek, for instance, was Christian, and during the Cold War period he used his Christianity to garner American support for Taiwan. We are grateful to Richard Madsen for calling our attention to this point.

41. Kim Han-Sik, "The Influence of Christianity on Modern Korean Political Thought," *Korea Journal* 23, no. 12 (December 1983): 6, 10.

42. Hong Kyong-Man, "Formation of Korean Protestantism and Its Political Nature," *Korea Journal* 23, no. 12 (December 1983): 20.

43. Andrew E. Kim, "A History of Christianity in Korea: From Its Troubled Beginning to Its Contemporary Success," *Korea Journal* 35, no. 2 (Summer 1995), 41.

44. Daniel J. Adams, "Church Growth in Korea: A Paradigm Shift from Ecclesiology to Nationalism," in Mullins and Young, *Perspectives on Christianity in Korea and Japan*, 17; Clark, *Christianity in Modern Korea*, 36.

45. Park, *Protestantism and Politics in Korea*, 33, 35.

46. Adams, "Church Growth in Korea," 24.

47. Clark, *Christianity in Modern Korea*, 52.

48. Scott M. Thomas, *The Global Resurgence of Religion and the Transformation of International Relations: The Struggle for the Soul of the Twenty-First Century* (New York: Palgrave MacMillan, 2005), 45.

49. Orville Schell, "Hu Jintao," *Time*, December 18, 2007.

50. Joseph Kahn, "In China, Talk of Democracy Is Simply That," *New York Times*, April 20, 2007.

51. The Chinese government, however, does not consider Confucianism a religion. Its White Paper on religious beliefs only discusses five religions, namely, Buddhism, Taoism, Islam, Catholicism, and Protestantism, as officially recognized religions in China. *Freedom of Religious Belief in China* (White Paper, Chinese Embassy, Beijing, October, 1997), http://www.china-embassy.org/eng/zt/zjxy/t36492.htm (accessed January 13, 2010).

52. François Bougon, "Confucius Resurfaces in New China," *Agence France-Presse*, April 22, 2007.

53. Eric Teo Chu Cheow, "How to Stabilize China, According to Hu," *Japan Times*, April 1, 2005; Maureen Fan, "Confucius Making a Comeback In Money-Driven Modern China," *Washington Post*, July 24, 2007.

54. Herbert P. Bix, "Emperor, Shinto, Democracy: Japan's Unresolved Questions of Historical Consciousness," *Japan Focus*, June 13, 2005.

55. Michiko Maekawa, "The Politics and Culture of Contemporary Religion in Japan," *Nanzan Bulletin* 26 (2002): 45.

56. Daiki Shibuichi, "The Yasukuni Shrine Dispute and the Politics of Identity in Japan," *Asian Survey* 45, no. 2 (March/April 2005): 204.

57. Toyota and Tanaka, "Religion and Politics in Japan," 281.

58. Shibuichi, "The Yasukuni Shrine Dispute," 200. The membership of local branches of some of these conservative groups tends to overlap with that of LDP branches. Ibid., 200–201.

59. Ibid., 210; Maekawa, "The Politics and Culture of Contemporary Religion in Japan," 44.

60. Howard W. French, "A Sect's Political Rise Creates Uneasiness in Japan," *New York Times*, November 14, 1999.

61. Toyota and Tanaka, "Religion and Politics in Japan," 284.

62. Don Baker, "World Religions and National States: Competing Claims in East Asia," in *Transnational Religion and Fading States*, ed. Susanne Hoeber Rudolph and James Piscatori (Boulder, CO.: Westview, 1997), 163; French, "A Sect's Political Rise Creates Uneasiness in Japan"; Charles Scanlon, "Risky Alliance for Japan's Ruling Party," *BBC News*, June 22, 2000.

63. Jim Frederick, "Japan's Holy Wildcard," *Time*, Nov. 23, 2003.

64. Ibid. In the 2003 parliamentary elections, for example, approximately 80 percent of LDP candidates with the Komeito endorsement were elected

65. Kim, "A History of Christianity in Korea," 47; "Yeokdae Daetongryung-gwa Jonggyo" [Past Presidents and Religions], *Seoul Shinmun*, August 28, 2008.

66. Clark, *Christianity in Modern Korea*, 42.

67. Park, *Protestantism and Politics in Korea*, 204.

68. During this period, however, the Rhee administration oppressed married monks (*daecheo-seung*), forcing them out of Buddhist temples. The monks later established a separate order called Taegojong, which remains one of the largest Buddhist orders in South Korea ("Yeokdae Daetongryung-gwa Jonggyo" [Past Presidents and Religions]).

69. Park, *Protestantism and Politics in Korea*, 170.

70. Ibid., 180, 204.

71. It is worth pointing out, however, that Asian states' efforts to utilize religion for national cohesion are not always successful and sometimes may backfire. For instance, the Singaporean government's efforts to include Confucian ethics in the school curriculum in the 1980s failed due in large part to the fact that "Confucian values are clearly identified with the Chinese race and hence touched off certain ethnic sensitivities" in a multiethnic country. John Wong, "Promoting Confucianism for Socioeconomic Development: The Singapore Experience," in *Confucian Traditions in*

East Asian Modernity: Moral Education and Economic Culture in Japan and the Four Mini-Dragons, ed. Tu Wei-Ming (Cambridge, MA: Harvard University Press, 1996), 288. Concerned about possible interreligious tensions, the Singaporean government eventually decided to phase out the Confucian ethics course. But the government continued to promote what were called "national ideology" and "shared values," a set of ideas fully compatible with Confucianism and other Asian traditions. See Eddie, C. Y. Kuo, "Confucianism as Political Discourse in Singapore: The Case of an Incomplete Revitalization Movement," in Tu, *Confucian Traditions in East Asian Modernity*, 307–309. We are indebted to Katharine Moon on this point.

72. François Bougon, "Confucius Resurfaces in New China," *Agence France Presse*, Apr. 22, 2007.

73. "Religion in China: When Opium Can Be Benign," *Economist*, Feb 1, 2007.

74. "China to Build Harmonious Society with Wisdom of Taoism," *People's Daily*, April 23, 2007.

75. "CPC Constitution Mentions 'Religion' for First Time," *People's Daily*, October 21, 2007; "Full Text of Resolution on Amendment to CPC Constitution," *People's Daily*, October 22, 2007.

76. Harootunian, "Memory, Mourning, and National Morality," 153.

77. Ibid., 154.

78. N.J. Demerath and Karen S. Straight, "Religion, Politics, and the State: Cross-Cultural Observations," *Cross Currents* 47, no. 1 (Spring 1997).

79. Akiko Takenaka, "Enshrinement Politics: War Dead and War Criminals at Yasukuni Shrine," *Japan Focus*, June 7, 2007; Herbert P. Bix, *Hirohito and the Making of Modern Japan* (New York: HarperCollins Publishers, 2000), 683.

80. Shibuichi, "The Yasukuni Shrine Dispute," 206.

81. Inken Prohl, "Religion and National Identity in Contemporary Japan," in Steunebrink and van der Zweerde, *Civil Society, Religion, and the Nation* (Amsterdam: Rodopi, 2004), 144.

82. "Japan's Abe Made Secret War Shrine Visit: Report," *People's Daily*, August 5, 2006; "Japan Rivals in Row Over Yasukuni." *BBC News*, August 4, 2006; "Aso Sparks Warnings with Gift to Yasukuni," *Japan Times*, April 22, 2009.

83. Clark, *Christianity in Modern Korea*, 25.

84. Ibid., 25.

85. Seong-won Park, "A Survey on Mission Work in the Korean Churches, *International Review of Mission* 86 (July 1997): 330; Jennifer Veale, "Korean Missionaries Under Fire," *Time*, July 27, 2007.

86. The Web site of the Ministry of Culture and Tourism, South Korea, http://www .mct.go.kr/web/deptCourt/introService/introDept.jsp?pMenuCD=0702010000&pDept MenuCD=0702000000 (accessed January 14, 2008).

87. "Nambuk Jonggyoin-deul Ghinmilhan Gyoryu Hyupryuk Saup Jeongae" [North and South Korean Religious Leaders Initiated a Joint Project on Cooperation and Exchange], *Chosun Ilbo*, May 8, 2007, available at http://www.nkchosun. com/news/news.html?ACT=detail&cat_id=6&res_id=95381&page=1 (accessed June 15, 2010).

88. Euigeun An, "Cho Yongki Moksa Interview" [Interview with Pastor Cho], *Kookmin Ilbo*, December 6, 2007.

89. Chunki Chung, "Keumgangsan Sadae Myungchal Shingyesa Yetmoseup Doichatda" [Shingye Temple, One of the Four Famous Buddhist Temples on Mountain Keumgang, Has Been Fully Restored], *Hangyorye Shinmun*, October 13, 2007.

90. Baker, "World Religions and National States," 146.

91. Fan, "Confucius Making a Comeback."

92. Howard W. French, "Faith Sprouts in Arid Soil of China," *New York Times*, May 6, 2004.

93. Chang, *Falun Gong*, 4.

94. Danny Schechter, *Falun Gong's Challenge to China: Spiritual Practice or "Evil Cult"?* (New York: Akashic, 2000), 43.

95. Chang, *Falun Gong*, 7.

96. Schechter, *Falun Gong's Challenge to China*, 44–46; Chang, *Falun Gong*, 1.

97. Susan L. Shirk, *China: Fragile Superpower* (New York: Oxford University Press, 2007), 49–50.

98. Schechter, *Falun Gong's Challenge to China*, 46.

99. Chang, *Falun Gong*, 10.

100. Schechter, *Falun Gong's Challenge to China*, 123.

101. "China Bans Falun Gong," *People's Daily*, July 22, 1999. Similarly, the problem of Tibetan Buddhism, neglected here only for reasons of space, rests with the religion's search for political autonomy, which the Chinese state views as a brazen attempt to split the nation, disrupting social and political stability.

102. Matsumoto Shigeru, introduction to *Religion in Japanese Culture: Where Living Traditions Meet a Changing World*, ed. Noriyoshi Tamaru and David Reid (Tokyo: Kodansha International, 1996), 25–26; Ian Reader and George J. Tanabe Jr., *Practically Religious: Worldly Benefits and the Common Religion of Japan* (Honolulu: University of Hawaii Press, 1998), 100–103.

103. Ibid., 262.

104. Arai Ken, "New Religions," in Tamaru and Reid, *Religion in Japanese Culture*, 107.

105. Ian Reader, *Religious Violence in Contemporary Japan: The Case of Aum Shinrikyo* (Richmond, UK: Curzon Press, 2000), 8.

106. Peter J. Katzenstein, *Cultural Norms and National Security: Police and Military in Postwar Japan* (Ithaca: Cornell University Press, 1996), 72, and "Same War— Different Views: Germany, Japan, and the War on Terrorism," *International Organization* 57, no. 4 (Fall 2003): 731–60.

107. Reader, *Religious Violence in Contemporary Japan*, 225.

108. Ibid., 224–25.

109. Baker, "World Religions and National States," 164–165.

110. Ibid., 165.

111. Clark, *Christianity in Modern Korea*, 44.

112. Park, *Protestantism and Politics in Korea*, 183.

113. Ibid., 203.

114. Clark, *Christianity in Modern Korea*, 45.

115. Il Hyun Jang and Yong Won Yu, "Singoonbu Bihyupjojeok-in Jogyejong Son-boryo Jahaenghan Jonggyo Tanap" [The Military Regime Persecuted the Uncoopera-tive Jogye Order], *Chosun Ilbo*, October 26, 2007.

116. Baker, "World Religions and National States," 168.

117. Introduction to the "Confucius Institute" Project, Education Office of the Embassy of the People's Republic of China, http://www.sino-education.org/chinese/kongzijieeng.htm (accessed July 9, 2009).

118. Zhu Zhe, "Confucius Institutes Expanding Worldwide," *China Daily*, July 7, 2006.

119. Kazuo Ogoura, "China's Public Diplomacy," *Japan Times*, December 31, 2007; Baker, "World Religions and National States," 156.

120. "Confucius Institute in Seoul," Confucius Institute, January 18, 2007, http://www.hanban.edu.cn/en_hanban/content.php?id 2017 (accessed January 10, 2008).

121. Michael Robinson, "Perceptions of Confucianism in Twentieth-Century Ko-rea," in *The East Asian Region: Confucian Heritage and Its Modern Adaptation*, ed. Gilbert Rozman (Princeton: Princeton University Press, 1991), 218–219.

122. Park Chung-hee, *Reflections on our Nation's Past: Ideology of Social Recon-struction* (Seoul: Dong-a Publishing, 1962), 34–107, cited in Robinson, "Perceptions of Confucianism," 219.

123. "Buddhism and Confucianism," Korea Net, http://www.korea.net/korea/kor_loca.asp?code G0403 (accessed January 14, 2008).

124. Gi-Wook Shin, "The Paradox of Korean Globalization" (Working Paper, Asia-Pacific Research Center, Stanford University, January 2003), 11–12.

125. Ibid., 11–12.

126. Susanne Hoeber Rudolph, "Dehomogenizing Religious Formations," in *Transnational Religion and Fading States*, ed. Susanne Hoeber Rudolph and James Piscatori (Boulder, CO: Westview, 1997), 247.

127. *Chosun Ilbo*, August 6, 2009.

128. We are grateful to Katharine Moon for alerting us to this new development.

129. Baker, "World Religions and National States," 160.

130. Gerald Chan, "The Sino-Vatican Negotiations: Old Problems in a New Con-text," *China Quarterly* 153 (1989): 128–40; Beatrice Leung, "Communist Party-Vatican Interplay Over the Training of Church Leaders in China," *Journal for the Scientific Study of Religion* 40, no. 4 (2001): 657–73.

131. "Vatican Condemns Chinese Arrests," *BBC News*, June 23, 2004, http://news.bbc.co.uk/go/pr/fr/-/2/hi/asia-pacific/3833861.stm (accessed June 30, 2009).

132. "China Names New Catholic Bishop," *BBC News*, May 7, 2006, http://news.bbc.co.uk/go/pr/fr/-/2/hi/asia-pacific/4982530.stm (accessed June 30, 2009).

133. "China Defends Ordination of Catholic Bishops," *China Daily*, May 7, 2006, http://www.chinadaily.net/china/2006–05/07/content_583379_2.htm (accessed June 30, 2009).

134. "In China, Another Catholic Bishop," *New York Times*, May 14, 2006.

135. Jim Yardley and Keith Bradsher, "China Installs Bishop with Approval of Vatican," *New York Times*, May 8, 2006.

136. Jeff Israely, "The Pope Reaches Out to China," *Time*, July 3, 2007.

137. Maureen Fan, "Catholic Bishop Ordained in Beijing," *Washington Post*, September 21, 2007.

138. Elisabetta Povoledo, "China Orchestra Plays for Pope for First Time, Hinting at Thaw," *New York Times*, May 8, 2008.

139. "Catholic Bishop Carries Olympic Torch in China Relay," Catholic News Agency, August 3, 2008, http://www.catholicnewsagency.com/new.php?n 13426 (accessed July 8, 2009).

140. Norimitsu Onishi, "Korean Missionaries Carrying Word to Hard-to-Sway Places," *New York Times*, November 1, 2004.

141. Anthony Faiola, "An Act of Subversion, Carried by Balloons: A Korean Missionary Sends Aerial Messages of Faith Over Border to North," *Washington Post*, August 10, 2005.

142. David D. Kirkpatrick, "Christian Groups Press Bush About North Korea," *New York Times*, August 9, 2005.

143. Harootunian, "Memory, Mourning, and National Morality," 147.

144. "Hu's Protests Over Yasukuni Have No Effect on Koizumi," *Japan Times*, November 23, 2004, "Hu Warns of 'Instant' Diplomatic Damage," *Japan Times*, May 23, 2005, Reiji Yoshida and Kanako Takahara, "Wu Cancels Koizumi Meeting, Flies Home," *Japan Times*, May 24, 2005.

145. Tanaka Nobumasa, "Yasukuni Shrine and the Double Genocide of Taiwan's Indigenous Atayal: New Court Verdict," *Japan Focus*, http://www.japanfocus.org/-Tanaka-Nobumasa/1928 (accessed July 9, 2009).

146. "Taiwan Natives' Yasukuni Protest Unfulfilled Due to Obstruction," *People's Daily*, June 15, 2005.

147. The Korean Committee of Anti-Yasukuni Joint Counteraction, http://www.anti-yasukuni.org (accessed January 14, 2008).

148. Francis Ching-Wah Yip, "Protestant Christianity in Contemporary China," in *Chinese Religions in Contemporary Societies*, James Miller (Santa Barbara, CA: ABC-CLIO, 2006), 180; Goldman, "Religion in Post-Mao China," 148.

149. Yip, "Protestant Christianity in Contemporary China," 180–81.

150. Goldman, "Religion in Post-Mao China," 149. In a similar fashion, the Communist regime in North Korea virtually wiped out religion from the public realm and filled the spiritual void with the worship of its dictator, Kim Il Sung.

151. Mullins and Young, *Perspectives on Christianity in Korea and Japan*, xv.

152. William P. Woodard, *The Allied Occupation of Japan 1945–1952 and Japanese Religions* (Leiden: E.J. Brill, 1972), 201.

153. Richard Madsen, "Discerning the Religious Spirit of Secular States in Asia," *The Immanent Frame: Secularism, Religion, and the Public Sphere*, Social Science Research Council blog, http://blogs.ssrc.org/tif/2009/02/05/discerning-the-religious-spirit-of-secular-states-in-asia/ (accessed July 14, 2009).

154. We are grateful to David Leheny for clarifying our thoughts on this point. For the Asian values debate, see Fareed Zakaria, "Culture Is Destiny: A Conversation with Lee Kuan Yew," *Foreign Affairs* 73, no. 2 (March/April 1994): 109–126; Kim Dae Jung, "Is Culture Destiny? The Myth of Asia's Anti-Democratic Values," *Foreign Affairs* 73, no. 6 (November/December 1994): 189–194; Paul Krugman, "The Myth of Asia's Miracle," *Foreign Affairs* 73, no. 6 (November/December 1994): 62–78; Tu, *Confucian Traditions in East Asian Modernity*; Francis Fukuyama, "Asian Values and the Asian Crisis," *Commentary*, February 1998.

155. Tu Wei-Ming, "Multiple Modernities: A Preliminary Inquiry into the Implications of East Asian Modernity," in *Culture Matters: How Values Shape Human Progress*, ed. Lawrence E. Harrison and Samuel P. Huntington (New York: Basic Books, 2000), 257.

156. Terry McCarthy, "In Defense Of Asian Values: Singapore's Lee Kuan Yew," *Time*, March 16, 1998.

157. "Indonesia Calls for Countries to Bear Asian Values," *People's Daily*, December 1, 2006.

158. Byrnes and Katzenstein, *Religion in an Expanding Europe*.

159. Madsen, "Embedded Religion in Asia."

8. CONCLUSION

Religion's Contribution to International Relations Theory

EMILY COCHRAN BECH AND JACK SNYDER

With the political salience of religion on the rise, international relations scholars must consider how religious belief systems, movements, and authority structures affect the international system and our approaches to understanding it. This theoretical task is long overdue, notwithstanding a handful of recent pioneering works, most of them by contributors to this volume. Here and elsewhere, they have shown that religion has played a significant role in shaping the modern state system from its inception to the contemporary period.

Taking account of the preceding chapters' contributions, this chapter lays out some considerations for continuing that research. We examine the challenges that religion poses to conventional ways of thinking about international politics as well as potential contributions that a focus on religion might make to invigorating theoretical debate in that field. In particular, we ask what explains religion's rising salience in contemporary international politics, whether religion is a distinctive realm that requires dramatically new approaches and methods, whether religion challenges the centrality of the state, and how the role of religion can be fit into existing theories.

WHY THE RESURGENCE OF RELIGION?

Assuming, as most of our contributors do, that religion has reemerged as a force in global politics in the past several decades, why has it done so? Drawing on our contributors' insights, we conjecture that the rising prominence of religion in world politics reflects an increasing demand for mass political participation in response to the perceived failure of secular institutions to satisfy mass expectations.

First, waves of democratization around the globe have given a greater voice to all kinds of actors, including religious ones. More citizens in more states than ever before are articulating the political demands that are anchored in their belief systems, and can organize, vote, and engage in broader advocacy in pursuit of those goals.[1]

Second, secularization has ironically proved to be religion's protector in many settings. Over the past two centuries, secular toleration and democratization have provided freedom of religion for many states' citizens.[2] This has led to increasing political expression of existing religious diversity. It has also led to increasing religious diversity as individuals exercise their right to adopt, convert to, or renounce religious beliefs and identities, and as religious groups exercise their freedom to form new religious communities based on points of doctrine and practice.

Third, migration has increased religious diversity in many states. This new reality has challenged the post-Westphalian status quo of national religions and corresponding secularist arrangements, especially in Western Europe. Western patterns of interaction between states and specific majority religious heritages have been "normalized" by Western powers and scholars over two centuries.[3] The entry of other religious groups and other forms of religiosity into those societies has challenged status quo arrangements by demanding renegotiation of religion-society-state relations. This has fueled social and political conflicts over a range of religious, ethnic, cultural, and economic diversity issues.

Fourth, the fall or perceived failure of many secular regimes and nationalist movements left many societies or groups with legitimacy vacuums for political authority. Religiously based political movements and ethnoreligious causes resonated with citizens in this political environment.[4] Some governments, realizing that secular ideologies were wearing thin as bases of legitimacy, tried to strengthen their hold on power by integrating religious symbolism and authority into national ritual and rhetoric.[5]

Finally, dissatisfaction with secularist establishments long incumbent in national governments and international institutions has fueled political opposition by religious actors and movements. This opposition takes many forms. Religious opposition parties, advocacy groups, or armed insurgent groups struggle to change national political structures. Religious humanitarian, advocacy, and issue-based movements make political appeals to international courts and organizations. Transnational religious networks coordinate political appeals across systems. Antisystemic religious insurgent networks attack the dominant actors and state-centric assumptions of the entire interstate system.

This analysis of the origins of religious resurgence has important implications for international politics. These populist religious actors display widely divergent political goals and strategies in their struggles against secular orders that they think have failed them. Diverse doctrines on the moral legitimacy—or even necessity—of extreme tactics shape contrasting political programs. Conflicts on the domestic, regional, and global levels affect one another through the transfer of ideas, fighters, and funding, posing a challenge to analyses that compartmentalize international and comparative domestic politics.[6] That said, transnationalism is hardly a new topic in international relations theory, so we still need to ask what difference religion, including religious transnationalism, makes for international relations scholars' choice of conceptual tools.

IS RELIGION DISTINCT FROM OTHER BELIEF SYSTEMS, INCLUDING SECULARISM?

A key question of this book has been whether religion is distinct enough from other legitimizing belief systems to warrant its own analytical space in international relations frameworks, and whether its resurgence signals the need for a reconsideration of ideology and transnational social movements more generally. The book's contributors are not agreed on this point.

Daniel Nexon does not believe that studying religious beliefs and networks requires a complete retooling of international relations theory. He argues instead that "in many respects, religion provides a new vehicle to cover rather familiar terrain in disciplinary debates about the significance of, for instance, ideational forces and non-state actors."[7] Il Hyun Cho and Peter Katzenstein argue that religion plays a particularly important role as a legitimizer of political goals in East Asian societies and in the region more broadly. They call for theoretical and methodological imports from the field of comparative politics to help understand how this works. Nonetheless, legitimation is familiar terrain for at least some existing approaches to international relations theory.

Timothy Shah and Daniel Philpott stake out a more ambitious view, arguing that religion is unique in its potential to unify and mobilize for political action. Since globalization has enabled growing numbers of religious communities to establish effective transnational networks and organizations, religious actors "can increasingly muster resources, mobilize constituencies, and apply pressure on governments and international organizations in ways that other non-state actors—and even some states—can only dream of."[8] International relations theorists, they write, must recognize (1) the distinctive ends of religious actors and how those ends translate into politics, and (2) that religious movements and actors cannot be "easily subsumed into the state." They cannot be so subsumed, Shah and Philpott argue, because the world's major religions are older and more broadly legitimate than modern states, and because both their populations of adherents and their authority structures flow over borders. The historical permanence, legitimizing capacity, and transnational nature of religion, in their view, give it the potential to make significant impacts on world politics.

Several contributors compare the impact of religious and secular belief systems. For Michael Barnett, it is not sufficient to tack on religion as a "modifier" expressing one source of identity, norms, and values to be analyzed in abstract terms, as many constructivist international relations theorists do. Instead, he writes, scholars must recognize and explore the constitutive role of both religious and secular belief systems, often in combination, in social and political processes. Extending this view, Elizabeth Shakman Hurd argues that it is a mistake to treat religion and secularism as antithetical from an analytical point of view. She notes that secularisms, like religions, are a source of norms and behavior on individual, societal, and international levels.

In practice, the similarities between religious and secular organizations—whether they are humanitarian, ethnonationalist, diasporic, issue-oriented, or insurgent—may be more important for some analytical purposes than their differences. Indeed, organizations such as Christian Democratic parties have some characteristics that are secular and some that are religious, and this mix may change over time. Organizations of both types engage in political strategies ranging from party mobilization to extreme violence. Both may have cosmopolitan leaderships. Both are based on deeply held norms and even transcendent ideologies including, as Barnett points out, universalist secularized doctrines of liberal international order. Both can become the basis of identity for their adherents, as Michael Ignatieff has written about secular humanists in the field of human rights.[9] Activists in both religious and secular organizations display the entire range of commitment levels, including in some cases a willingness to die for their cause. Both can mobilize supporters transnationally. Though Shah and Philpott may be right that religions hold the largest and longest-standing cross-border constituencies of adherents, organizations based on secular appeals can boast impressive transnational mobilizations as well.

Still, some significant differences remain. It may be that religious organizations can appeal for legitimacy and political mobilization on a deeper and more persistent existential basis than most secular organizations can, since people who believe their goals are divinely inspired may be impervious to earthly discouragements. Further, as Monica Duffy Toft highlights, religious and secular movements often differ in the time horizons of actors' expected payoffs for themselves (e.g., salvation versus contribution to a desired social order) and their societies (e.g., promotion of an eternal order versus promotion of some specific political structure or group). But actors' ends rarely differ so greatly as such extremes suggest. In most cases, political and ultimate goals merge, in both individual reasoning and movement ideologies. Secular actors may not believe they will benefit after death from sacrifice for a cause. But they can, as Barnett notes, see their actions as promoting an order that advances the progress of humanity. Finally, religious and secular actors may differ in perceived sources of norms: while religious adherents may claim divine inspiration, secular groups can point to established group identity and interests, or more broadly to a norm respecting the dignity of human life. While secular actors do not claim divine inspiration, norms held by both types of actors will be shaped by a mix of practical experience, parochial interests, social functions, and rational thought, which may reduce the differences between religious and nonreligious normative orders.

The geographical reach, normative sources, and perceived ultimate ends of religion can make it a distinctive mobilizer. Yet for most purposes we suspect that common frameworks for analyzing religious and secular movements will offer greater theory-building leverage than separate frameworks tailored to the supposedly distinctive nature of religious movements.

RELIGIOUS MOVEMENTS:
CHALLENGE TO STATES OR CHANNELED THROUGH STATES?

Traditional approaches to studying international relations remain centered on states, notwithstanding some attention to transnational groups and processes. The rising role of religion in world politics might be seen as challenging state-centered conceptual frameworks if religious movements were to take a heavily transnational form and play a major role in shaping the kinds of outcomes that concern international relations scholarship, notably global patterns of cooperation and conflict. We argue that state-centered paradigms remain highly relevant to studying many of the impacts of politicized religion, though our conceptual frameworks also need to be flexible in encompassing some processes that are more strictly transnational.

Only three of this book's chapters take clear positions on this question. Although Nexon wants greater consideration of structures constitutive of states and their policies, he concurs with Jack Snyder's introduction that there is some support for the assumption that transnational and substate politics will largely continue to be funneled through states to world politics. Shah and Philpott, however, argue that religious movements and actors wield greater potential for mobilization than other transnational and non-state actors, so "new assumptions are needed" for the study of religion and world politics.[10]

How, then, do religious beliefs and structures affect the international system? Following the recommendation of several contributors to examine religion's role in constituting actors and interests at all levels of world politics, we propose five key channels of influence. First, the beliefs of religious individuals affect their choices as constituents and leaders of local and state governments; as donors or activists for local, national, or transnational advocacy organizations; and as staff of intergovernmental institutions and programs. Since the majority of individuals act politically through institutions and groups that target local and national political arenas, religious influence on the system through individual actors is primarily channeled through states. However, availability of rapid communications brings increasing numbers of individuals into direct contact with transnational organizations attempting to influence international processes directly, so individual transnational engagement—some of it shaped by participants' religious beliefs—is on the rise.

Second, religious influence affects international politics indirectly through religiously based organizations that target political appeals to local and national decision makers. The use of this approach seems to be increasing. Muslim parties, for example, have found increasing success since the 1990s in Bangladesh, Pakistan, Malaysia, Indonesia, and Turkey.[11] While these groups often focus their political action on intrastate processes, they may also affect international processes by influencing the individual states in which they operate. As Shah and Philpott highlight, this can include appeals over interstate affairs, as when the U.S. Conference of Catholic Bishops condemns the Iraq War, India's BJP pushes for a stronger Hindu homeland, and the Russian Orthodox Church urges state intolerance of foreign Protestant missionaries. Armed insurgencies involving religion, a focus of Toft's chapter, also influence world affairs by challenging governments and the very legitimacy of states, and include majority-religion rebel groups like the GIA in Algeria, resistance movements with armed wings like Hamas in the Palestinian Territories, and parties to ethnoreligious conflict such as the IRA in Northern Ireland. All these organizations may also exchange ideas and resources with similar groups in other states. Cho and Katzenstein point out, in addition, that government responses to religious groups within a state may affect that state's international reputation.

Third, explicitly religious transnational networks and organizations influence international processes both directly and indirectly through multiple states. These include aggregate bodies that promote religious unity and coordinate campaigns such as the network of Orthodox Churches, political and social movements like the Muslim Brotherhood, humanitarian organizations like World Vision, and militant networks like Al Qaeda.[12] They engage in cross-border recruitment and fund-raising, influence citizen appeals to their states, and appeal directly to multiple governments and intergovernmental organizations themselves. Appeals to states are often concerted through individual members, national subsidiary organizations, and international leadership groups that raise issues of global concern on which policy is to be shaped within states, or on issues to be decided by member states in IGO structures and by IGO agencies and international courts. These networks or organizations vary widely in scope and strength, some holding continual political-religious legitimacy for citizens in multiple countries, while others are formed ad hoc for the purpose of making appeals on a particular issue. Their influence thus flows partially through states, though often through concerted campaigns, and they also attempt to influence international processes directly.

Further, supranational religious organizations (e.g., the Roman Catholic Church, the World Council of Churches, and the World Hindu Council) exercise influence in the international system with almost state-like diplomacy to affect state policy and with appeals through representatives directly to international institutions. While such organizations exercise influence through states by way of individual adherents and through constituent organizations, they also seek direct influence on international processes and institutions.

Finally, religious influence flows into the international system through religiously based intergovernmental organizations. There are few of these (the most obvious may be the Organization of the Islamic Conference, or OIC), but they make a significant impact by (1) shaping some interactions between constituent states, (2) providing a platform through which leading national and transnational actors can influence member states and a world audience on issues of religious concern, and (3) forming (or at least giving the appearance of) a concerted front of states around issues of concern in the face of the broader international system and its leading states. The OIC, for example, was the site of appeals by religiously driven individual, non-state, and state-level actors for a joint statement of condemnation of a Danish newspaper's 2005 publication of the now-famous "Muhammad cartoons," driving the issue onto the world stage.[13]

While the first two dynamics described above flow overwhelmingly through state-based political hierarchies, the final three have direct transnational influence on interstate relations and international institutions. The question then remains to be researched: is the religious influence flowing into the system through these channels significant enough to warrant a rethinking of conventional approaches to international politics, at least in some issue areas?

DOES RELIGION POSE A CHALLENGE TO TRADITIONAL WAYS OF CONCEPTUALIZING INTERNATIONAL RELATIONS?

Our contributors see a number of tensions between religious subject matter and the philosophical presumptions of traditional approaches to international relations. Though these tensions do not correspond exactly to the three canonical paradigms, religion does give rise to distinctive problems for each paradigm.

One tension with realism lies in religion's transnational character. Although some religions are congruent with the borders of a nation-state, most are not. Another is the tension between the logic of the sacred and the logic of power politics. Nexon shows, however, that these two logics often interpenetrate at the nexus of the state, which is a central location for organizing collective action through which the activities of substate and transnational actors translate into outcomes in world politics. Exactly how this works, and how it should work, has long been a subject of philosophical and empirical analysis. At the philosophical level, there is a long Christian realist tradition running from Augustine through Luther to Reinhold Niebuhr recognizing dual logics of the divine realm and the realm of temporal power: the city of God and the city of man, the two kingdoms, moral man and immoral society. At the political level, the decidedly realist formula of the pre-Westphalian Peace of Augsburg, *cuius regio, eius religio*, provided a formula for sorting states neatly among transnational religions. And yet none of these formulas succeeded in banishing religion to an apolitical realm, insulating realpolitik from the impact of transnational religion, or subordinating either type of authority to the other. As Nexon argues, we need theory that can comprehend these realms' interpenetration and interaction.

A tension with liberalism lies in religion's sacred and transcendental qualities, which are at odds with liberalism's interest-based rationalism. But this tension is also found within liberalism, between those who emphasize the normative underpinnings of the liberal order and those who stress the mechanical workings of institutions that check and channel self-interest. Explanations for the democratic peace that stress common norms and identities arguably have more in common with religious modes of understanding than they do with rationalist self-interest explanations based on institutionalized accountability to the average voter. Indeed, Hurd and other contributors discuss the ways in which Kantian liberalism provides a link between the West's Christian traditions and its more secular present.

Canonical statements of the liberal international relations paradigm have not emphasized these connections to religion in part because the most prominent of these liberal manifestos are implicitly grounded in a one-track theory of modernization, in which the rise of the rationalized bureaucratic state, capitalist markets, and liberal democracy go hand in hand with the triumph of secularism. If liberal international relations scholars were more explicit about the grounding of their assumptions in modernization theory, they would have to acknowledge the reality of multiple paths of historical development leading to multiple modernities in which religion may play different roles. Sudipta Kaviraj points out, for example, that the elements of modernity were introduced in a different sequence in many late-developing societies than they were in Great Britain, with mass democratic politics institutionalized in India before the urbanization and secularization of society.[14] If so, we need not just a single, invariant account of liberalism's role in world politics, but a more variegated, contextualized theory that considers paths other than Western-secularist forms but nonetheless stays true to liberalism's basic assumptions.

A tension with constructivism, Barnett notes, lies in the implicit secularist bias in the way that the paradigm's central concepts of identity, values, norms, and beliefs are understood. Religious lifeworlds comprise all of these elements, but for at least some believers, they do so as an all-encompassing totality infused with the presumptions of sacredness and transcendence. In contrast, constructivist understandings of these terms are typically less totalizing and not turbocharged with the divine. While constructivists may acknowledge that identities, norms, and values may have religious sources, they tend to treat those grounded in religion as functionally the same as those of other types. Recognizing the differences between religious and nonreligious social constructions of reality would arguably enrich constructivism's contribution to international relations studies rather than undermine it.

In short, religion presents analytical challenges to all three of the traditional international relations paradigms, but incorporating religion would in each case enhance the subtlety, accuracy, and power of these approaches rather than undermine them. Some of our contributors, furthermore, urge that international relations theorists should seize upon the study of religion as an opportunity to loosen the grip of the traditional paradigms, use them more eclectically, and import ideas and methodological habits from the field of comparative politics. One crucial area in which comparative politics can play such a role is in the study of religious resurgence as a phenomenon of contemporary political development that features rising demands for mass political participation. Since these demands have major consequences for international relations, it is important to study the societal and transnational forces impelling them. We hope that the varied models presented in this collection will stimulate thinking about the way forward in theorizing the role of religion in international politics.

NOTES

1. Monica Duffy Toft, chapter 5 of this book.

2. As in the third and fourth concepts of secularism outlined by Timothy Samuel Shah and Daniel Philpott, chapter 2 of this book.

3. Elizabeth Shakman Hurd, chapter 3 of this book.

4. Mark Juergensmeyer, *The New Cold War? Religious Nationalism Confronts the Secular State* (Berkeley: University of California Press, 1993).

5. Il Hyun Cho and Peter J. Katzenstein, chapter 7 of this book, describe such a development in China in recent years.

6. Mark Juergensmeyer's *The Global Rebellion: Religious Challenges to the Secular State, from Christian Militias to Al Qaeda* (Berkeley: University of California Press, 2008) expands on his earlier work by suggesting that conflicts between religious activism and secular nationalisms have escalated into a global confrontation, but this may blur the different grievances and goals of a diverse set of militant actors.

7. Daniel Nexon, chapter 6 of this book.

8. Shah and Philpott, chapter 2 of this book.

9. Michael Ignatieff, "Human Rights as Politics and Idolatry," *Human Rights as Politics and Idolatry*, ed. Amy Gutmann (Princeton: Princeton University Press, 2001), 3–98.

10. Shah and Philpott, chapter 2 of this book.

11. Vali Nasr, "The Rise of 'Muslim Democracy,'" *Journal of Democracy* 16, no. 2 (2005): 13–27.

12. Shah and Philpott, chapter 2, and Barnett, chapter 4 of this book.

13. Hassan M. Fattah, "At Mecca Meeting, Cartoon Outrage Crystalized," *New York Times*, February 9, 2006; Organisation of the Islamic Conference, "Final Communiqué of the Third Extraordinary Session of the Islamic Summit Conference" (Mecca, December 7–8, 2005).

14. Sudipta Kaviraj, "An Outline of a Revisionist Theory of Modernity," *Archives Européennes de Sociologie* 46, no. 3 (2005): 497–526.

CONTRIBUTORS

Michael Barnett is University Professor of International Affairs and Political Science at George Washington University. His book *Confronting the Costs of War: Military Power, State, and Society in Egypt and Israel* won the ISA's Quincy Wright award. His other major books include *Dialogues in Arab Politics: Negotiations in Regional Order* (Columbia University Press, 1998); *Security Communities*, which he coedited with Emanuel Adler; *Eyewitness to a Genocide: The United Nations and Rwanda*; *Rules for the World: International Organizations in World Politics* with Martha Finnemore; and *The Empire of Humanity: A History of Humanitarianism*.

Emily Cochran Bech is a PhD candidate in political science at Columbia University specializing in the politics of religious minorities in Europe.

Il Hyun Cho is assistant professor of political science at Cleveland State University. He has conducted field research in China, Japan, and South Korea, and has written about national missile defense and the North Korean missile program. His current research projects include global rogues and regional orders, the politics of nuclear restraint, national identity politics in democracies, East Asian regionalism, and religious politics in East Asia. He has held fellowships and research affiliations at Yonsei University, Seoul; the University of Tokyo; and the Belfer Center for Science and International Affairs, Harvard University.

Elizabeth Shakman Hurd is an international political theorist and assistant professor of political science at Northwestern University. She is interested in the history of the modern category of religion and its demarcation from politics and law. Central to her research interests are the politics of religious difference, religious pluralism, and religious freedom and their legal management and regulation at the global level. She is the author of *The Politics of Secularism in International Relations* and coeditor of *Comparative Secularisms in a Global Age*.

Peter J. Katzenstein is the Walter S. Carpenter, Jr., Professor of International Studies at Cornell University, president of the American Political Science Association (2008–9), and a member of the American Academy of Arts and Sciences and the American Philosophical Society. He is the author, coauthor, editor, and coeditor of more than thirty books and monographs and over one hundred articles and book chapters. Recent books include: *Beyond Paradigms: Analytical Eclecticism in World Politics*; *Civilizations in World Politics: Plural and Pluralist Perspectives*; *Religion in an Expanding Europe*, coedited with Timothy A. Byrnes; and *Rethinking Security in East Asia: Identity, Power, and Efficiency*.

Daniel H. Nexon is an assistant professor and the codirector of undergraduate studies at the Edmund A. Walsh School of Foreign Service at Georgetown University. He is the author of *The Struggle for Power in Early Modern Europe: Religious Conflict, Dynastic Empires, and International Change*.

Daniel Philpott is associate professor of political science and peace studies at the Kroc Institute for International Peace Studies at the University of Notre Dame. He is a senior associate at the International Center for Religion and Diplomacy in Washington, D.C. His books include *Revolutions in Sovereignty: How Ideas Shaped Modern International Relations* and he is the editor of *The Politics of Past Evil: Religion, Reconciliation, and the Dilemmas of Transitional Justice*. He also trains political and religious leaders in reconciliation in Burundi and the broader Great Lakes region of Africa under the auspices of the Catholic Peacebuilding Network.

Timothy Samuel Shah is an adjunct senior fellow for religion and foreign policy at the Council on Foreign Relations. Shah's research and expertise is in the areas of religion and foreign policy, religion and the theory and practice of democracy, global democratization, Third World religion and politics, South Asia, and religion and domestic politics. He is also a senior research scholar at the

Institute on Culture, Religion, and World Affairs at Boston University; a principal researcher at the Religion in Global Politics Project at Harvard University; and a research director at the Project on Evangelicalism and Democracy in the Global South. Formerly, he was Senior Fellow for Religion and World Affairs at the Pew Forum on Religion and Public Life.

Jack Snyder is the Robert and Renée Belfer Professor of International Relations in the political science department and the Saltzman Institute of War and Peace Studies at Columbia University. His books include *Electing to Fight: Why Emerging Democracies Go to War*, coauthored with Edward D. Mansfield; *From Voting to Violence: Democratization and Nationalist Conflict*; *Myths of Empire: Domestic Politics and International Ambition*; and *The Ideology of the Offensive: Military Decision Making and the Disasters of 1914*. He is a fellow of the American Academy of Arts and Sciences.

Monica Duffy Toft is associate professor of public policy and director of the Initiative on Religion in International Affairs at the Harvard Kennedy School of Government. She was a research intern at the RAND Corporation and served in the U.S. Army. Toft is director of the Belfer Center's Initiative on Religion in International Affairs, which was established with a generous grant from the Henry Luce Foundation. She is the author of three books: *The Geography of Ethnic Violence*, *Securing the Peace*, and an edited volume, *The Fog of Peace: Strategic and Military Planning Under Uncertainty*.

INDEX

Waltz, Kenneth, 2, 7–8, 10, 12–3, 35, 106, 148
Wars of Religion, 6, 11–2, 70, 93, 147–9, 154
Weber, Max (Weberian), 9, 18, 27, 77, 107, 127–8, 134, 171
Weber-Troeltsch axis, 77
Wendt, Alexander, 2, 14–7, 51
Wertrationalität (values rationality), 127–8, 134
Westphalia (Westphalian), 6, 10, 15, 31–4, 37, 52, 69–70, 128, 201, 207; Peace of Westphalia, 25, 31, 63, 70, 94, 129, 168
Wilcox, 156
World Council of Churches, 52, 206
World Missionary Conference (WMC), 99–100

World Vision, 48, 52, 110, 206
World War I, 45, 95, 102
World War II, 29, 37, 45, 79, 92, 95, 125, 177, 183, 188

Yasukuni Shrine, 177, 179–80, 187–8
Yemen (North and South), 124
Yi Taejo, 172
Yoido Full Gospel Church, 181
Yongki Cho, 181
Yugoslavia, 120–2
Yushin Constitution, 178

Zendavest, 73
Zweckrationalität (instrumental rationality), 127–8, 134
Zwingli, Heinrich, 150